D1592570

Economics of Employment

ECONOMICS HANDBOOK SERIES

SEYMOUR E. HARRIS, Editor

ADVISORY COMMITTEE: Edward H. Chamberlain, Gottfried Haberler, Alvin H. Hansen, Edward S. Mason, and John H. Williams. *All of Harvard University.*

Economics
of Employment

Abba P. Lerner

Professor of Economics
Roosevelt College, Chicago

NEW YORK   TORONTO   LONDON

McGRAW-HILL BOOK COMPANY, INC.

1951

ECONOMICS OF EMPLOYMENT

VII
37205

To Harold J. Laski and Ludwig von Mises, and the millions of lovers of freedom in between who are addicted to baiting "capitalism" or "socialism": dedicated in the hope that they will cease to tolerate "anticapitalist" tyranny as "progressive" or to fight full employment policies as "socialist," but will focus their efforts on practical measures for enlarging human freedom and dignity.

Preface

WHENEVER I mentioned, while working on this book, that I was writing on the economics of employment, the first question, three times out of four, was "Did you say the economics of unemployment?" or "Do you mean the economics of full employment?" Nevertheless, the title of the book is exactly as it appears on the title page.

The refusal of my friends to believe that they had heard aright is, I think, significant of just the kind of attitude that this book hopes in a slight measure to correct. I was expected to write a book devoted to attacking the evil of unemployment or to write a book indicating how one could achieve the desirable state of full employment. I think I have done both of these things, but neither can be done properly if primary attention is directed at what we want to avoid or at what we want to achieve. Primary attention must be directed at understanding and explaining the way things work. Understanding comes first. Only when we understand the nature of the machinery that determines any level of employment can we hope to be able to avoid what we do not like and achieve what we do like. The primary concern of this book is, therefore, to provide an understanding of what makes employment high or low. I think I have done this in nontechnical language so that any intelligent person who is willing to pay a little attention can understand it. No previous study of economics is necessary.

To make sure of this, I asked some of my friends and colleagues who were completely innocent of economics, and even shamefully lacking in interest in economic and social affairs, to read the manuscript chapter by chapter. I was of course most gratified when they declared they could understand all of it and even found it interesting.

In doing all this I have not found it necessary to leave out any part of the heart of the argument. Many alleged popularizations of difficult subjects fail because they leave out what they promise to simplify. Such a procedure leaves unsatisfied the reader's hunger for understanding and adds to this injury the insult of implying that he is really not up to understanding the true explanation of the matter. This book does, I think, go to the bottom of things. Although it is written so that the noneconomist can follow it, it can be read with profit by the student of economics or by the teacher of economics or even by the advanced research worker in economics. But those trained in economics will have the additional sport of looking out for and recognizing many old technical concepts disguised by the only too unfamiliar garb of plain English.

In spite of all efforts some parts of the book are a little harder to read than others. There are seven parts. Part I indicates the nature of the problem to which the book is devoted, and the first chapter is a kind of preview of the thesis of the whole book.

Part II is probably the most difficult. Geometrical figures and diagrams are used here for the convenience of those who find them helpful, but these have been imprisoned in the appendixes to the various chapters so that those who are frightened rather than helped by them can safely ignore their existence. In the text of these chapters there are some lines of what looks like algebra or even mathematics. The reader is hereby assured that anyone can follow these who can add, subtract, multiply, and divide small numbers and who realizes that a letter (like C, which indicates consumption) can also stand for a number (like the number of dollars spent on consumption in some period). Those who are still frightened by such algebra can omit it without losing the thread of the argument, because it is there only to make clearer, by this kind of repetition, what has already been said in an English which, while far from fancy, is unavoidably cumbersome. It is even possible to skip these chapters (4 through 7) altogether without running into serious difficulties in the rest of the book. Readers who skip Chapters 4 through 7 would be wise to skip

Chapter 17 too. No one should skip Chapter 8 on Functional Finance.

Part III deals with the resistances that prevent the immediate application by society of the solution made clear in Part II. It is put here to answer the inevitable response that the solution cannot be so simple and clear or we would have put it into practice long ago. It seems to be necessary to remind almost everyone that the human race is not noted for the promptness with which it acts collectively to adopt reasonable methods of dealing with its problems.

Part IV goes into some of the problems that would face a society which would adopt a policy for maintaining satisfactory employment and indicates some ways of going about solving them. This is important both to combat the idea that achieving full employment would solve all problems and to counter the objection to employment policies on the ground that they would *not* solve all problems.

Part V digs a little more deeply into the issues raised in Part II and begins with Chapter 17 on Saving and the Multiplier which depends so much on Chapters 4 through 7 that it should not be read if these have been skipped. The rest of Part V is, however, not particularly difficult.

Part VI brings in international aspects which up to this point have been deliberately and artificially left out in the interests of simplicity.

Part VII consists of only one chapter and is primarily devoted to the thesis that while it is not true that human society acts quickly to adopt reasonable policies as soon as they are clearly presented, it is equally false to rush to the opposite view that society will never do that which is reasonable. Although society learns slowly, it nevertheless does learn, so that there is room for a guarded optimism.

I am deeply indebted to Dorothy Welker of the English Department of Roosevelt College for taking great pains in reading the manuscript and criticizing it in detail. Any remaining lack of clarity or murkiness of style is due to my disregarding some of her advice. I have benefited much from theoretical discussions with Professor Armen Alchian of the University of California at Los Angeles on the nature of full-employment equilibrium and with Professor Fritz Machlup of Johns Hopkins University, who has been working along parallel lines on this problem. I am grateful to Sara Landau of Roosevelt College for criticisms of Chapter 22, some of which I have tried to meet, to Jennifer Forsyth of the ECE for painstaking editorial help at the page-proof stage, and to Winifred Turnbull of the ECE for stalwart assistance with the index.

The basic ideas of this book are, of course, derived from the work of the late Lord Keynes.

Acknowledgments are due to *The University Review* of the University of Kansas City for permission to reprint "The Economic Steering Wheel" as Chapter 1 and to *The New Yorker* for permission to reprint the excerpt on page 316.

ABBA P. LERNER

CHICAGO, ILL.
February, 1951

Contents

xii CONTENTS

Editor's Introduction

FOR YEARS many teachers of economics and other professional economists have felt the need of a series of books on economic subjects which is not filled by the usual textbook or by the highly technical treatise.

This present series, published under the general title, the Economics Handbook Series, was planned with these needs in mind. Designed first of all for students, the volumes are useful in the ever-growing field of adult education and also are of interest to the informed general reader.

The volumes are not long—they give the essentials of the subject matter within the limits of a few hundred pages; they present a distillate of accepted theory and practice, without the detailed approach of the technical treatise. Each volume is a unit, standing on its own.

The authors are scholars, each writing on an economic subject of which he is an authority. In this series the author's first task was not to make important contributions to knowledge—although many of them do—but so to present his subject matter that his work as a scholar will carry its maximum influence outside as well as inside the classroom. The time has come to redress the balance between the energies spent on the creation of new ideas and on their dissemination. Economic ideas are unproductive if they do not spread beyond the world of scholars. Popularizers without technical competence, unqualified textbook writers, and sometimes even charlatans control too large a part of the market for economic ideas.

In the classroom the Economics Handbook Series will serve, it is hoped, as brief surveys in one-semester courses, as supplementary reading in introductory courses, and in other courses in which the subject is related.

Professor Abba P. Lerner's volume on employment is a lucid, elementary account of Keynesian economics. The editor knows of no more skillful presentation of Keynesian economics for the student or informed layman. The author deals with the components of income, consumption, and investment and with their relationships; the determinants of income and notable, the rate of interest, and the marginal efficiency of capital; the relation of money and the rate of interest, of the latter and savings; and the international aspects of Keynesian economics.

The objective of the Handbook Series is a clear presentation of available material. But Dr. Lerner cannot write a book of a few hundred pages without making important contributions. The treatment of the multiplier in process analysis, of low- and high-level full employment, the conflicts of private and social interests with attendant danger to stabilization objectives, the handling of Say's law—in these and other areas Lerner shows much originality. One cannot but be impressed by the author's resoluteness in refusing the easy road to expediency.

The arrangement of Dr. Lerner's book is eminently practical. Aware that many readers are averse to graphic presentation, Lerner has not encumbered the text with charts. Though these diagrams are included and will help the average student, the material is presented in a manner to allow omission by those who prefer the literary exposition.

Professor Lerner has had a distinguished career as student, teacher, and writer. He ranks in the top echelon of economic theorists and yet can present difficult ideas in simple language. As a student at the London School of Economics, in the years 1930 to 1932, he virtually cornered the prize market. He remained there as a research fellow and lecturer. Later he migrated to the United States, teaching successively at Columbia University, the University of Virginia, University of Kansas City, Amherst College, the New School of Social Research, and Roosevelt College, where he is now Professor of Economics.

Lerner's best-known writing is his volume *The Economics of Control*. Greatly influenced by Lord Keynes, Lerner has made numerous contributions to Keynesian economics, and particularly a large proportion of about 100 articles were devoted to the clarification and advancement of the new economics. In fact, I can attest at first hand the importance of Lerner's work on the subject, for when in the course of other editorial duties, *i.e.*, launching the volume *The New Economics*, I combed the available published material, Lerner's articles on this subject were most rewarding.

SEYMOUR E. HARRIS

Part I
The Problem

CHAPTER 1

The Economic Steering Wheel
or The Story of the People's New Clothes[1]

OUR ECONOMIC system is frequently put to shame in being displayed before an imaginary visitor from a strange planet. It is time to reverse the procedure. Imagine yourself instead in a Buck Rogers interplanetary adventure, looking at a highway in a City of Tomorrow. The highway is wide and straight, and its edges are turned up so that it is almost impossible for a car to run off the road. What appears to be a runaway car is speeding along the road and veering off to one side. As it approaches the rising edge of the highway, its front wheels are turned so that it gets back onto the road and goes off at an angle, making for the other side, where the wheels are turned again. This happens many times, the car zigzagging but keeping on the highway until it is out of sight. You are wondering how long it will take for it to crash, when another car appears which behaves in the same fashion. When it comes near you it stops with a jerk. A door is opened, and an occupant asks whether you would like a lift. You look into the car and before you can control yourself you cry out, "Why! There's no steering wheel!"

"Of course we have no steering wheel!" says one of the occupants rather crossly. "Just think how it would cramp the front seat. It is worse than an old-fashioned gear-shift lever and it is dangerous. Suppose we had a steering wheel and somebody held on to it when we reached a curb! He would prevent the automatic turning of the wheel, and the car would surely be overturned! And besides, we believe in democracy and cannot give anyone the

[1] This chapter is reproduced (with minor changes) from *The University Review* (University of Kansas City, Mo.), June, 1941.

3

extreme authority of life and death over all the occupants of the car. That would be dictatorship."

"Down with dictatorship!" chorus the other occupants of the car.

"If you are worried about the way the car goes from side to side," continues the first speaker, "forget it! We have wonderful brakes so that collisions are prevented nine times out of ten. On our better roads the curb is so effective that one can travel hundreds of miles without going off the road once. We have a very efficient system of carrying survivors of wrecks to nearby hospitals and for rapidly sweeping the remnants from the road to deposit them on nearby fields as a reminder to man of the inevitability of death."

You look around to see the piles of wrecks and burned-out automobiles as the man in the car continues. "Impressive, isn't it? But things are going to improve. See those men marking and photographing the tracks of the car that preceded us? They are going to take those pictures into their laboratories and pictures of our tracks, too, to analyze the cyclical characteristics of the curves, their degree of regularity, the average distance from turn to turn, the amplitude of the swings, and so on. When they have come to an agreement on their true nature we may know whether something can be done about it. At present they are disputing whether this cyclical movement is due to the type of road surface or to its shape or whether it is due to the length of the car or the kind of rubber in the tires or to the weather. Some of them think that it will be impossible to avoid having cycles unless we go back to the horse and buggy, but we can't do that because we believe in Progress. Well, want a ride?"

The dilemma between saving your skin and humoring the lunatics is resolved by your awakening from the nightmare, and you feel glad that the inhabitants of your own planet are a little more reasonable. But are they as reasonable about other things as they are about the desirability of steering their automobiles? Do they not behave exactly like the men in the nightmare when it comes to operating their economic system? Do they not allow their *economic* automobile to bounce from depression to inflation in wide and uncontrolled arcs? Through their failure to steer away from unemployment and idle factories are they not just as guilty of public injury and insecurity as the mad motorists of Mars?

Depression and inflation can be prevented by regulating the rate of spending.

The outstanding problem of modern society is just this. All the other really important problems, such as wars and fascism, are either caused or aggravated by the failure to solve this one. What is needed more than anything else is a mechanism which will enable us to regulate our economy so as to maintain a reasonable degree of economic activity: on the one hand to prevent any considerable unemployment of resources and on the other hand to prevent the stresses of the overemployment of resources and the disorganization that we know as inflation. We need a regulator of employment—a mechanism for the maintenance of prosperity.

The instrument that can do this is as readily available as the steering wheel for automobiles, yet it has not been installed and put into operation. Instead, all our universities are engaged in studying and adding to the enormous literature about the path traveled by the economy when no steering wheel is used—the study of the business cycle.

In our present moderately competitive economy based on moderately free enterprise the level of economic activity is determined by how much money is being spent on the goods and services that can be produced. The immediate effect of a decrease in spending is that the goods accumulate on the shopkeeper's shelves. The shopkeeper may reduce the price in an attempt to move the goods, but this is not necessarily the case. He may prefer to let his stocks increase, especially if he believes that he will be able to sell them soon at the normal price. But whether he lowers the price or not, he will reduce his orders to the wholesalers and the manufacturers and there will result a reduction in output (and in the number of workers employed in making the goods). A reduction in the rate of spending is thus followed, after this adjustment, by a smaller supply of goods to be purchased, and if the price was lowered in the first place it will rise again to the normal level when the supply has been reduced in response to the reduction in demand.

The same thing happens in reverse when there is an increase in demand. The shopkeeper's stocks are reduced below normal and he may take advantage of the increase in demand to raise the price. But whether he raises the price or not he will increase his orders to the wholesalers and the manufacturers. There will then be an increase in the amount of goods produced (and in the number of people employed in making them). After this adjustment there will be a greater supply of goods corresponding to the greater demand for them, and if the price was raised when the demand first increased, it will fall again to the normal level when the supply has caught up with the demand. The important effect of an increase or of a decrease in spending is essentially, therefore, to increase or decrease the supply. The effect on prices is only temporary.

But if there are no unemployed resources available when spending increases, it is impossible for employment or output to increase. Prices then *must* be raised and they do not fall back again to normal. They stay higher. The increased spending cannot be absorbed by an increase in the supply of goods. It then shows itself in higher prices for the same supply of goods.

Nor is this the end of the story. Although the manufacturer cannot increase output where there are no unemployed resources available, the increased orders at higher prices induce manufacturers to *try* to increase their output to take advantage of the unusually high profits. In so doing they try to get men and materials away from each other by offering higher wages and prices (or merely agreeing to demands for higher wages and prices). This raises the money incomes of labor and of the owners of materials and results in a further increase in spending. Increased spending increases incomes, and increased incomes increase spending, and so the process becomes cumulative, with prices rising (and the value of money falling) faster and faster. If this process is permitted to continue by a monetary authority which provides the increasing amount of money that is needed as prices rise, we have an inflation. Inflation disorganizes the economy, works great hardship on persons whose money incomes are fixed or only slowly adjustable, and ruins persons whose savings are cautiously tied to the depreciating money.

The aim of any reasonable regulation of the level of economic activity (which we may call "employment" for short) must be to arrange for the rate of spending to be neither too small (which would cause unemployment) nor too great (which would cause inflation). A satisfactory level (or range) of employment must be chosen, and the total rate of spending must be raised when employment is too low and curtailed when employment rises too high.

There are three rules governing the economic steering wheel.

If the rate of spending happens to satisfy this criterion, employment is adequate and there is no need for any special measures. If there is not sufficient spending, so that employment is too low, then the difference can be made up by the government. The government can spend money *directly* on public works or *indirectly* by reducing taxes, thus permitting the taxpayers to increase their spending, or by paying out more to people who would be only too glad to spend it, such as pensioners or people on relief. If there is too much spending, so that there are signs of the beginnings of inflation, the government can correct this either *directly,* by reducing its own spending, or *indirectly,* by collecting more in taxes and thus leaving less for the taxpayers to spend. This gives us the first rule for the regulation of employment:

1. The government shall maintain at all times a reasonable level of total spending in the economy. If there is not enough spending, so that there is excessive unemployment, the government shall increase total spending by lowering taxes or by increasing its own expenditures or both. If there is too much spending, so that there is inflation, the government shall reduce total spending by cutting its own expenditures or by increasing taxes or both.

Most of the time our present economy seems to suffer from too little rather than from too much spending, so that to correct this disposition it would be necessary for the government on the whole to spend more or to decrease its tax revenues or both. Where is the money to come from?

The simplest answer is "from the printing press." After giving this answer it is usually necessary to wait for the listener's eyebrows to fall back a little. This movement can be helped by pointing out four things: (1) an increase in the amount of money is not identical with inflation; (2) an increase in the amount of money in existence is of no importance for the economy unless it leads to an increase in *spending* by somebody; (3) an increase in spending is just what is needed to bring about an increase in employment; and (4) as long as it is possible for the supply of goods to increase along with the increase in spending, there will be no (permanent) increase in prices.

This does not mean that the government would have to keep on printing more new money forever week by week and year by year to maintain prosperity. As the stock of money increased, it would in various ways lead to an increase in spending by private individuals and corporations. This would reduce the gap in spending that has to be made up by the government. When there is so much money in existence that the rate of private spending is enough to provide a satisfactory level of employment, the government will not have to spend any more than it raises in taxes and the printing presses can be stopped.

Thus an adjustment of the stock of money can, through its influence on the rate of spending, be the equilibrating factor which keeps employment at a reasonable level. Nevertheless, it might not be considered desirable to reach this particular equilibrium. Such a policy might perhaps be considered to entail overinvestment—too large a portion of the resources of society devoted to investment for the future and too little left to provide for current consumption.

If the stock of money increases, the members of society will find themselves holding larger and larger amounts of money (since the money that is in existence or "in circulation" is always held by somebody).

They will consider it wasteful to keep such increasing quantities of their wealth in the form of idle money, making no profit and earning no interest. They will therefore attempt to make some profit by lending it out at interest or by buying interest-yielding forms of wealth, such as securities, with the idle money. The increased availability of money for borrowers directly lowers the rate of interest that they have to pay. The attempt to buy more securities, constituting an increase in demand for securities in relation to their supply, raises the price of securities. Since the issue of securities by business firms or by the government is a method by which business firms or the government borrow money, the higher price means that more money can be borrowed for the same interest payments or that the same amount of money can be borrowed for smaller interest payments. This is nothing but another aspect of the reduction of the rate of interest. In this way by more direct or by less direct methods an increase in the amount of money reduces the rate of interest.

At the lower rate of interest it becomes worth while to borrow money to undertake investments in new productive equipment and the like even if they do not yield very much. As the amount of money keeps on increasing and the rate of interest keeps on falling, marginal investments with very low yields, which were not worth making before, now become worth while. Investment will thus keep on increasing. A situation might be reached in which this produces enough spending to prevent depression. But the government might feel that the resources absorbed by these not very effective marginal investments for raising productivity in the future could be put to much better use for the benefit of the present generation. It might think it better to bring about the required increase in spending by, say, providing children's allowances.

But the government cannot undertake the children's allowances *on top* of the marginal investments because there would then be *too much* spending—there would be inflation. The marginal investments must therefore be stopped if the children's allowances are to come into effect without causing inflation. The marginal investments would be stopped if the rate of interest were to stay high enough to prevent them from being profitable. But the spending of money on the children's allowances out of deficits keeps on increasing the stock of money and this keeps on pushing down the rate of interest. Somehow the government must *prevent* the rate of interest from being pushed down by the additions to the stock of money coming from its own expenditures on children's allowances.

There is an obvious way of doing this. The government can *borrow back* the money that it is spending.

In different circumstances the government might wish to encourage private investment, and in that case it could do the opposite. It could *lend* rather than borrow money on the capital market (or repay some of the national debt in cash, which comes to the same thing) and in this way increase the amount of money, lower the rate of interest, and increase investment. This brings us to the second rule, which is not so fundamental as the first but helps to complete the sketch of the economic mechanism:

> 2. The government shall maintain that rate of interest which induces the optimum rate of investment, bor-

rowing money when the rate of interest is too low and lending money (or repaying loans) when the rate of interest is too high.

These two rules provide the mechanism for guiding the modern economy—the missing steering wheel. The principles are not really very difficult. Why have they not been applied long before now?

First there is the breach with tradition. The approach is unorthodox. Spending by the government must be regarded not as something to be done when it can be "afforded" or when it is essential to prevent starvation, but as a regular and painless way of maintaining prosperity. It should be undertaken when the society is poor on account of unemployment rather than when it is prosperous and appears to be able to afford luxuries. Taxation must be regarded not as the government's way of earning its living, but as a device for reducing the incomes and thereby the expenditures of members of society. The quantity of money must be regarded not as something sacred to be governed by the rules of some gold standard with which the government has no right to interfere, but as a mere instrument for maintaining the right amount of spending. Government borrowing must be regarded not as a measure of last resort to be undertaken only in extreme emergency and in limited degree, but as a matter of very little consequence, the national debt and the rate at which it is being increased or repaid being completely subjected to the rules for maintaining the optimum rate of investment. It is only to stress this breach with tradition that the third "rule" is provided:

> 3. If either of the first two rules should conflict with the principles of "sound finance" or of balancing the budget or of limiting the national debt, so much the worse for these principles. The government press shall print any money that may be needed in carrying out these rules.

Traditionalism, misunderstanding, and vested interests by themselves could not have prevented the use of the economic steering wheel.

The conflict with tradition does not seem by itself a sufficient explanation of the failure of modern society to regulate the level of economic activity. The fundamental logic of the new position is quite easily demonstrable. It is almost self-evident that, while the individual can be sent to prison for manufacturing money, the government need not fear the police. It may thus be guided by different principles in this respect. A firmly established modern state is perfectly well able to borrow money or print money if it is in need of money. It is foolish for it to behave like a bankrupt monarch whose credit is so low that he can hardly borrow, who has little or no power over the scarce metal that is used for money within his realm, and who must perforce limit his private spending to the taxes that his parliament or his rudimentary fiscal machinery permits him to collect. Since the modern state can obtain the money needed for state purposes by borrowing it or by printing it, the modern state can decide to tax or not to tax according to which has the better effect on the body politic. Policy can be directed in accordance with the *effects* of taxing, which are undoubtedly to decrease the money in the hands of the taxpayer and to permit him to spend less. The advisability of taxation depends only upon whether this reduction in income or wealth and the consequent reduction in spending is socially desirable.

Similarly with the national debt. In spite of newspaper editorials, it is being recognized more and more generally that a nation does not get poorer any more than it gets richer when the internally owned national debt increases. All that happens is that the citizens as members of the state owe more to themselves (*i.e.,* to each other) as holders of government stock. While a debt by one nation to other nations or to the citizens of other nations is a burden comparable to the debt of a man to other men, the debt of a nation to its own citizens is not comparable in this way and is not a "burden" on the nation in the same way.

These arguments are simple to pose and difficult to argue against. They easily convince the unsophisticated and are accepted after a struggle by almost all economists who have not grown too old to change their habits of thought. Something more than ignorance, therefore, must be sought as an explanation of the general failure to apply them to practical government.

Nor does the resistance from vested interests seem to be strong enough to overcome the pressure of all who would gain from the maintenance of prosperity. Workers would be secure in their jobs and in the knowledge that other jobs are not difficult to get. Capitalists would be making profits on a scale that in the past has been experienced only in short periods of boom. This gain need not involve any man's loss, for it can all come out of the avoidance of waste from underemployment—waste that for the United States during the single decade 1930–1939 is estimated at over 500 billion dollars' worth of real goods and services that failed to be produced.

Apart from such specialists as bankruptcy lawyers, the only people who *might* lose by the maintenance of prosperity would be the insurance companies, the banks, and the endowed institutions who live on the pure interest from safe investments. These would find their incomes cut if maintaining prosperity necessitated a reduction in the rate of interest. The insurance companies and the banks, in so far as they do not make it up in the greater volume of business that goes with prosperity, would have to find other ways of making ends meet, such as investing in industry or charging higher premiums and service charges, but they are in a position to look after themselves. The endowed institutions—universities, research foundations, hospitals, and the like—might encounter difficulties if private gifts are not sufficiently increased as a result of general prosperity, but even a most generous compensation by the government to such institutions would be a negligible cost compared with the benefits of prosperity. There should be no strong resistance here.

*The main obstacles in the way of an economic steering wheel
are dogma (rightist and leftist) and timidity.*

There are ideological resistances which are to some extent
bound up with the dead weight of tradition. These are less sus-
ceptible to change through enlightenment because they are based
on dogma rather than on mere inertia. There is a dogma of the
right and a dogma of the left.

The dogma of the right says that it is improper for the government to go into business or to interfere with business. It is all but
blind to the concept of business activity as a way in which the
needs of society come to be provided. It looks upon a business
simply as a privately owned source of income—a "racket" to which
the businessman is entitled by virtue of discovery or conquest.
Usually this is covered up by some rationalization, but there can
be no other explanation of the idea that it is unfair for the government to compete with business even in cases where it is shown
that the consumer would benefit. The consumer is not the person
considered when it is a question of somebody "muscling in" on
one's racket.

It is possible for the government to regulate prosperity without
competing with anybody besides the banks, and it is even possible
to compensate the banks for any loss without making any appreci-
able inroads into the benefits of prosperity. But the principle of
having the government regulate the level of business activity is
bad for the morale of the captains of industry, who could no
longer be regarded by themselves or by others as the source of all
blessings of our age of progress. Furthermore, any interference by
the government is a dangerous precedent. It might lead to other
actions being demanded of it in the general interest, some of
which definitely would conflict with the private interests of mo-
nopolists and others. This seems to be the reason why the ideological champions of the extreme right have denounced as bol-
shevism the first hesitating (not to say wobbly) steps of the New

Deal in the direction of maintaining prosperity by governmental regulation of total spending.

The dogma of the left says that it is improper for private business to compete with the government. It is based upon a belief that only 100 per cent collectivism can solve the problems of society and that private enterprise for the sake of profit is not only unjust and exploitative but must inevitably bring with it the wastes, the disorganization, and the unemployment that has been associated with capitalism in the past. This seems to be the reason why the New Deal was in the beginning so foolishly labeled "fascistic" by many communists and socialists. There would seem to be little force behind either of these ideological oppositions in so far as businessmen prefer profits to principles, workers prefer employment to empty theories, and neither group is easily swayed by the professional interests of the organizers of communist parties or of associations of manufacturers.

All these resistances would be of little avail were it not for a weakness in the camp of the proponents of organized prosperity. A kind of timidity makes them shrink from saying anything that might shock the respectable upholders of traditional doctrine and tempts them to disguise the new doctrine so that it might be easily mistaken for the old. This does not help much, for they are soon found out, and it hinders them because, in endeavoring to make the new doctrine look harmless in the eyes of the upholders of tradition, they often damage their case. Thus instead of saying that the size of the national debt is of no great concern, it has been argued that the increase in the national income will permit the interest on the national debt to be raised without increasing taxes. Instead of saying that the budget may have to be unbalanced and that this is insignificant compared with the attainment of prosperity, it is proposed to disguise an unbalanced budget by having an elaborate system of annual, cyclical, capital, and special budgets as in Sweden.

But infinitely more depressing than these particular timidities, which weaken the forces working for the organization of prosperity, is a more general capitulation before the prejudices of the public. Many of the people to whom the theory of controls is explained will say, "I can see that you are right but most people will not be able to see it, so that there is no chance of anything being done." The number of people who take this attitude is most alarming. This is the attitude of the more intellectual members of the public. Equally discouraging is the attitude of less intellectual (or rather less self-confident) members of the public, who will say, "It seems all right to me, but I am not an expert and I suppose there is something wrong that I can't see." And in this way policy is stalled. The intellectuals are afraid to push the proposal because of unjustified contempt for the public (or perhaps because of subjective doubts as to their own superiority), and the public is afraid to accept arguments that they understand perfectly well because the "intellectuals" (for whom they have an unjustified reverence) have not come out for them.

With one important difference the situation is like that of the famous emperor in the story who was tricked by charlatans into parading before his people in his underwear. The charlatans claimed that the imaginary new clothes they had made for him were so fine that no one could feel them and so beautiful that no one who was foolish or dishonest or unfit for his office could see them. And so neither the emperor nor any of his courtiers or his people would admit that they saw no clothes until they were betrayed by an unintimidated child.

So it is with the problem of organizing prosperity. The scholars who understand it hesitate to speak out boldly for fear that the people will not understand. The people, who understand it quite easily, also fear to speak out while they wait for the scholars to speak out first. The difference between our present situation and that of the story is that it is not an emperor but the *people* who are periodically made to go naked and hungry and insecure and discontented—a ready prey to less timid organizers of discontent for the destruction of civilization.

CHAPTER 2

The Meaning of Full Employment

THE PRIMARY objective of the "steering wheel" of Chapter 1 is to prevent inflation and deflation. This is a rather negative formulation, but the same thing can be expressed positively. The objective, in positive terms, is *full employment*.

Full employment is difficult to define.

It is necessary first of all to guard against some common misinterpretations by pointing out some of the things that full employment does *not* mean.

In the first place it does not mean that everybody must work as many days in the year or as many hours in the day as he is able to work. Any number of people may refuse to work or refuse to do more than a certain amount of work at the current rates of pay, and we may still have full employment. It is not part of the objective to compel people to work if they prefer leisure.

In the second place, full employment does not even mean that everybody is working who wants to work at the current rates of pay, even if he is reasonably efficient in his work and even if he is available at a place where such work is being done.

Full employment means only that those who *want* to work at the prevailing rates of pay are able to find work without undue difficulty.

This is not very satisfactory. What is "undue" difficulty? The word "undue" looks as if it is inserted because of its vagueness—to permit the economist to squirm out of any difficult situation. But the vagueness cannot honestly be avoided. It is in the nature of our problem, and any attempts to provide greater precision

17

than is to be found in the subject matter dealt with can only turn out to be illusory and disappointing.

This may seem rather paradoxical. Why should we define full employment in a way which permits the term to be used to describe a situation in which millions of people are looking for jobs and do not have them? These people will certainly regard themselves as unemployed and will think, it very strange for economists to say that the economy is enjoying full employment.

Deflationary unemployment must be distinguished from frictional unemployment.

The explanation is that economists have to distinguish between the unemployment which exists because there are not enough jobs available in the economy as a whole and the unemployment which exists because the unemployed men and the unfilled jobs do not fit each other—their special qualifications, skills, and locations do not match. This includes those workers who at any time are on their way from one job to another.

The unemployment which results from a general insufficiency of jobs may be called "deflationary unemployment," and the unemployment due to workers having the wrong skills or being located in the wrong places to get jobs is called "frictional unemployment." The frictional unemployment is the unemployment which exists when there is "full employment."

The distinction between deflationary and frictional unemployment may seem pedantic to the unemployed person. He does not see how he is helped by being told that his unemployment is not deflationary but frictional.[1] But the distinction must be made

[1] In the economic literature on the subject, deflationary unemployment is often called "involuntary unemployment." The use of this term is likely to make "frictionally" unemployed workers even more bitter, for they will insist, and quite rightly, that from their personal point of view their unemployment is by no means voluntary. If it were, it would not be called unemployment at all but a holiday or simply the enjoyment of leisure.

because the two different kinds of unemployment call for quite different kinds of treatment. The solution for deflationary unemployment lies in measures for increasing the total spending on goods and services in the economy. This is because deflationary unemployment is caused by too small a demand for workers. The demand for workers is too small because there is not enough spending on goods and services in general. Deflationary unemployment and its treatment are the subject of the parable of the steering wheel.

Frictional unemployment, on the other hand, is due to difficulties in getting workers and jobs together and must be dealt with by special devices for overcoming the particular frictions that are in the way. The relationship can be seen if we consider how the application of measures for increasing the total of money spending can eliminate all the deflationary unemployment and leave a great deal of remaining unemployment. This remaining unemployment is what we must call frictional unemployment.[2]

If we start from a very severe depression, with a general insufficiency of spending and with severe unemployment, both deflationary and frictional, throughout the whole economy in every region and in every branch of economic activity, the measures needed are such as will increase the over-all money expenditure on goods and services of all kinds. Such measures increase the number of available jobs, and since there are workers available in all parts of the economy, the newly available jobs are filled and the number of unemployed is reduced.

As this process continues, the newly created job opportunities are not quite so easy to fill. They call for workers of special skills in special localities and it is more and more difficult to find them. We begin to find jobs looking for men as well as men looking for jobs.

As long as the number of men looking for jobs is greater than

[2] In Chap. 13 below and further on in the book, an important distinction will be made between unemployment due to economic frictions and unemployment due to technical frictions.

the number of jobs looking for men, it is still possible to increase the volume of employment (and reduce the number of unemployed) by continuing to increase total spending and the number of vacancies. Some of the vacancies are filled, and to that extent employment is increased. But as the process continues, more and more vacancies must be created for each job actually found, since many vacancies remain unfilled. Finally a situation is reached in which an increase in spending does not do any good at all. It does not increase the number of jobs actually found and does not reduce any further the number of unemployed. The remaining unemployed—they may still be a very large number—will then be those suffering from frictional unemployment.

Frictional unemployment is compatible with inflation.

But a very serious trouble emerges long before the increasing spending completely loses its efficacy in reducing unemployment. As the number of jobs looking for men increases and the number of men looking for jobs decreases, we reach a more and more inflationary situation. Employers compete with each other more and more keenly for the scarce labor supply in many parts of the economy. They offer to pay higher wages or agree to demands for higher wages, because they are able to raise the prices of the products sufficiently to cover the increased cost (and perhaps even a little extra). This raises the cost of living, and workers demand further wage increases to meet the increased cost of living or perhaps simply because they are in a strong bargaining position. Employers agree to the increases because prices are rising together with wages in a cumulative inflation.

We have seen that severe widespread unemployment can be reduced by measures which work through a simple increase in spending. But if this remedy is pressed beyond a certain point, the increased spending comes up against frictions, and instead of increasing employment it increases wages and prices in an inflationary spiral.

The recognition that the remaining, frictional, unemployment constitutes a different kind of problem from deflationary unemployment has led to the suggestion that full employment be defined as the situation in which there are as many jobs looking for men as there are men looking for jobs. But this will not do. We would have two opposite evils, the evil of men not being able to find jobs and the evil of employers not being able to find men to do jobs which need to be done. The two evils do not add up to a good thing. They do not even cancel each other out. There is therefore no special merit in having them exactly equal. It does not give us what we are after.

Men without jobs is worse than jobs without men.

At the point where the number of jobs looking for men is equal to the number of men looking for jobs, any increase in spending makes the number of vacancies greater than the number of unemployed. The increased spending creates a certain number of opportunities for employment, not all of which are filled. The number of vacancies is therefore increased while the number of unemployed is decreased. The equality is upset, but the new situation nevertheless shows a definite improvement. It is an improvement to have employment increased even if this makes the number of vacancies greater than the number of unemployed. Failing to fill a vacancy is much less serious than failing to find a job, because it means merely the loss of an apparent opportunity for some extra profit.

Furthermore, the profit opportunity which appears to be lost is not even a *real* opportunity from the point of view of society. It rests on the error of supposing the economy to have more productive resources than are really available. That there is no man available for the job means that it is not really possible for the production to be undertaken which would have yielded the imagined profit. Only if a man were taken away from some other activity would he be made available. But the fact that the alternative occupation keeps the man is prima-facie evidence that he would be missed even more in this alternative occupation than in the one in the mind of our potential employer. There would be a loss rather than a gain from the point of view of society if he were to be moved from his actual occupation to the unfilled job.

On the other hand, the failure to find a job involves one of the most serious of human frustrations—a man is deprived of the opportunity of earning his own living and of finding a meaningful place for himself in society. It is therefore a great improvement to enable an unemployed man to find work, even if it means having more jobs looking for men than men looking for jobs.[3]

[3] There is a position, somewhere between the extremes of inflation and depression, at which the *sum* of the two evils—unemployed men and unfilled jobs—is at a minimum. At this point there is equality not between the *size* of the two items but between their *sensitivity* to a change in the money demand for goods and services.

In depressions the job opportunities created by an increase in spending are filled very quickly, so that the decrease in the number of unemployed is greater than the increase in the number of vacancies. The sum of the two numbers is *diminished* by an increase in spending. In inflationary situations the opposite is the case. The new vacancies created by an increase in spending are very difficult to fill, so that the increase in vacancies is greater than the decrease in unemployed. The sum of the two numbers is increased by an increase in spending. Somewhere between the two extreme situations an increase in spending increases vacancies just as much as it reduces unemployment. At this point the sum of the two numbers is at a minimum.

It seems likely that those who would like to adopt as a standard the point at which unemployment *equals* vacancies are confusing that point between inflation and depression with this other intermediate point at which the *sum* of unemployment plus vacancies is minimized. But this more reasonable middle point is still not what we want. We do not want to minimize the *sum* of vacancies plus unemployed because it is a much more serious problem for a man not to be able to find a job than it is for an employer not to be able to fill a vacancy. (Unless, of course, the failure to fill a vacancy, by curtailing the supply of materials or of tools or of demand for the product, indirectly destroys the opportunity of many other men to find jobs. In this case the importance of the vacancy is derived from the indirect unemployment for which it is responsible.)

It does not follow from this that it is always desirable to increase spending as long as it increases employment—it does not follow that we need not be concerned at all about the increase in the number of unfilled vacancies. If we go too far in the direction of permitting unfilled vacancies to increase in order to decrease unemployment, we find that the scarcity of labor makes the bargaining power of workers too great. Any further increase in their scarcity enables them to obtain wage increases so widespread that there result a general increase in prices and a further increase in wages. A cumulative upward spiral of wages and prices is set in motion. We have inflation.

Full employment is where inflation begins.

We can now give more precision to the phrase "undue difficulty in finding employment." As long as it is possible, by increasing the total of money spending, to increase the number of jobs available without causing inflation, the difficulty of finding employment is not "undue." Some of the difficulty of finding jobs can in this way be removed, not only costlessly but with a clear and undoubted benefit to society. But when the number of unfilled vacancies is so great that an increase in the total money spending would result in inflation, the difficulty in finding employment is not so easily reduced and one can no longer say with such finality that difficulty in finding employment is "undue."

This means that full employment, where it is no longer "unduly" difficult to find employment, is that level of employment at which inflation begins. A full-employment policy is one which aims at that rate of total spending which brings about this level of employment. A lower level means unnecessary unemployment, which can be cured by an increased rate of spending. A higher level means inflation, with all its disagreeablenesses and with no certainty that it will increase the volume of employment. As long as any increase in money demand can increase employment without leading to a general inflationary spiral, we have not reached the full-employment level of spending.

Full employment is therefore that level of employment at which any further increase in spending would result in an inflationary spiral of wages and prices.

It may seem too obvious but it is nevertheless necessary to state that a full-employment policy does not *always* call for an increase in the rate of spending any more than a "full-pitcher policy" in a restaurant would call for always pouring more water into the pitcher. Just as a pitcher which is already full does not get any fuller if still more water is poured into it, so obviously if there is already full employment, the level of employment is not raised by any further increase in the general rate of spending. An increase in spending merely spills over in the increased prices and increased money wages of inflation. This remark may seem uncalled for. It is, however, not unnecessary. Some of the most frequently heard arguments against a full-employment policy seem to be based squarely on the unfounded belief that such a policy calls for a perpetual increase of the rate of spending no matter what the circumstances.

Frictional unemployment can be decreased by increasing labor mobility.

There still seems to be something profoundly unsatisfactory about our definition of full employment. There may be millions of people who are unable to find work and who would not be very much comforted by being told that full employment has been reached and that their own unemployment is "only frictional." They may be out of work because there is no longer a sufficient demand for their particular skills. There may be a shortage of the raw materials they must use in their work, due to a scarcity of the kind of labor which makes them. There may be similar shortages in the supply of other products without which their product cannot be used. They may be in seasonal trades or in industries in which a system of casual employment is responsible for their plight. They may not be aware of existing opportunities for employment in other places where there is a scarcity of their particular skills, or they may know of them but not have the means of going there. Or opportunities for employment in fields somewhat different from their own may be blocked for them by discriminations in employment or by restrictions which those in the field organize against the entry of others.

These are only a few of the thousands of particular reasons why a particular person or group of persons may be unable to find work. Yet they cannot be helped by any general increase in spending. That would merely cause inflation. In all such cases the remedy is to be found in dealing with the particular situation—providing information as to the availability of employment opportunities, providing financial help to enable people to seek employment a little farther from home, helping people to retrain themselves when their skills become obsolete, removing discriminations and restrictions of entry to particular occupations, improving the hiring practices of industries employing casual labor, encouraging employers to increase the regularity and continuity of the employment they offer, coordinating seasonal industries so that different products can be made by the same men in different seasons, or diminishing seasonality in other ways.

Increased mobility raises the level of full employment.

All such improvements in the functioning of the economy in particular situations are ways not of moving toward full employment, but of *raising the full-employment level itself.* Every one of these particular improvements converts some frictional unemployment into deflationary unemployment. It permits a greater level of employment to be attained before the inflationary point is reached. The full-employment level comes to mean a greater level of actual employment. There is less residual *frictional* unemployment. The increase in the mobility of labor (which is what all these improvements basically amount to) makes it possible for an increase in total spending to enable some of the unemployed men to fill some of the vacancies for which they were previously unsuitable or unavailable.

The relevant difference between increasing employment by increasing spending (which is the way to move from depression to full employment) and permitting employment to be increased by increasing the mobility of labor (which is the way to raise the full-employment level itself) is in the different effects on the relation between unemployed men and unfilled jobs. Whenever employment is increased by simply increasing the rate of spending, the number of jobs looking for men is increased at the same time as the number of men looking for jobs is reduced. Vacancies increase in relation to unemployment and the bargaining power of workers is increased. When the bargaining power reaches the critical level beyond which it would bring about inflation, we have full employment and cannot increase employment any more by simply increasing the rate of spending.

But when an increase in employment is made possible by increasing the mobility of labor, there is no change in the relationship between vacancies and unemployment. The jobs looking for men and the men looking for jobs are brought face to face with each other so that it merely requires some additional spending for the men to fill the vacancies. There will then be fewer vacancies and fewer unemployed than before and no change in the bargaining power of labor. Making it possible for workers and employers to get together does not increase the bargaining power of the workers any more than it increases the bargaining power of the employers. This is why it permits an increase in spending to raise the volume of employment instead of causing inflation, even if there is already full employment. If achieving full employment (by raising the rate of total spending) is like filling a vessel with water, improving the mobility of labor is like increasing the size of the vessel so as to permit more water to be poured into it.

No matter how hard we try to increase the mobility of labor by as many special devices as there are special situations and special resistances to overcome in different parts of the economy, we shall never make labor *perfectly* mobile. Full employment will always leave substantial numbers of people unable to find work immediately. But we can increase the level of money demand so as to reach full employment and we can increase the mobility of labor so as to minimize the remaining frictional unemployment.

Achieving full employment is prior to diminishing frictional unemployment.

In this book we shall primarily be concerned with the first of these two tasks. We shall be more concerned with the task of achieving full employment by bringing about the proper level of money demand than with the task of raising the level of full employment by measures for increasing the mobility of labor. This emphasis can be justified by the fact that more unemployment can be prevented by working on monetary demand than by increasing the mobility of labor. It can also be justified by the fact that the hindrances to the mobility of labor are of so many different forms in different situations that special measures can be recommended only after careful study of the nature of the particular resistances and not very much can be said of a general nature. But the chief justification for our concentration on the achievement of full employment rather than on devices for raising the full-employment level itself lies in the logical priority of achieving full employment. Only if full employment is achieved and money demand is adequate can the various measures for increasing the mobility of labor be of much use.

Perhaps this can be put more strongly still. We have been considering the possibility of raising the level of full employment by reducing the immobility of labor and spoke of such an increase in mobility permitting an increase in employment. This must not be understood to mean that an increase in mobility can increase employment by itself without any help from an increase in total spending. Increased spending and increased mobility are not al-

ternative means for increasing employment. Without an increase
in spending, an increase in mobility would raise the level of
full employment without raising the level of *actual* employment.
It would merely change some of the frictional unemployment
into deflationary unemployment, thereby enabling an increase in
spending to increase employment instead of causing inflation.

Of course if there is more than enough spending to reach full
employment, so that there is some inflationary pressure, an increase in mobility will increase employment without calling for
any further increase in total spending. By raising the level of
full employment it enables the excessive spending to achieve a
higher level of actual employment. But here, too, the increase in
employment depends on the existence of excessive spending which,
without the increase in mobility, would have caused some inflation. Except in an inflationary situation an increase in mobility
cannot increase the level of employment unless it is accompanied
by an increase in total spending. And if there is less than full
employment the increase in total spending would bring about
the increase in employment without the increase in mobility.
It is only when the economy is just at the level of full employment that the level of full employment has to be raised, by an
increase in mobility, if an increase in spending is to result in an
increase in employment rather than in inflation. Only if the
pitcher is quite full does it have to be enlarged to enable more
water to be poured into it.

Indeed this recognition of the futility of rushing about to find
jobs which do not exist or are not easy to find is one of the chief
reasons for one of the most important frictions—the general immobility of labor. Workers are reluctant to leave the little security
they enjoy in being with friends and relatives. They are naturally
and reasonably afraid of going to strange places where their tiny
savings may be exhausted before they find work. Immobility is
itself due in a large measure to the failure to achieve full employment and would be greatly diminished if full employment
made movement less risky.

What is perhaps even more important is that in the absence of full employment the breaking down of barriers to movement can have the effect only of permitting newcomers to displace some of those who are already in the field. In such circumstances it is understandable that those workers who are first in a field will do all in their power to keep the scarce jobs for themselves and will fiercely resist any attempt to remove the protective restrictions. Even though full employment is not enough by itself and should be supplemented by all possible measures for increasing the mobility of labor, thereby raising the full-employment level (and the efficiency of the economy in general), the achievement of full employment is the first objective.

Later in this book (Chapters 13 to 16), more detailed attention will be given to techniques for raising the full-employment level itself.

Summary.

Full employment is defined as the condition where those who want to work at the prevailing rates of pay can find work without undue difficulty. The vagueness of "undue difficulty" lies in the nature of the phenomenon and in the possibility of moving the line which demarks *deflationary unemployment,* which is absent when there is full employment, and *frictional unemployment,* which is compatible with full employment. The two different kinds of unemployment call for quite different forms of treatment. Deflationary unemployment can be removed by making the total spending on goods and services in the economy adequate. Frictional unemployment cannot be removed but some of it can be transformed into deflationary unemployment by lessening the frictions that prevent unemployed workers from getting together with unfilled vacancies.

If spending is increased, employment is increased too, but long before all unemployment has disappeared scarcities of particular kinds of workers result in an increase in the number of jobs looking for men in relation to the number of men looking for jobs, and this results in increasing inflationary pressure. There is no particular interest in making the number of vacancies equal to the number of unemployed or even in minimizing the sum of the unemployed and the vacancies. This is because an unemployed man is an infinitely more objectionable social phenomenon than an unfilled vacancy. But once full employment has been reached, attempts to increase employment by increasing total spending lead to inflation rather than to increased employment. "Undue difficulty" is therefore defined so that full employment is reached at the level where inflation begins.

Employment can be increased above this level only by reducing the frictional unemployment and thereby raising the level of full employment itself. Removing frictions permits some of the unemployed men to get together with some of the unfilled jobs, so that an increase in total spending can increase employment without strengthening the bargaining power of workers any more than that of employers.

Achieving full employment by arranging for an adequate total flow of spending is prior to measures for raising the level of full employment by increasing the mobility of labor, because in the absence of the provision of the total flow of spending which is necessary for reaching full employment, measures to raise the potential level of full employment by removing frictions are fruitless and would be resisted by those whose jobs are protected by the frictions from competition.

Techniques for raising the achievable level of full employment will be discussed later in the book.

CHAPTER 3

The Importance of Full Employment

THE MOST obvious benefit from full employment is the addition to the goods and services which we can enjoy by having prosperity instead of depression. This benefit is so great that we are inclined at first to be surprised by its magnitude and then to suppose that it must be the most important reason for having a full-employment policy. In the depression of the 1930's we lost about 500 billion dollars' worth of goods and services which we failed to produce but could have produced if we had had full employment. Some recent estimates make the loss as high as 1,000 billion dollars while some earlier and extremely conservative ones go as low as 200 billion.

The economic gains from full employment are enormous.

The wide range in these estimates results from a change which took place during the war in our idea of what it is possible for the economy to produce if it is working at full capacity. Before the war (and its preparatory armament activities), our national income was running at between 50 and 80 billion dollars per annum, and those who spoke of the possibility of producing 100 billion dollars per annum were often regarded as irresponsible, optimistic dreamers. The war showed that we could produce more than twice the 1935–1939 average and that the optimistic dreamers had been far too conservative.

One reason why economists underestimated the potential output of full employment was that they figured this from the number of people actually out of work. Insufficient attention was given to potentialities of increased output by people who were engaged

31

in relatively wasteful occupations but could be shifted to more productive occupation when there is a need for the product.

In full employment workers are not tempted to go slow for fear of working themselves out of a job. More effective use is made of equipment which otherwise would be idle a large part of the time. Much of the unemployment in depression is the "disguised unemployment" of people who stay on the payroll but who are not really pulling their full weight. It is the elimination of these wastes that brings about much of the great increase in output that comes with full employment.

Another contributing factor to the great increase in output in full employment is the greater efficiency in the use of resources that flows from the increase in the mobility of the factors of production. Because of the greater security of finding jobs in the new position as well as because many restrictions are relaxed when workers are scarce, factors move more easily from where they are less productive to where they can be more productive.

For our purpose we do not have to go into the problems connected with getting an exact measure of the loss from having a depression. We need not examine the difficulties of measurement connected with such things as changing price levels or the relative productivity of the employed and the unemployed. We are interested here only in getting a rough idea of the gain that would have accrued from having full employment. There is no doubt that it comes to a very large amount, of the same order of magnitude as the cost to the United States of World War II.

Even if the loss during the depression should come to no more than the amount of the present American national debt, it represents something infinitely more important. The national debt, as we shall see in detail in a later chapter, does not constitute a national impoverishment such as would be represented by the goods that the money measure of the national debt would be able to buy. But the loss from not having had full employment in the 1930's can legitimately be expressed in real terms. Real houses and automobiles and food and clothes—$6,000 worth at the least

for every American family—could have been produced in the depression years as a net addition to the useful goods and services
that actually were produced.

Full employment yields individual economic security.

The tremendous gain in potential goods and services is far
from being the most important of the benefits that would have
been derived from a full-employment policy. The higher real incomes of full employment may indeed not add very much to the
real welfare of the people. The benefits may all be absorbed in
the creation by advertising of greater needs so that people will
be no happier with the larger real incomes than with the smaller
real incomes (although it is difficult to imagine that this is true
for people really suffering from want of basic necessities in the
depths of a depression).

What cannot be destroyed by such an artificial increase of
wants is the feeling of individual security which would accompany
full employment. The knowledge that one is able to keep his
present job, or find another one easily if it should be lost, creates
an improvement in one's state of mind—involves a relief from
anxiety—that is much more important than the increase in real
income of goods and services. A similar security will be felt
by businessmen and investors, who will not have to worry about
the possibility of their plans being spoiled by a general business
depression. They will be able to concentrate on such causes of
loss or failure as are due to their own inadequacies or to particular misfortunes, and this concentration will further increase the
over-all efficiency of the economy.

Security promotes progress.

One extremely important result of the confidence and security of the individual that full employment affords is its effect on
the smoothness of operation and the progress of our economy.

In a world of unemployment, with alternative jobs hard to find, men naturally seek security in tying up the jobs they have so that they cannot easily be fired. This substitution of job security for employment security is not only a source of particular in-efficiencies, in business and in government, but the basis for the growth of bureaucracy—another serious peril to our general effi-ciency and to our freedom.

The matter would not be helped by eliminating the formal tying up of jobs. Security of the job would then depend even more on not upsetting one's superior too much. Enterprise and initiative are very dangerous for the individual in search of security. It is better to do nothing except on proper authoriza-tion and then you are safe—you can produce a piece of paper as a comeback and pass the buck to someone else. But if jobs are easy to get, men of ability and initiative do not permit themselves to be tied down to such depressing conditions, and the resulting increase in enterprise and experiment greatly enriches our society.

Such a freeing of initiative and of progressive change is not limited to bureaucratic organizations but spreads throughout the economy. One of the greatest inhibitors of progress is the recogni-tion that some people will be displaced, and those who would suffer from the change are often able to mobilize sufficient sym-pathy to prevent the improvement from taking place. The best remedy is, of course, to give adequate compensation to those who suffer from something done in the general interest. If the change is really worth while there must remain some benefit even after full and generous compensation has been paid. But frequently the machinery for making the compensation is too elaborate to be practicable, and more often still there are other difficulties, political or technical, in the way of arranging such compensation. The change is still in the social interest and should be undertaken even if it means that there will be a different constellation of privileges, no more objectionable in general than the old constel-lation. But such a change is often prevented by reluctance to impose severe and undeserved hardships. If there are full employment and a state of business prosperity, nobody need be made to suffer too much, and so this obstacle to progress is considerably diminished. Those who are unlucky are not destroyed—they have another chance and the game can go on.

Full employment contributes to human dignity.

Even the security of the individual is less important than yet another psychological benefit that each individual would obtain. This is the feeling that he is a significant and useful member of society—that there is a place for him where he is needed. During the depression of the 1930's most of the unemployed in the United States were fed and housed better than full-time workers in many other countries, but the stigma of charity or relief resulted in their being psychologically much worse off and much unhappier than persons with far lower standards working hard in other parts of the world. More important than the material gains and the security is the feeling of significance in the social setting.

There will be other benefits for individuals. When workers are hard to get, the conditions under which they work will be improved. Employers competing for workers will apply to this part of their activity some of the ingenuity and resourcefulness which in the past has been entirely employed in serving the whims of the customer. In the war and in the immediate postwar prosperity we came across the strange sight of employers, in their attempts to get workers, advertising the cleanliness and other attractive conditions of work. These first attempts are clumsy and inefficient and often applied in a spirit of resentfulness. Employers are so conditioned that they believe it only right, or at least inevitable, for them to have to apply themselves to meeting the desires of customers, but they consider it strange, and sometimes even outrageous, to have to be concerned in a similar way for the well-being and even for the secondary preferences of their employees. Continued full employment would get employers accustomed to having to please their workers and would increase their efficiency in discovering the things that really matter to the workers and in actually bringing them about. Ultimately it will become clear to all that the time spent by workers at their work and the strains and pains and the happinesses of work constitute a most important part of the lives of the great majority of the population. It will cease to seem strange for the welfare of its workers to be considered one of the most important, if not actually the most important, of any factory's products.

At the same time, or rather as the most significant element in this improvement of conditions, there will develop an attitude of respect of the foreman or employer for the worker. The dignity of the worker as a human being will be more often and more generally recognized, for if any worker is not treated decently he can go away somewhere else. The worker's greatest protection is his power to go somewhere else, but only if it is a real power based on the existence of satisfactory alternative jobs and not a mere legal right rendered worthless by a condition of unemployment which makes alternative jobs doubtful or difficult to find. The power to go somewhere else will do more to improve conditions of work than any amount of legislation of conditions or of participation of workers' representatives in factory management, useful as these might be for many purposes.

Full employment weakens nonfunctional discrimination.

Full employment would serve to enhance the dignity of the worker by weakening and ultimately eliminating discrimination along nonfunctional lines such as race, creed, and color. With workers hard to get, employers will not be able to indulge their own prejudices or reflect other people's prejudices in hiring workers. Competition will force them to be liberal, as indeed it did to some extent during the war.

Perhaps more important than simple prejudices in fostering racial, religious, and other nonfunctional discriminations in hiring workers is the economic interest of a group of workers in protecting their scarce jobs against competition from outside. With full employment, the scarcity of jobs being eliminated, there is no longer the economic drive for such protective utilization of these discriminations.

Full employment further raises the dignity of the individual by indirectly improving the distribution of income and wealth. By weakening restrictions of all kinds it does much to remove the inequality between pay in different occupations. It helps more than any direct legislation to remove the evils of sweated trades and by making enterprise easier diminishes the inequalities between the incomes of businessmen and those of managers and other employees.

Full employment is essential to protect democratic society against fascism and communism.

But even these benefits for the dignity and the welfare of the individual are not the most important gain to be obtained from a full-employment policy. For it is not only the security of the individual that is destroyed by unemployment. At the present moment in history the security of our whole social order and of those freedoms which remain to the individual even in depression are in serious danger. The democratic society developed in the last two hundred years was almost destroyed by the rise of fascism. We were successful in one war against fascism, but we may not be so lucky if the same thing happens again.

An essential ingredient for the rise of fascism is the failure of capitalist society to provide full employment. Hundreds of reasons have been given for the rise of fascism in Germany, and there is probably some truth behind most of them, but there can be no doubt that severe and prolonged unemployment was a necessary condition without which fascism could not have conquered Germany and then almost conquered the rest of the world. Fascism was able to grow only because there were millions of men and women who saw no place of significance and dignity for themselves in the existing order and were thus more easily persuaded by the Nazis that they had nothing to lose by a new order. Great as is our attachment to freedom and democracy, their importance fades for people who are continually harassed by the anxieties and the humiliations of economic insecurity. Full employment is a necessary condition for the safeguarding of our democratic way of life.

Some of the critics of capitalism, seeking a society with a greater freedom, a deeper democracy, and a more consuming concern for the dignity of the individual, see in the failure of capitalism to provide full employment not only a reason for trying to change the state of affairs but also a means for engineering the necessary change. The Marxists frequently speak as if an inevitably increasing severity of capitalist depressions will be the key to a better society. Increasingly severe depressions are supposed to be scheduled to bring about the proletarian revolution and the establishment of a better society based on the brotherhood of man. The believers in such a program for world history tend to be extremely suspicious of any plans to prevent or even alleviate severe unemployment. Such plans would remove a fundamental force that is cast for the role of moving the world into their utopia. They are therefore to be found together with the most die-hard of reactionaries in opposition to schemes for dealing with the problem of unemployment. They are strongly opposed to "making capitalism work" and are more concerned about their "escalator" to the better society being destroyed by full employment than is consistent with their dogma that it is impossible to achieve full employment under capitalism.

Liberal reformers, progressive democrats, and non-Marxian socialists (like those in the British Labor party), on the other hand, have no patience with doctrines about the revolution and the thereafter but prefer to concentrate on practical measures whose effects can be seen and tested in the here and now. They are very much concerned with policies which would succeed in providing employment and prosperity even if they should incidentally be helping capitalism by making it more satisfactory to workers.

Until recently it was possible to believe that these two groups— revolutionary Marxists on the one hand and democratic reformers on the other—represented two alternative approaches to the improvement of our society. But the experience of fascism and of the development of the Russian "proletarian revolution" into a totalitarian slave state have made it impossible to maintain a scholarly neutrality between two such methods. A policy of letting things grow worse so that they may then grow better, apart from the immorality of the preventable human suffering that it deliberately accepts, would almost certainly put the reins of the future not in the hands of the utopian revolutionists but rather into the hands of unscrupulous fascists, as happened in Italy and Germany. And even if power should be seized by the minority which professed belief in a "dictatorship of the proletariat" whose "destiny" it was to widen the field of human freedom and dignity, its first consideration would be to consolidate its power against the majority without.

It is vain, and at this hour in history supremely foolish, to suppose that in a democracy liberty can be spread by a party which has to resort to revolution by a minority because it is unable to convince the majority. Such a minority will have to apply more and more force to maintain itself in power against the majority. The result is a progressive limiting and destruction of human freedom and dignity such as happened in Russia. Whichever the course of events, a failure to apply a full-employment policy in the existing "capitalist" society will lead to one form of fascism or another.

Full employment may prevent war.

Fascism is not the most immediate and pressing of the dangers from which our full-employment policy can deliver us. Since the end of the war it has become clear that behind all the talk of peace and of the United Nations, the significant development has been the squaring off of the two remaining great powers of the world, America and Russia, in preparation for a possible third world war. This war is not inevitable, but the greatest influence working for its probability is the Russian dogma that it *is* inevitable. The Russian dogma says that capitalist countries cannot maintain prosperity, that inevitably they will fall into economic crises and depressions, that however well-intentioned may be the present leaders of capitalist states, the inevitable depression will bring fascists into power, and that these fascists will then lead their countries in a holy crusade against the Russian communist fatherland. The Russian dogma that such a course of development is inevitable forces them to prepare for this eventuality and to resist any attempts at organizing world peace. It forces them to interpret every proposal for preventing the war as a trick devised only for the purpose of lulling their suspicions and weakening their preparedness. The preparedness of the Russians forces the Americans to be prepared, and with both sides prepared, what they are preparing for becomes almost inevitable. The only escape from this conflict lies in persuading the Russians that the United States can and will maintain prosperity and thus prevent the rise of fascism. Only by the actual demonstration of such permanent prosperity through a full-employment policy can we hope to convince the Russians of the falseness of their dogma and to avoid the catastrophe of a third world war.

This list of the benefits from full employment is so impressive that many others of considerable importance must be omitted because they would seem picayunish in comparison with these essential conditions for survival. Indeed the blessings of full employment might even seem to be embarrassing in their plenitude and their importance. But their ubiquity will cease to embarrass us if we consider unemployment as a serious organic disturbance which would naturally have innumerable repercussions in our extremely complex society. Each one of these repercussions would be a symptom of the same basic illness, and nearly all of them would be socially harmful.

If we had been living in a world of full employment and were then transplanted to a world of unemployment, we would look for the symptoms of the malady and would not be in the least surprised to find them all over the place. But because we start with the world of unemployment and consider what would be the symptoms of the *absence* of the disease, the process of cataloguing the qualities of health looks suspiciously like an undiscriminating list of everything desirable.

Full employment revives the spirit of liberalism.

Any remaining surprise at the constellation of benefits from full employment will be relaxed when it is realized that the state of healthy full employment is nothing else than the kind of society that the liberal thinkers of the eighteenth and nineteenth centuries had in mind. Their great mistake was to assume the existence of an automatic tendency toward full employment and no need for a full-employment *policy*. Because of this mistake they were unable to persuade the nations to accept free trade. Because of this mistake the freedom of the individual, undermined by economic insecurity, was subjected to the perils that have so nearly wrecked our free society and that may yet succeed in wrecking it if we do not soon remedy the great defect. All the benefits we have considered and innumerable others that can be discovered are no new dreams. They are the same lines in the development of a free society which were seen by the great prophets of liberalism and which, from a slightly different angle, were glimpsed anew by the prophets of democratic socialism. To raise these prophecies from the dust we need only be sure that the missing foundation of full employment is there to provide the economic basis on which alone the other virtues of a free society can stand.

The arrival of the atom bomb has complicated this picture somewhat and may have taken away the time necessary for a long-term demonstration of the possibility of permanent prosperity under capitalism. Atomic preparedness may result in a preventive war breaking out before such a demonstration can be made. There is also the possibility, as many people believe, that it is not merely suspicion which is responsible for the Russian sabotaging of the peace but an ambitious determination to spread the Russian empire over the whole planet—an ambition disguised as a crusade for the dictatorship of the proletariat in the name of a religion which finds adherents throughout the world.

It may be that atomic preparedness or Russian imperialism will yet bring about a third world war even if we do have a full-employment policy. Other and more dangerous action may be necessary in attempts to prevent the destruction of civilization by nuclear energy. But as long as it is not certain that atomic preparedness or Russian imperialism will bring the catastrophe, there is still a chance that it will be prevented, and for that chance a full-employment policy is essential. The chance that it may prevent the atomic war is still the most important of all the reasons for having a full-employment policy.[1]

Summary.

The first visible benefit from full employment is the purely economic gain of the goods that the unemployed could produce if put to work. This includes the benefits from the elimination of the "disguised unemployment" of those who, while employed, are not properly utilized in a depression and the benefits from the more efficient use of productive resources because of the greater mobility of labor that full employment makes possible. Second, and more important, is the increase in each worker's economic security from knowing that it is easy for him to leave his job and get another one, his freedom from the fear of being thrown into a mad competition for nonexistent jobs.

[1] Several paragraphs in this chapter have been adapted from my article "An Integrated Full Employment Policy," published in *International Postwar Problems,* January, 1946, and reprinted in *Planning and Paying for Full Employment,* Princeton University Press, 1947.

The individual's economic security is most important as a safeguard against oppression or exploitation. With the individual able to find other occupations, his employer will have to compete to keep him, and this will do more than anything else to improve the conditions of work. Then there is the value to the individual of knowing that he is needed and has a place in the economy. Nothing is more important for a man's self-respect and happiness. Full employment is in this way the greatest safeguard of the dignity and the feeling of worthiness of man.

Full employment indirectly reduces economic inequality and is indispensable as a safeguard of the democratic way of life against totalitarian adventurers. Finally, full employment is needed to demonstrate our possible peacefulness to the Russians so that they will not feel constrained to prepare for and thereby to make inevitable a third world war.

The extreme importance of full employment and the enormous number of ways in which it seems to be important might make one suspicious. But the suspicion disappears if we consider these benefits as the manifold symptoms of social health restored by the removal of a basic malady. The benefits are the same as those envisaged by the old prophets of liberalism and of socialism.

Part II
The Solution

CHAPTER 4[1]

Employment and Spending

THE BASIC principle of the theory of employment is simple. A worker can find work if an employer decides to employ him, and the employer will decide to do so only if he is able to sell the worker's product for a sufficiently high price.

The question: "How high is enough?" raises many problems which we must leave until later. All we need consider here is that in any situation there is some price of the product, related in some way to the costs of production, which is just enough to make the employer decide to employ a worker to make the product. This is the "adequate" price.

How many workers the employer will employ depends on how much of the product he decides to have produced, and this depends on how much of it he can sell (at an adequate price, of course). If more can be sold, more will be produced and more workers will be employed in making it. If less can be sold, less will be produced and fewer workers will be employed.

[1] The first four chapters of this part (Chaps. 4 to 7) are somewhat more difficult to read than the rest of the book. Geometrical figures and diagrams are kept to the appendixes to these chapters and those who do not find diagrams helpful can merely disregard the references to the appendixes. The algebra in the text can be followed by anyone who can add, subtract, multiply, and divide small numbers and who realizes that a letter can stand for a number which we are in the process of figuring out. It is possible to skip this algebra without missing any of the argument in these chapters. The only purpose of this algebra is to make the text easier to follow. Readers who are allergic to algebra are hindered rather than helped and should skip it. Readers who still find these chapters difficult can skip them altogether and go on to read Chap. 8 on "Functional Finance" at this point. They will not be hindered by this in following the rest of the book (except for Chap. 17).

The volume of employment depends on the rate of spending.

How much can be sold depends on how much money the customers are spending in buying it. Many considerations influence their eagerness to buy any particular product—the state of fashion, the prices and availability of all the other products that might be bought instead, the prices and availability of all the items that are ordinarily used in conjunction with the product in question, and so on almost ad infinitum.

But since we are concerned with employment not in some particular industry but in the economy as a whole, we do not have to go into all these complications. The amount sold in the economy as a whole, and hence employment in the economy as a whole, depends not on the amount of money spent in buying one product rather than another, but on the amount of money spent altogether on all currently produced goods and services. For our purpose it does not matter very much if consumers give up buying one thing in order to buy something else instead. This may be devastating for the employment in the manufacture of the item given up, but since employment will increase in the manufacture of the newly fashionable item, total employment need not change at all.

The general or over-all level of employment thus depends on the total rate at which money is being spent in buying all kinds of currently produced goods and services. A full-employment policy must therefore consist of measures for getting and keeping the proper rate of total money spending.

It is assumed here, for simplicity, that the spending, the paying, and (in the case of consumption expenditure) the consuming all take place at the same time. But really significant here, and throughout this argument, are the *purchases* (or from the other side the *sales*), even if some or all of the payment (or some or all of the consumption) should take place in some other period.

*Employment depends on spending in socialist as well as in
capitalist economies.*

The dependence of the volume of employment on how much of
the product can be sold at an adequate price is not peculiar to
capitalist society, as is sometimes suggested by sentimental socialists who think that this problem, together with almost every
other problem, would disappear if we stopped using a "profit
system." It is true that in a profit system the adequate price is
one which provides an adequate profit for the employer. Whenever the requisite profit is not forthcoming, the employer will
not want to produce the product or to employ the worker. In a
nonprofit socialist economy there would be no consideration of
profit. The worker would nevertheless still find that whether he
is employed depends on whether his product can be sold at an
adequate price.

In any reasonably efficient society of free men, capitalist or
socialist, the citizen must be free to spend his income according
to his own preferences. He must have a money income so that
he can go into a store with it and decide which things he wants
to buy and how much of them and which things he does not think
worth buying at the prevailing prices. Since the purpose of the
economy is to produce the goods and services that the citizen,
as a consumer, wants and not merely to make him consume the
goods that the producer happens to have produced, there must
be some way of letting the producer know what the consumer
wants and what he does not want. To do this is the function of
the prices that the goods which have already been produced can
fetch in the stores.

If some goods have been produced which the consumer does
not fancy, the shopkeeper will have to cut their price to get
rid of them. The low price then indicates to the manufacturer
just how low is their usefulness to the consumer. The cost of
producing an article (if properly reckoned) represents the value

and the usefulness of other things which can be made with the productive resources involved. A price below this cost is evidence that the product is valued less by the consumer than the alternative products. It is therefore an appropriate signal to the manufacturer to reduce output, in the social interest, so as to set free the resources to be used for something else that the consumer would prefer to have.

The rules for determining the adequate price in a socialist society may be quite different from those applicable to a capitalist society. There may be no whisper of a suspicion of anybody being concerned with seeking a profit. But as far as the worker is concerned he loses his job, exactly like the worker in the profit system, whenever his product cannot be sold for an adequate price.

In a socialist society, just as in a "profit system," the number of workers who can find employment in each industry depends on how much of the particular product can be sold at an adequate price. In the same way the total volume of employment in the economy depends on the total amount of money spent on currently produced goods and services of all kinds.

Socialists never worry about the volume of employment in a socialist society because they assume, if they ever think about it at all, that there will be some authority which will see to it that enough money is spent to permit enough goods and services to be sold at adequate prices, so that there will be work for all who want to work. This is a perfectly reasonable assumption for a socialist society, in which the authorities know that it is their responsibility to keep the economy running in good order. But just as the dependence of employment on sufficient spending is not limited to "profit systems," so the possibility of having an authority to see that enough money is spent is not limited to socialist economies. There is no reason whatsoever why there cannot be an authority doing exactly the same thing in a capitalist society or profit system.

We see, therefore, that the problems of employment are the

result not of a profit system particularly, but of any money-using system, irrespective of whether it permits, encourages, or prohibits the seeking of profits. Employment problems can arise in any money-using system simply because in any money-using system the rate of total spending can depart from the level required for full employment.

The flow of spending must not be confused with the stock of money.

Experience shows that it is necessary to stress the obvious fact that the flow of spending is not the same thing as the stock of money in existence in the economy and that the level of employment depends on the former and not on the latter. The level of employment depends on the *flow* of acts of *payment* involved in the spending, not on the *stock* or amount of *money* in existence.[2]

It also is necessary to declare emphatically and to repeat frequently that there does *not* have to be a dollar in existence for every dollar's worth of goods in existence or even for every dollar's worth of goods that is produced in the course of a year or any other arbitrarily chosen period of time. What matters is only the rate at which dollars are being spent—how much per annum or how much per week or per month.

This emphatic injunction not to confuse the flow of spending with the stock of money is necessary because the same rate of money spending can take place whether the stock of money in existence is larger or smaller, and greater or smaller flows of spending can take place without there being any change in the amount of money in existence. If the stock of money is 120 billion dollars while the flow of expenditure is 240 billion dollars a year, we say that the velocity of circulation of money is 2 per annum, meaning that each dollar in existence is used twice, on the average, in the course of a year. If the stock of money is 80 billion dollars we say that the velocity of circulation of money is 3 per annum

[2] See appendix to Chap. 4, sec. 1.

because each dollar is spent three times, on the average, in the course of a year.

Of course some dollar bills will change hands (be spent) hundreds of times in the year, while others will be used only once or perhaps not at all. The *average* number of times is obtained by dividing the total of payments (in dollars) by the total number of dollars in existence. We divide the 240 billion dollars of money payments by the 80 billion dollars of money in existence and get the figure 3, which we call the average velocity of circulation of money. If we multiply the stock of money (80 billion dollars) by the velocity of circulation (3 per annum), we naturally get back to the number we started with, which was the flow of spending (240 billion dollars per annum).[3]

This digression would not be necessary were it not for a common notion that there should be some sort of correspondence between the goods of a society and its money—that for every dollar's worth of goods there ought to be a dollar in existence somewhere if the economy is to work properly. Economists escaped from that notion a long time ago but find it difficult to get out of the habit of speaking about the stock of money even though they know that it is the flow of spending and not the stock of money that really matters. The velocity of circulation is the device which permits them to keep mentioning the stock of money while really considering the flow of spending, since the stock of money, *when multiplied by the velocity of circulation,* is nothing but the rate or flow of spending.

The traditional procedure for describing the course of economic activity is to begin with a stock of money (M), multiply this by the velocity of circulation (V), thus getting a complex symbol (MV) to represent the flow of spending. It would be much simpler and less confusing to consider only the flow of spending and not to pay any attention to the stock of money at all (except when considering the possible effects of changes in the stock of

[3] See appendix to Chap. 4, sec. 2.

money on the flow of spending—which we shall be doing in a later chapter). There would not be much harm in keeping to the more complicated traditional procedure, but many noneconomists still have something of the old idea that there ought to be a dollar somewhere for every dollar's worth of goods (in existence or produced in the course of a year). No such direct relationship exists or is desirable. The only thing that matters is the *flow* of money spending. The stock of money can be of significance only to the degree that it *may* influence the flow of spending, never as something apart from or in addition to the flow of spending.[4]

Spending consists of consumption and investment, by business, by individuals, and by government.

Since the volume of employment depends on the flow of money spent on currently produced goods and services, it is necessary to consider what this flow of spending itself depends on. Since it is only by working on the forces which govern the flow of spending that we can hope to develop any effective employment policy, we must divide up the total flow of spending into such parts as may be governed by different forces which can be worked on in different ways.

The first distinction we must make is between spending on goods and services that are currently consumed (*i.e.*, consumed in whatever period we are considering) and spending on goods which are not currently consumed.[5] The first part of the flow of spending—that part directed to currently consumed goods and services on the items that make up the daily necessities and luxuries of the population—is called "consumption." The second part—that directed to goods not currently consumed—is therefore necessarily spent on goods added to stocks of material, machines, factories,

---

[4] See appendix to Chap. 4, sec. 3.

[5] Services, since they have no durability and have to be consumed currently or not at all, cannot enter the second category.

houses, and all the other things which constitute our real wealth. This spending on additions to our real capital is called "investment." The total flow of spending thus consists of consumption and investment.[6]

The word "consumption" is used to represent not only the flow of *money* spent on goods and services currently consumed (*money* consumption) but also for the corresponding counterflow of *goods and services* received and consumed by the people who spend the money for them (*real* consumption). In the same way the word "investment" is used to represent both the flow of money spent on goods not currently consumed (*money* investment) and also the flow of goods bought with the money investment and added to the capital stock (*real* investment). To prevent confusion it is sometimes necessary to make explicit whether we are talking about money consumption (the dollars spent in buying goods and services to be currently consumed) or about real consumption (the actual goods and services consumed), and similarly, it is sometimes necessary to state explicitly whether we are talking about money investment (the dollars spent in buying additions to stocks of all kinds) or about real investment (the actual additions to the various stocks). But in most cases this is unnecessary, either because what we have to say applies equally to both the real and the money flow (of consumption or of investment) or because the context makes it clear which we are talking about.[7]

Since all spending which is not for goods which *are* currently consumed must be for goods which are *not* currently consumed, consumption and investment make up the whole of the flow of spending. This total can, however, be divided not according to what the money is spent on but according to who does the spending. If we look at this we can divide all spending into spending by individuals, by businesses, and by the government.

[6] See appendix to Chap. 4, sec. 4.
[7] See appendix to Chap. 4, sec. 5.

Businesses can invest but cannot consume.

Spending by businesses is never for consumption, because businesses are not consumers. Only human beings can consume. The owners of businesses are consumers, of course, as are the managers and workers employed by businesses, as well as the shareholders and creditors. These do spend on consumption most of the money which they obtain from the businesses, but that consumption is counted in the spending by individuals and cannot be counted again in the spending by businesses. The contribution by businesses to the total flow of spending must therefore consist entirely of investment.

Disinvestment must be subtracted from investment to show net investment.

Investment, we have seen, means buying goods that are not currently consumed. Such purchases are called investment because anything that is bought and not currently consumed constitutes an addition to stock. But most of the things bought by businesses do not remain in stock; they are currently used up (or worn out) in the normal course of the business. How can they then be considered investment?

When a business buys things and yet does not add to its stock of capital goods, this is because at the same time, in the course of producing the goods or services that constitute its output, it *uses up* (or wears out) the goods bought or other goods which it had in stock. Such a using up of materials, semifinished goods, equipment, etc., is just the opposite of investment and can be called "disinvestment." It is a *subtraction* from capital stocks just as investment is an addition to capital stocks.

If the goods and services bought by the business are just sufficient to balance the goods used up, the investment and the disinvestment just cancel. The capital stocks are neither increased nor depleted and there is neither *net investment* nor *net disinvestment*. If the business buys more than enough to replace what is used up (including what is worn out) then there is an addition to capital and there is that amount of net investment. On the other hand, if the business uses up more than it buys for replacement, there is a net disinvestment measured by the excess of the disinvestment over the investment.

Individuals and the government can both consume and invest.

While businesses can only invest and disinvest, leaving a balance of net investment or net disinvestment, individuals can spend either for consumption by themselves or their families or for investment. Strictly speaking, most of the expenditures by individuals on consumption, when examined microscopically, look much more like the expenditures by businesses. Many things are bought which are not instantaneously consumed by the individual or by his family but which merely replace other things that are being consumed out of previously existing stocks. In other words, they are investment, being canceled by disinvestment for consumption. When clothes or furniture are being bought they replace others which are being worn out. Even when the housewife buys a loaf of bread, this is an addition to the household stock of capital which is being canceled by the consumption during the day of some bread that was bought yesterday. In the matter of groceries we can almost completely eliminate the complication by considering a week or a month instead of a day, so that almost all of the bread bought in the period is actually eaten in the same period. To insist on distinguishing between newly bought bread which is added to capital and old bread which is eaten out of previously acquired capital becomes rather pedantic. In the case of things like clothing or furniture the distinction is much more sensible, but it is still not considered worth while. But in the cases of houses or automobiles bought by individuals it is necessary to consider the purchases as investment and to count the act of using them up as disinvestment just as we do with business purchases.

The government, like any individual, can spend money either on providing goods and services for current consumption by the population or on providing goods that are added to the stock of capital of the economy. Businesses, however, as we have seen, can spend money only on investment. This gives us five elements in the total money demand for currently produced goods and services which constitute the income of the economy and which determine the volume of employment. The five elements are consumption and investment by individuals, consumption and investment by the government, and investment by businesses. Any full-employment policy must influence the volume of spending in the economy as a whole. To do this it must operate on one or more of these five elements.

Summary.

The volume of employment depends on the rate of spending. This is true for any money-using economy whether capitalist or socialist—whether it encourages or discourages or is neutral to the seeking of profits. Whether a worker finds a job depends on whether an employer can sell the product at an adequate price. Thus the number of workers that an employer will employ depends on how much of the product he can sell at an adequate price and therefore on how much is being spent in buying the product. The total volume of employment thus depends on how much is being spent on currently produced goods and services throughout the economy.

It is important to avoid confusion between the flow of money spending and the stock of money in existence, only the former being significant directly for our purposes. The flow of spending may be separated into spending for consumption and spending for investment and into spending by individuals, by businesses, and by the government. Businesses cannot spend for consumption but can only invest (or disinvest). There are, therefore, five elements in the total spending of the economy: consumption and investment by individuals, consumption and investment by the government, and investment by businesses. Any policy for full employment has to work on one or more of these five elements which make up the total spending on currently produced goods and services.

<h2 style="text-align:center">Appendix to Chapter 4</h2>

1. The relationship between the stock and the flow is illustrated in Fig. 1. The *stock* of water in the tank at any point of time is measured on the scale that tells by the height of the water how many cubic feet there are in the tank. The *flow* of water out of the tank is measured by means of the meter which tells you how many cubic feet have

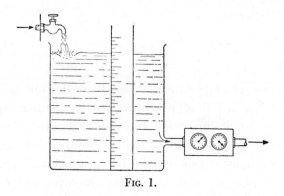

Fig. 1.

passed through the meter in the period that has elapsed since the last time the meter was read. The stock refers to a *point* in time and is measured simply as so many cubic feet. The flow always refers to a *period* and is measured not as so many cubic feet, but as so many cubic feet *per hour* or *per month* or other period.

2. Figure 2*A* shows a stock of 120 billion dollars going round and round through the meter at the rate of 240 billion dollars per annum. The flow through the meter in the course of a year is twice as great as the stock in the tank so that every dollar could pass through the meter twice if no dollar passed through more than twice. The velocity of circulation is 2 per annum. In Fig. 2*B* there is the same *flow* of 240 billion dollars per annum going through the meter,

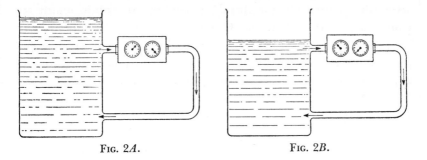

FIG. 2A.   FIG. 2B.

but the *stock* is only 80 billion dollars. All the money in the tank could pass through the meter three times in a year so that the velocity of circulation is 3 per annum.

3. In the last three figures (and in others following) MV is represented by the flow through the meters. M is represented by the stock (of water or of money) in the tank. V is the number obtained by dividing the flow MV by the stock M.

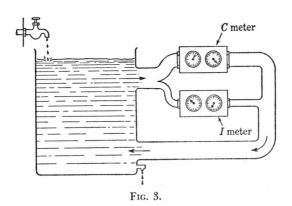

FIG. 3.

4. Figure 3 illustrates the division of the flow of spending into consumption and investment. The large flow above represents consumption and the small flow below represents investment, each of these flows being measured by its own meter. The two flows together add up to the total of spending.

5. It is possible to imagine the flow of *real* consumption and *real* investment as moving through the same meters in the opposite direction to the flow of money payments, since the goods do in fact move

across the counters in the direction opposite to that in which the money passes. It is, however, best not to do that because there is no corresponding tank in which the goods are held. The money goes round and round but the goods are mostly consumed as they are produced. Some of the money may get worn out or otherwise lost to the system (as represented by the leak in Fig. 3) and this can be made up by additional money being added (as represented by the tap dripping into the tank). But most of the money can be used again and again and goes round and round within the system many times.

CHAPTER 5

Spending, Consumption, and Income[1]

THE LEVEL of employment depends on the total rate of spending and the total rate of spending consists of the five elements distinguished in the last chapter: consumption and investment by individuals, consumption and investment by the government, and investment by businesses. Any employment policy, therefore, must operate by influencing one or more of these five elements. To be able to work on them effectively we must know what are the main forces which govern their magnitudes. (We are leaving until Part VI the complications of international economic relations arising from the spending by ourselves on foreign products and the spending by foreigners on our products.)

The five elements, as we have seen, fall into two groups: consumption and investment. Consumption may be undertaken by individuals or by the government. Investment, too, may be undertaken by individuals or by the government and may also be undertaken by businesses.

Spending depends on income.

Consumption by individuals is the largest of the five elements. It comes to more than all the other four together. Its magnitude depends on many things. Individuals will consume more if they expect their incomes to increase, or if they expect prices to rise, or if they believe that the goods will be unavailable later, or if it is more fashionable to be seen consuming more, or if they believe that what they do not consume will be lost, and so on. But the most important influence that determines how much people

[1] See the note at the beginning of Chap. 4.

61

spend on consumption is how much income they have. The larger a man's income the more he will consume, *i.e.*, spend on consumption.

There are, of course, some individuals with large incomes who consume very little and there are other individuals with smaller incomes who consume much more. But it is still true that both kinds of people as well as all those of intermediate temperament would consume more than they do if their incomes were greater than they are and would consume less than they do if their incomes were smaller. Their response to a change in income may be very large or very small and it may be very rapid or very slow, but it is difficult to think of anyone who would consume less just because his income is larger or who would consume more because his income is smaller. For different people there will be different relationships between their income and their consumption, but for all of them the relationship will be positive—a larger income will result in a larger consumption in one degree or another.

The relationship between any individual's income and his consumption is called his *propensity to consume*. If we know his income and his propensity to consume we can figure out his consumption. His propensity to consume is the formula or the table which enables us to calculate the corresponding consumption for every income that he might have.

There is also a propensity to consume for a group of people or for all the people in a country. It depends on the propensities to consume of the individuals in the group or the nation, on how the income is divided among the individuals, and on how much is consumed by the government. If we know the propensity to consume of any society, we can figure out its consumption from its income in the same way as we can figure out the consumption of any individual from his income and his propensity to consume. If, for example, the propensity to consume of the nation is $\frac{5}{6}$ (to take an oversimplified example in which the proportion remains the same for different levels of income), then an income of 240 billion dollars would result in 200 billion dollars being spent on consumption goods and services, and out of an income of 246 billion dollars 205 billion dollars would be consumed.

Income is earned by selling services.

The propensity to consume directs our search from consumption to income. Knowing the propensity to consume we now need to know the income in order to be able to find out how much will be consumed.

Any individual's income is what he earns. He may earn income by working, in which case his income consists of what is paid for his work. (At least that is the case if he is himself the owner of his own labor power and is not a slave. What is paid for the work of a slave constitutes income not for the slave but for the owner of the slave.)

An individual may also earn income from the ownership of property of the kinds which (unlike slaves) are now legally permitted—land or machines or houses or money. The payment for the services of any piece of property constitutes income for the owner of the property just as the payment for work done constitutes income for the free worker who owns his own labor power.

There is no moral implication in the concept of earning income by work. It is frequently assumed that income obtained by the sale of labor power is better justified morally than income obtained by the sale of the services of other kinds of property. This is not necessarily the case. Income from the sale of some specialized kind of labor involving skills from which outsiders are barred in one way or another may result in very high incomes that reflect a special and unjust privilege much more than some incomes from the sale of the services of property. The relatively high income earned by one who is lucky enough to become a member of, say, the New York Scene Shifters Union is certainly not easier to justify morally than the income obtained from the renting of a house belonging to a retired worker who has built it with his own hands. But in any case we are not concerned here with the moral implications and so need not distinguish between income which is morally justified and income which is the result of a special and unjustified privilege unfairly held at the expense of others. We need not inquire whether such unfairness is connected with the distinction between income earned by work and income earned by property.

The earning of income is thus identical with the selling of services or of goods incorporating such services. But nothing can be sold unless there is somebody who spends money in buying what is being sold. The earning of income is itself dependent on spending.

Here we seem to be back where we started. It was in order to find out what determines the total of spending that we divided it into the five different kinds of spending of which the first and the largest was the consumption of individuals. Now we find that this item itself depends on income and thus on spending.

Income is equal to spending.

The relationship between income and spending is really much closer than mere dependence. The *income* earned in any period of time is always *exactly equal* to the *spending* in that period of time. Income must be exactly equal to spending simply because the two words refer to the same thing looked at from different points of view. Every receipt of a dollar of income is also the outlay of a dollar of spending. Which we call it depends only on whether we are looking at it from the point of view of the person receiving the dollar or whether we are looking at it from the point of view of the person paying out the dollar. The equality thus turns out to be a somewhat disguised form of saying that the total sum of dollar payments (looked at from the front) is equal to the total sum of dollar payments (looked at from behind). This kind of proposition is difficult to dispute.[2]

[2] See appendix to Chap. 5, sec. 1.

The equality between income earned and money spent is one of the most fundamental propositions in the theory of the determination of income and employment. A failure to recognize the equality or a supposition of the possibility of even a momentary inequality between them involves error and contradiction and completely destroys any arguments that permit it.

This may seem rather strange because the equality between income and spending is one of those unconditional and inevitable equalities that are sometimes called identities or tautologies. It does not really make any statement about the actual world in the sense that it tells something about it which we might have supposed to be otherwise. But although the equality or identity of spending and income does not give us any information about the actual world, it is extremely useful in checking on arguments which do purport to tell us something about the actual world. If any argument should imply that income was greater or smaller than spending, even if only for the smallest period or only by the smallest amount, then that argument is no good. What it tries to show us may still be true, but an argument which either explicitly or implicitly assumes an inequality between income and spending is disqualified as thoroughly and in exactly the same way as if it depended on assuming somewhere in the course of the argument that 2 and 2 are equal to 17.

The equality between spending and income does not apply to any individual or to any group of individuals constituting less than the whole of the economy. We are talking about a free country in which anyone can spend less than his income if he wishes to and can spend more than his income if he has any other source of cash or credit. The equality is not between anyone's income and his own spending. It is between anyone's spending and the income that *someone else* earns because of this spending. It is therefore only when we include *everybody* in the community without exception that every dollar counted in spending is also counted in income earned, and vice versa, so that the sum of all the spending comes to exactly the same as the sum of all the income earned.

The necessary equality between spending and income holds only for the economy as a whole.

Only spending on currently produced goods and services creates income.

In applying the identity we must, however, be careful to count only such spending as is directed to buying *currently produced* goods and services, for it is only the sale of currently produced goods and services which constitutes income to the seller. If I sell you my house for $10,000, that $10,000 does not constitute any part of my income. I have not earned the $10,000. I have merely received it in exchange for the house which I previously possessed. If I spend any part of that money on consumption, I shall be eating up a part of my capital. If I spend none of the money on consumption but keep all of it, I shall not be adding anything to my capital. All that has happened is a swap between us. Before the exchange you had the money and I had the house. Now, after the exchange, you have the house and I have the money. Your buying has been canceled by my selling (which must be counted as negative buying). No income has been created.

It might be thought that this tries to prove too much. Does not every purchase imply a sale? Would not that prove that no income is ever created by anybody's buying anything? Is it not always true that if *A* buys from *B, B* must be selling to *A,* so that there is a similar canceling out and no income is ever created?

The argument does not try to prove too much. If I am a house-builder and *currently produce* the houses I sell, I *earn* the money I get for them and it *is* a part of my income. I am not impoverished by consuming it, and if I save any of this money it will constitute an addition to my capital or wealth. The difficulty is thus avoided by counting only the sales of *currently produced* goods and services.

We can sometimes get the same result more conveniently if we start by counting *all* sales and then subtracting those sales which involve a reduction in the stock of goods possessed by the seller. These sales are subtracted because if the goods came out of previous stocks, as they must have done if their sale caused the stocks to decline, they could not have been currently produced. Since all goods either are currently produced or are not currently produced, if we subtract from our grand total of sales those which are of goods out of stock (and so not currently produced), we obtain the value of the sales of goods that *are* currently produced and whose sales do constitute the income currently earned.

Money obtained from the sale of goods not currently produced is not currently earned and does not constitute current income to the recipient any more than would money received as a gift or as a loan. Such money may possibly come out of income earned by the donor or lender or by the purchaser of goods out of stock, but it does not constitute income for the person who receives them. Only money received from the sale of currently produced goods or services is *earned* by the seller and constitutes his *income*.

Spending and income depend on each other.

At the beginning of this chapter we set out to examine the elements that constitute the total of spending so that we might know more about how to work on these in any employment policy. We found that consumption (*i.e.,* spending on consumption) depends primarily on income. But we went on to observe that income in turn depends on spending. This looks rather like a vicious circle. Can it be that we have to know the size of income in order to obtain the figure for consumption and that we have to know the value of consumption in order to figure out the size of the income? Can we thus have been caught in an eternal run-around?

When the theory of employment was first developed by Lord Keynes it did seem to many economists that the argument was circular, endlessly chasing its own tail. But this was an illusion resulting only from the unfamiliarity of the argument. If we know how A depends on B and also know just how B depends on A, it is perfectly possible to find out the actual values of both A and B. For instance, if we are told that a father is twice as old as his daughter and that the daughter is 20 years younger than the father, we do not have to wait until somebody tells us how old the father is in order to find the age of the daughter or until somebody tells us how old the daughter is in order to be able to find the age of the father. We can solve this problem immediately because it provides two equations to determine the two unknowns: $F = 2D, D = F - 20$. By substitution it is easy to show that $F = 40$ and $D = 20$. Or even without using any explicit algebra we can consider that if the father is twice as old as the daughter, the excess of his age over his daughter's must be the same as his daughter's age. We are told that this excess is 20 years; the daughter must therefore be 20 years old and the father 40.

In exactly the same way if we know how consumption affects income and how income affects consumption we have two unknowns and two equations and we can solve them. To simplify our example to the extreme, let us suppose that no investment takes place at all so that we can for the time being leave it out of the picture Income is then created only by the spending on consumption goods and is equal to consumption. This gives us our first equation, $Y = C$, where Y stands for income and C stands for consumption. (The letter Y is used to represent income because the initial I has traditionally been used for investment and some other letter had to be substituted.)

The second equation is provided by the *propensity to consume,* which is the way in which consumers adjust their consumption to their income. Let us suppose that $C = 40 + \frac{2}{3}(Y - 40)$. This means that the propensity to consume is such that the people in the country will consume 40 billion dollars a year plus two-thirds of any excess of their income over 40 billion dollars.

We have two equations:

(1) $$Y = C$$

(2) $$C = 40 + \tfrac{2}{3}(Y - 40)$$

The first equation enables us to substitute Y for C in (2) obtaining an equation with a single unknown:

$$Y = 40 + \tfrac{2}{3}(Y - 40)$$

Solving this by easy steps we have

$$Y = 40 + \tfrac{2}{3}(Y) - \tfrac{2}{3}(40)$$

$$Y - \tfrac{2}{3}(Y) = 40 - \tfrac{2}{3}(40)$$

$$\frac{Y}{3} = \frac{40}{3}$$

$$Y = 40$$

Or, without algebra, we can see without much difficulty that it is impossible for any income other than 40 billion dollars to satisfy both the equality of income to consumption and the propensity to consume which is supposed to rule. For if income were supposed to be anything over 40 billion dollars, only two-thirds of this excess would be consumed. Consumption would be 40 billion dollars plus only two-thirds of the excess of income over 40 billion dollars, and so it would be less than income by one-third of the excess. Since such an inequality between income and spending (consumption here being the sole element in spending) is impossible, any income over 40 billion dollars is impossible. The same is true for any income less than 40 billion dollars (*i.e.*, if the excess of income over consumption is *negative*). For every $3 that income is below 40 billion dollars, consumption will be only $2 below 40 billion dollars, and again spending (which here is identical with consumption) would not be equal to income. This is impossible, so that income cannot be less than 40 billion dollars.[3] Only if income is exactly 40 billion dollars is spending (consumption) exactly equal to it.[4]

When we say that it is impossible for income to be either greater or less than 40 billion dollars, we merely mean that it is impossible as long as the other conditions of the problem are true. One of these, the equality of Y to C (when there is no investment), is always true. There can never be any departure from this. But there can be a departure from the other equation. Consumers may on occasion behave erratically, not following their propensity to consume, or they may be forced off it. When they discover this they will try to change their ways, but meanwhile the second equation will not hold and income will meanwhile not be equal to 40 billion dollars. The public may, for instance, have been led to believe that they were earning 46 billion dollars and therefore, in accordance with their propensity to consume, spent 44 billion dollars on consumption $[40 + \frac{2}{3}(6)]$. If they do that their income will in fact be not 46 billion dollars but 44 billion dollars, and they will be consuming more than is indicated by their propensity to consume. They will be consuming 44 billion dollars instead of the $42\frac{2}{3}$ billion dollars $[40 + \frac{2}{3}(44 - 40)]$ that they should spend out of an income of \$44 according to their propensity to consume.

It is similarly possible for consumption to be less than 40 billion dollars. A belief that income was being earned at the rate of 37 billion dollars would cause the population to consume at the rate of 38 billion dollars. Their income would then be 38 billion dollars and not 37 billion and they would not be consuming the $38\frac{2}{3}$ billion dollars which the propensity to consume tells us they should consume if their income were 38 billion dollars $[40 + \frac{2}{3}(40 - 38)]$. Whatever happens their income cannot be different from their consumption (as long as there is no invest-

---

[3] If we interpret the propensity to consume to mean that consumption cannot fall below 40 billion dollars whatever the income, it is even clearer that spending and therefore income cannot fall below this figure.

[4] See appendix to Chap. 5, sec. 2.

ment), but unless their income is exactly 40 billion dollars they will not be behaving in accordance with their propensity to consume. Only at this level of income are they consuming the amount that they think right (according to their propensity to consume) in relation to their income. At any other level of income the population will not be satisfied with their consumption, contracting it whenever it is above 40 billion dollars and expanding it when it is below 40 billion dollars until the satisfactory or equilibrium income of 40 billion dollars is reached at which the relation between their income and their consumption (namely, the relation of equality) is in accordance with their propensity to consume.[5]

So far we have been assuming that there is no investment by anybody—that all expenditure is for consumption. We found that income could be in equilibrium only at the level at which the propensity to consume prescribes that it must all be consumed. It should be noted that saving, which is defined as the excess of income over consumption, is thus equal to zero. Since investment is also equal to zero, saving is equal to investment.

Income is made up of consumption and investment.

We can now bring in the other set of elements in total spending. These elements consist of *investment*. Investment, it will be remembered, is spending on goods which are not currently consumed but added to the stock of goods or of productive equipment. For our present purpose it does not matter whether the investment is undertaken by individuals, by businesses, or by the government, just as in the earlier part of this chapter it did not matter whether consumption was by individuals or by the government.

If in addition to the spending on consumption there is an expenditure on investment of 10 billion dollars per annum, this

[5] See appendix to Chap. 5, sec. 3.

creates an additional 10 billion dollars of income. But this does *not* mean that income will simply be 50 billion instead of 40 billion dollars. The extra 10 billion dollars of income created by the 10 billion dollars of investment results in some *additional* consumption, which creates still more income, which results in still more consumption, and so on. What will be the level of income and consumption that will be reached now that we have 10 billion dollars of investment?

Again we can solve the problem either algebraically or by simple reasoning. Algebraically we now have three equations:

(1) $Y = C + I$ (*I* stands for investment. The consumption and the investment between them create all the income.)

(2) $C = 40 + \frac{2}{3}(Y - 40)$ (The propensity to consume.)

(3) $I = 10$ (The assumed level of investment.)

Again we can proceed to solve the simultaneous equations by simple steps. Combining (3) and (1) we get

$$Y = C + 10$$

Substituting this value of Y in (2) we get

$$C = 40 + \frac{2}{3}(C + 10 - 40)$$

$$= 40 + \frac{2}{3}(C - 30)$$

$$= 40 + \frac{2}{3}(C) - \frac{2}{3}(30)$$

$$C - \frac{2}{3}C = 40 - \frac{2}{3}(30)$$

$$\frac{C}{3} = 40 - 20$$

$$C = 60$$

and Y, which is equal to $C + I$, is 70.

If we do not like to use algebraic symbols we can say instead that if investment is 10 billion dollars instead of zero, income will tend to be at the level at which people will consume 10 billion dollars less than their income. This consumption will create an amount of income that is 10 billion dollars less than total income, leaving the remaining 10 billion dollars to be created by the investment. What this level of income is can be figured out from the propensity to consume. The propensity to consume is such that for every $3 of income over and above 40 billion dollars, only $2 will be consumed. This leaves a gap of $1 of income to be filled by investment. Since investment is 10 billion dollars, this must be the size of the gap. A gap of 10 billion dollars needs an income that is 30 billion dollars above the 40-billion-dollar level, since it takes $3 of income above 40 billion dollars to create each dollar toward the gap to be filled by investment. Income must therefore be 70 billion dollars. Out of such an income, consumption will be 60 billion dollars (40 billion dollars plus two-thirds of the excess of 70 billion over 40 billion dollars) which, together with the investment of 10 billion dollars, creates the income of 70 billion dollars.[6]

It is indeed possible for income to be greater or less than 70 billion dollars, but in that case the propensity to consume will not be satisfied. An income different from 70 billion dollars can come about only if the public is mistaken about the size of its income. If they believe their income to be 73 billion dollars, they will consume 62 billion dollars. But their income in that case will be 72 billion dollars out of which, according to the propensity to consume, they should be consuming not 62 billion but 61⅓ billion. Similarly if they are led to believe that their income is less than 70 billion dollars they will consume less than 60 billion but more than is indicated by the propensity to consume. Seventy billion dollars is the only income level which satisfies all the conditions laid down: the assumed propensity to consume, the

[6] See appendix to Chap. 5, sec. 4.

assumed investment of 10 billion dollars per annum, and the identity between total spending and total income.[7]

Saving is equal to investment.

It will be observed that in this case, as in the previous case, saving is equal to investment. Income is 70 and consumption is 60, so that the amount saved by all the members of society is 10, which is also the amount of investment.

This equality is not an accident. The amount saved in the whole economy must always be equal to the amount that is invested. This follows very simply from the proposition we have already considered which tells us that total income must be equal to total spending because they are two different views of the same happenings. Total spending and therefore total income consist of consumption plus investment. This is seen when we look at income to see how it is created. If we look at what is done with the income, we see that a part of it is consumed. The remainder is what we call "saving." Income is then also equal to consumption plus saving. Consumption plus investment is thus equal to consumption plus saving, both being equal to the same thing—income—and so equal to each other. It follows that the investment that takes place in any period is always equal to the saving that takes place in the same period. In algebraic symbols: $C + I = Y = C + S \therefore I = S$.

The necessary equality between saving and investment, like the necessary equality between spending and income, applies only to the economy as a whole and not to any individual or to any combination of individuals short of the economy as a whole. Each individual is perfectly free to save more than he invests or to invest more than he saves. But total income can be greater than total consumption only to the extent that investment creates income in excess of the income created by (and equal to) the

[7] See appendix to Chap. 5, sec. 5.

consumption, and this excess of income over consumption is what we call saving. It is only for the economy as a whole, when we count everybody without exception, that the sum of all the saving is necessarily exactly equal to the sum of all the investment.

The equality between investment and saving enables us to discover the level of income in a less mathematical and, for some people, an easier way. Investment now being 10 billion dollars instead of zero, income will move toward the level at which the economy as a whole wants to save this amount. Saving is equal to this investment, *i.e.*, to 10 billion dollars per annum. From the propensity to consume we can easily derive the *propensity to save*. We do this by subtracting the appropriate consumption, at each income level, from the income itself, leaving the part of income which, according to the propensity to consume, would not be consumed but saved. The propensity to save is equal to 1 *minus* the propensity to consume. The economy we have been discussing has the propensity to consume two-thirds of the excess of income over 40 billion dollars; it therefore has the propensity to save the remaining one-third of the excess of income over 40 billion dollars.

$$S = \frac{Y - 40}{3}$$

If $I = 10$, also

$$S = 10 \qquad \frac{Y - 40}{3} = 10$$

$$Y - 40 = 30 \qquad \text{and so} \qquad Y = 70$$

Or, without algebra, since saving must be equal to investment, which is 10 billion dollars, and saving, according to the propensity to save, is equal to one-third of the excess of income over 40 billion dollars, the excess of income over 40 billion dollars must be 30 billion, so that income must be 70 billion dollars.[8]

It is not impossible for income to be other than 70 billion dollars in the sense in which it is impossible for saving to be different

[8] See appendix to Chap. 5, sec. 6.

from investment. But if the income is not equal to 70 billion dollars, the amount actually saved (which cannot be other than 10 billion dollars, the amount actually invested) will not be in correspondence to the propensity to save. Only when income is 70 billion dollars does the propensity to consume direct a saving of 10 billion dollars. Any level of income other than 70 billion dollars will therefore not be stable and will result in changes in consumption until the equilibrium level of 70 billion dollars is reached, when saving will be in accordance with the propensity to save and the propensity to consume.

Summary.

The largest of the five elements constituting total spending is consumption by individuals. The most important influence determining how much anyone will consume is his income. The larger his income the more he will consume. The relationship between income and consumption is called the "propensity to consume." This concept is applicable to groups and nations as well as to individuals. A knowledge of the propensity to consume enables one to derive a figure for consumption from a knowledge of the size of the income.

Income in turn depends on spending, being exactly equal to it because it is created by the spending. Income is merely the other side of the act of spending. In figuring income one must, however, count only the spending on goods and services that are currently produced.

The dependence of consumption and therefore of spending on income and the dependence of income on spending look like a circular argument, but a knowledge of the manner in which these depend on each other enables us to solve the problem of the determination of the level of income. Given the amount of investment and the propensity to consume for the economy as a whole (which includes consumption by the government) it is possible to figure out the corresponding level of the national income that will tend to be reached. It is that level of income at which the economy finds that the relation between its consumption and its income is in accordance with its propensity to consume.

Another way of arriving at the same result is provided by the use of the concept of the propensity to save, which is easily derived from the propensity to consume. The amount actually saved can never be different from the amount actually invested. There is one level of income at which this amount of saving is in accordance with the propensity to save. That will be the level which the national income will tend to reach.

APPENDIX TO CHAPTER 5

1. The necessary equality of spending to income can be shown in Fig. 3 (page 59) by considering the dollars flowing *into* the meters as spending and the dollars flowing *out* as income. The dollars flowing into the C (consumption) meter are the dollars spent on consumption, and the dollars flowing out of the C meter are the dollars earned by people engaged in making and selling the consumption goods and services. The dollars flowing into the I (investment) meter are the dollars spent on investment and the dollars flowing out of the I meter are the dollars earned by the people engaged in making and selling the investment goods. The flow of dollars out of the meters (the total income) cannot be greater or smaller than the flow of dollars into the meters (the total spending). It is important to observe that the dollars passing through the meters do not constitute income to the man who is spending them but always to *somebody else,* since one does not pay dollars for things bought from oneself. It is only when we stop thinking of the individual payments and consider the whole that we need remember that all the spenders are the same people as all the income receivers because they are simply all the people.

2. The relationship between the level of income and the propensity to consume, in the absence of any investment, can be shown in Fig. 4. In this diagram the horizontal distance of any point from the vertical

axis OC to the right represents a level of income as measured on the scale along the horizontal axis OY. The vertical distance of any point from the horizontal axis OY upward represents a level of consumption as measured on the scale along the vertical axis OC. The 45-degree line $C = Y$ consists of all the points that are equidistant from both axes. Every point on this line therefore indicates a certain level

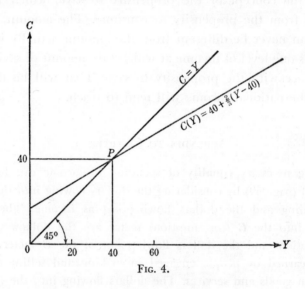

FIG. 4.

of income and an equal level of consumption. The curve marked $C(Y)$ represents the propensity to consume.

Since there is no investment, all the income that is earned is created by consumption. Total income must therefore be equal to total consumption and the point indicating the actual income and the actual consumption must fall somewhere on the line $C = Y$.

Since the propensity to consume is indicated by the curve $C(Y)$, which covers every point where consumption is equal to 40 billion dollars plus two-thirds of the excess of income over 40 billion dollars, the point we are looking for must lie on the curve $C(Y)$; the only point that lies on both the line $C = Y$ and the curve $C(Y)$ is the point P where income and consumption are each equal to 40 billion dollars.

3. Figure 5 illustrates what is meant by saying that consumption is determined by the propensity to consume. The curves in Fig. 5 are the same as those in Fig. 4 except that Fig. 5 concentrates on the

region where they intersect and shows them much magnified. Since there is no investment, income is created only by the consumption, income is equal to consumption, and the point describing any actual situation must fall on the 45-degree $C = Y$ line. If people believe that they are earning 46 billion dollars, they will consume 44 billion dollars. They will expect to be at the point represented by A, with

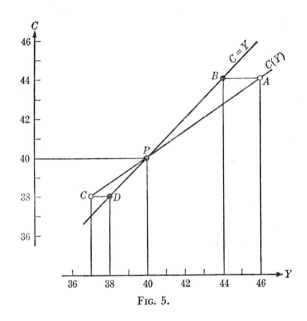

Fig. 5.

income 46 billion dollars and consumption 44 billion dollars, but they will in fact be at point B since, if they are spending only 44 billion dollars, they cannot be earning more than this sum. A is only an imaginary point; B is the point which genuinely describes the situation. When they discover that they are not earning as much as they thought they were they will reduce their consumption. This will reduce their income too. Points A and B will move down together. The gap between them represents the degree to which people are overestimating their incomes. As A and B move down along the curves the gap diminishes, but as long as there is any gap people keep on finding that they are overestimating their income and the imaginary point A and the real point B keep on moving down until they meet at P.

Consumption can be below 40 billion dollars if people believe that their income is less than 40 billion dollars. If people think that their income is 37 billion dollars, they will consume 38 billion dollars. They will believe themselves to be at *C* but in fact they will be at *D* because, if they consume 38 billion dollars, they will in fact be earning not 37 billion but 38 billion dollars. When they find out that they are underestimating their income they will increase their consumption. *C* and *D* will then move up and the gap between them will diminish. But as long as there is any gap they are still under-estimating their income and they will keep on increasing their consumption and their income until they reach *P*. The small hollow circles represent imaginary situations. The real situations are repre-sented by the solid circles connected with them.

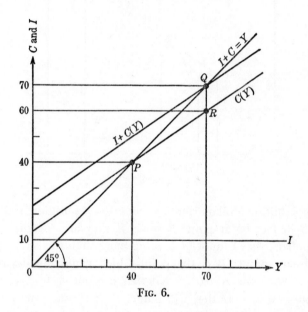

FIG. 6.

4. Figure 6 illustrates the effect of the introduction of a given invest-ment. With investment equal to 10 billion dollars the income created is now 10 billion dollars more than the consumption, which creates the rest of the income. The point indicating the new position will therefore be somewhere on the line $I + C(Y)$. It must also be some-where on the 45-degree line which now is called $I + C = Y$ because investment creates income as well as consumption and we no longer

are assuming that investment is zero. The only point that falls on both curves is Q. This then will be the income at 70 billion dollars while consumption will be at R directly beneath it showing a consumption of 60 billion dollars which is in accordance with the propensity to consume.

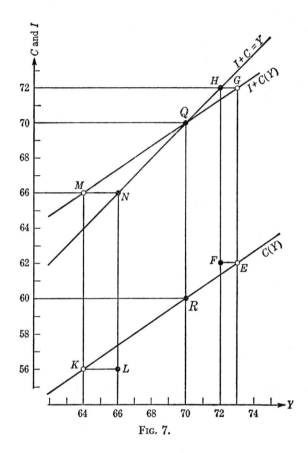

FIG. 7.

5. Figure 7 is an enlargement of part of Fig. 6. It shows how an expectation or belief that income is 73 billion dollars would result in consumption of 62 billion dollars. But with investment at 10 billion dollars the resulting income will be not 73 billion but 72 billion dollars. Consumers imagine they are at E but they are really at F. If we add the 10 billion dollars of investment we see the imaginary position at G while the real position is at H with income 72 billion

dollars and consumption 62 billion dollars instead of the 61⅓ billion dollars that would correspond to the propensity to consume. As consumers discover that their income is less than they imagined it to be they will cut their consumption until it reaches R when income will reach Q.

If consumers should be led to believe that they are earning only 64 billion dollars they will consume only 56 billion dollars thinking they are at K, but they will in fact be at L and the total position will be shown by N and not by M. When they discover that their income is not 64 billion but 66 billion dollars, they will increase their consumption and will keep on increasing it until consumption reaches R and income reaches Q.

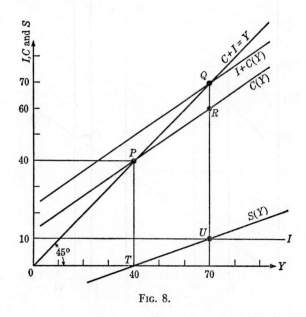

FIG. 8.

6. Figure 8 is the same as Fig. 6 except that there is added a line marked $S(Y)$ which represents the propensity to save. For each income level (measured horizontally to the right from the vertical axis) the corresponding point on $S(Y)$ is just as much above or below the horizontal axis as the 45-degree line $(C + I = Y)$ is above or below the $C(Y)$ curve. If there is no investment, that is to say, zero investment, the I curve would coincide with the horizontal axis. The point of

intersection of the S(Y) curve with the horizontal axis at T therefore shows the equilibrium position where S is equal to I, both being equal to zero and income is 40 billion dollars. Where investment is 10 billion dollars the point of intersection where I is equal to S is at U, where income is 70 billion dollars. Naturally this gives the same results as are reached if we work through the propensity to consume and arrive at points P and Q, but for some purposes it is more convenient to speak in terms of saving and investment.

With the same propensity to save and the same investment it is still possible for income to be greater or less than 70 billion dollars, but in that case the public will not be behaving in accordance with their propensity to save and will therefore be changing their behavior until they find themselves on it. Income may be at 73 billion dollars, 10 billion being created by our assumed 10 billion of investment and 63 billion created by consumption so that saving is 10 billion dollars and equal to the investment. This is represented by

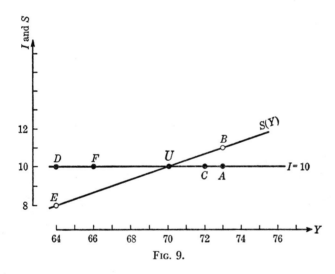

FIG. 9.

point A on Fig. 9. But A is not on the S(Y) curve. The public will want to save not 10 billion but 11 billion dollars. They will want to go to point B. In endeavoring to do this they will reduce their consumption by 1 billion dollars, but this will move them not to B but to C, where they are still saving no more than the 10 billion dollars that is being invested but have reduced their income by 1 billion dollars. They are still not on their $S(Y)$ curve and will continue to try to increase their saving by reducing their consumption. This never increases their saving but it keeps on reducing their income until they arrive at U where they no longer wish to increase their saving.

If income should be 64 billion dollars, the public is at D. They try to move to E in an attempt to reduce their saving below 10 billion dollars by increasing their consumption. This however moves them not to E but to F. They will therefore continue to try to decrease their saving by increasing their consumption. This keeps on increasing their income until they reach U at which point the 10 billion dollars of saving no longer seems excessive.

Throughout the whole of this process the amount actually saved cannot be different from the amount invested, but it is only at the equilibrium point U that the saving is in accordance with their propensity to consume.

CHAPTER 6

Investment[1]

IN THE last chapter we saw how the propensity to consume enables us to figure out the equilibrium level of income, *given the investment*. We must now turn to consider what determines the investment.

Investment depends on future benefits and present costs.

Investment was defined in Chapter 4 as spending on goods that are not currently consumed. Anything, therefore, which induces any individual or business or the government to spend money on anything that is not currently consumed qualifies as a determinant of investment. Like any other economic activity investment will be undertaken if the expected benefits from it outweigh the disadvantages or costs incurred in undertaking it. Since the benefits of investment, by definition, cannot be in the nature of current consumption, they must lie in the expected *future* enjoyment of the products or in their *possession* when completed. Possession of the product of the investment may begin currently (*i.e.*, within the period being considered). But the essential nature of *possession*, as distinct from *consumption*, is that the product is expected to continue into the future. The future thus always enters into the problem of any useful investment, whether the investor is thinking of the future consumption or is merely thinking of the immediate or current possession of the product of the investment.

This enables us to say that whether any investment by an

[1] See the note at the beginning of Chap. 4.

individual or by a business will take place or not depends on—
is determined by—whether the expected *future* benefit outweighs
the *present* cost of undertaking the investment.[2]

This formulation in terms of comparing *present* costs with
future benefits is not really quite exact because the present
does not really exist. What we mean by the present is the more
immediate future. A more exact formulation would be in terms
of the comparison of costs to be incurred in the more immediate
future with benefits which will accrue only in the more distant
future. The costs may have to continue over a considerable time
in the future and will usually overlap with some of the benefits.
Some of the benefits may be enjoyed before all of the costs will
have been incurred. But on the whole the costs, or the inputs or
sacrifices which have to be made in the course of the investment,
must come earlier in time than the benefits that flow from it.[3]
It is this more general priority in time of costs before benefits
that must be understood by the simpler statement that the costs
of an investment are incurred in the present for the sake of
benefits to accrue in the future.

*The future benefits depend on technical and on economic
elements.*

The expected future benefits depend in the first place on the
technical possibilities of increasing future outputs of goods and
services through the application of currently available productive

[2] Governments, as we shall see below, may take into account some *current*
benefits to society of the act of investment which would not be considered
by individuals or by businesses because they involve no direct private benefit
to the investor.

[3] This must be the case because if this were not so, that is, if the benefits
were in general prior to the outlays, we would have not an investment opportunity but a free gift, subject only to the provision that some of it
must be given back later. Such "investment opportunities" would so quickly
be snapped up that we need not suppose that there are any left.

resources. In any society which is not fully equipped with the very best of the known instruments of production it is possible, by directing productive resources to making goods for the future instead of for the present, to increase future output more than current output is curtailed. This is because the postponement of consumption permits better machinery to be built and better methods to be used, so that there is a greater future output from the same productive resources. This is the purely technical element in the effectiveness or "efficiency" of an investment.

In addition to the technical element, there are economic elements. Estimates have to be made by potential investors as to the state of future need or demand for the product to be yielded by the investment. Can the future demand for the product be counted on with sufficient certainty? What are the chances of some other product's displacing it in the consumers' demand? What are the chances of some other producers of the same product becoming even more efficient and, by undercutting its price, making the investment unprofitable?

Then there are the more general economic considerations. Will there be a sufficiently long and intense period of prosperity to make the investment worth while or will there be a depression?

And throughout all these there is the subjective element of the psychological feelings of the potential investors. Their natural optimism or pessimism is given great scope in determining actions where so many things are matters of guesswork.

Different expectations of costs can also affect investment.

Parallel to all these considerations are the considerations on the cost side. What are the chances that the costs in the near future will rise so far as to render the investment unprofitable? Or will an expected rise in costs rather act as a stimulus to investment in that it will be a protection of the investment from future competitors? This depends on the exact time of the rise in the costs of the various kinds, and again there is much scope for the subjective optimism or pessimism of the potential investors. An expected fall in costs may be a serious deterrent to investment. It may cause the investor to postpone his investment in order to take advantage of the lower costs in the future. He is more likely to do this if the availability of capital to the investor is limited so that he cannot invest in the future as well as in the present. Furthermore, the expectation of falling costs may make the investor wary of investing now, even though this would not interfere with his possibilities of investing more later when costs are lower, because he will be afraid of having to compete in the more distant future with others who will have invested more economically than he. The expected lower costs lead to an expected lower price of the product and here it is difficult and perhaps impossible to disentangle expectations about future costs from expectations about future benefits.

Subjective elements may be very important.

When we come to consider the determinants of the state of mind of the potential investors, their optimism or pessimism, we find ourselves lost in more and more vague influences. Obviously of importance is the current condition of the economy—whether there is a state of prosperity or of depression and whether there is a general expectation of good times or of bad times ahead. It will be of great importance whether people are looking forward to a period of peace or whether war is threatening. Also important is the attitude of potential investors to the activities of government in matters of social policy—whether they think the policy is good for society or for business (they are usually not very clear about the distinction between the two) and what they think will be the effects on the profitability of investments.

One of the effects of the time element in investment, the fact that the expected benefits are in the *future*, is that they are surrounded with risks and uncertainties which usually make them less worth while in view of the necessary costs or sacrifices than they would be if the benefits were completely certain.

The time element brings in the rate of interest.

All the considerations mentioned up to this point seem to emphasize the difficulties in the way of discovering the volume of investment rather than point to anything that would help us to make the necessary estimates. There is, however, one other effect of the time element about which we can make some more positive observations. Because of the time element in investment, because the benefits occur later than the costs, *interest* has to be taken into account. If the investor has to borrow the money with which to pay for the costs of the investment, he must get enough from the future benefits to return the borrowed money *with interest* for the period elapsed, and the higher the rate of interest the greater must be the returns in relation to the costs if the investment is to seem worth while.

The problem is by no means absent in the case in which the investor does not have to borrow money and pay interest but has his own money to invest. Interest is still important because he has the alternative possibility of lending out his money at interest instead of undertaking the investment. And if the rate of interest is high there is more temptation for him to do just that. The return on investment in either case has to be higher to appear worth undertaking when the rate of interest is higher in the market available to the potential investor, either as a lender or as a borrower.

If we suppose all the other determinants of investment to be given, we can consider the effects of different levels of the rate of interest. For each rate of interest there will be, in any period, a number of investments that are worth undertaking at this rate of interest (and which would be even more worth while undertaking if the rate of interest were lower). The lower the rate of interest the more potential investment will move from the category of investments that are not worth while into the category of investments that are worth while. This makes it possible to conceive of a table or chart which tells us just how much investment will take place at each possible rate of interest.[4]

*We now need the rate of interest to determine investment
and thereby employment.*

The investment curve, representing the existing conditions of cost, of expected future demand, and of expected future costs as they are expected to affect the efficiency of the investments, can tell us, in conjunction with the rate of interest, how much investment will take place. Given the rate of interest, we merely have to read off on the investment curve the corresponding horizontal distance which represents the volume of investment that will result from that rate of interest. This volume of investment, in conjunction with the propensity to consume, gives us the level of income and from this we can get what we are primarily interested in, the volume of employment. But at the beginning of this train of determinants is the rate of interest, which we have not explained at all. We must therefore do something about providing this initial link in the chain of influences determining the volume of employment. What determines the rate of interest? But we must leave this to the next chapter.

*Government may invest in unprofitable but socially
beneficial projects.*

So far we have spoken of the investment curve (or of the schedule of the marginal efficiency of investment, sometimes also called the marginal efficiency of capital) in terms of private investment by individuals or by businesses. The benefit from the investment in such cases is the money value of the products

---

[4] See appendix to Chap. 6, sec. 1.

that the investment will yield in the future. The money proceeds can then be compared with the money costs incurred and the efficiency of the investment compared with the current rate of interest to see whether the investment is worth undertaking.

Not all investment is undertaken by individuals or by businesses. Investment is also undertaken by the government. And the government can take into account benefits other than those which yield a money return. Investments can be undertaken by the government which show a money loss but which are considered worth while in the social interest because they yield benefits other than those which result in a money income. The government may build a road, for instance, because it believes that the benefits to the future users of the road are more than enough to compensate for the costs incurred in building it. And it can do so even though it decides not to charge anything at all for the use of the road.

Cases like these differ from private investment in that the benefit is not received by the investor in money payments for the output of goods or services in the future but are merely *attributed* or *credited* as desirable from a social point of view. Investments may be socially desirable even though there is no satisfactory way in which the beneficiaries can be made to pay for the benefits so as to render the investment privately profitable. It is just because there are many important investments where it would do more harm than good to try to make beneficiaries pay that social action by a government is necessary in general. These are the cases where the institution of private property fails to function satisfactorily in the social interest and other devices, such as public investment, have to be developed.

The government can take into consideration not only future benefits other than those which will result in money income but also some *immediate* benefits from investment that private investors have to ignore. In particular it can take into account the effect of the investment on the total volume of current investment and thereby on the level of income and employment.

If there is severe unemployment the immediate effect of the investment in creating employment may be much more important than the future benefits. In this case the investment is worth undertaking even if the future benefits would otherwise not be sufficient to justify the investment. The costs of the investment, the wages paid to workers who would otherwise be unemployed, are not really *social* costs since there is no real sacrifice involved in the workers working instead of pounding the streets looking for work. Rather the reverse, since working is usually much less painful than looking for urgently needed work which is unobtainable. And there are the indirect benefits of further employment and additional output of useful goods and services in response to the increased demand for consumption goods out of the incomes earned by those employed on the project. These benefits may indeed make an investment socially useful even if the expected future benefits from the investment itself should not materialize at all.

Even "wasteful" investments are socially useful in a depression.

More striking still is the consideration, which follows immediately from this analysis, that in time of depression it is worth while undertaking even "investments" that are not really investments at all but merely wasteful expenditures of money. For if an investment is socially useful even though the expected return fails to materialize, it will be socially useful if the future return was never even expected. If there is severe unemployment it is socially useful to have people paid for "digging holes and filling them in again." Since there is general unemployment no sacrifice in other output is involved in such activity. On the contrary there is an increase in the output of other goods and services because of the increased spending by the people employed in digging and filling up holes. Indeed it would even be socially useful in these conditions for people to be employed in doing things that were positively harmful so long as the direct harm was less than the indirect good brought about by the increased distribution of money income.

Of course, it is foolish to employ people to do harmful or even useless things as long as there are so many useful things to be done. But this is no criticism of employing people in these foolish ways in times of depression if there are difficulties in the way of real investment. It is rather a criticism of permitting a state of severe unemployment to come about in the first place through a failure to get everybody employed in doing useful things. It is this failure which is responsible for the ridiculous situation in which useless and even moderately harmful "investment" is an improvement on the unwanted idleness that it displaces.

Investment and consumption have repercussions on each other.

Any increase in investment—or in mock "investment"—results in a *greater* increase in income. This is possible although income is always equal to the sum of investment and consumption, because consumption does not stand still when investment increases.

Going back to our example in which the propensity to consume was equal to 40 billion dollars plus two-thirds of the excess of income over 40 billion dollars, we can see by just how much income increases when investment increases. We saw in Chapter 5 how an investment of 10 billion dollars per annum results in an annual income of 70 billion dollars out of which consumption is 60 billion dollars. What would be the effect of an increase in investment of 1 billion dollars over and above the 10 billion dollars assumed before?

With investment 11 billion instead of 10 billion dollars and with consumption staying at 60 billion dollars, income would be 71 billion dollars. But consumption would not stay at 60 billion dollars and so income would not stay at 71 billion dollars. The additional 1 billion dollars of income created by the additional investment would lead to more spending by those who earned the extra 1 billion dollars. The propensity to consume tells us that two-thirds of any increase in income would go for additional consumption. This would create an additional ⅔ billion dollars of income. But 71⅔ billion dollars of income is not the answer either because the additional ⅔ billion dollars of income would itself lead to more consumption and this would lead to still more income and so to still more consumption and so on.

The answer is that income will keep on increasing until it reaches the level where a gap equal to the additional investment is provided between income and consumption. An additional 3 billion dollars of income must be created out of which the recipients will want to spend an additional 2 billion dollars on consumption. This additional 2 billion dollars of consumption creates an additional 2 billion dollars of income, leaving a 1-billion-dollar gap to be filled by the additional investment. Consumption is 62 billion, investment is 11 billion, adding up to an income of 73 billion dollars. The propensity to consume is such that out of an income of 73 billion just 62 billion dollars will be consumed so that all the conditions are satisfied.[5]

An alternative way of getting the solution is to say that since saving must be equal to investment, income will keep on rising until it reaches the level where people *want* to save as much as is being invested. As long as income is less than 73 billion dollars, the economy as a whole wants to save *less* than 11 billion dollars. But they find themselves saving exactly 11 billion dollars because that is the amount which is being invested. The public will therefore increase their consumption in an attempt to reduce their saving to the amount indicated by their propensity to save (which is only another aspect of their propensity to consume). The effect of the increase in spending is, however, not to reduce the total saving (which cannot differ from the 11 billion dollars invested) but to increase total income. Since the propensity to save is such that the public wants to save one-third of any additions to income, income must increase by 3 billion dollars for

[5] See appendix to Chap. 6, sec. 2.

the public to want to increase their saving by 1 billion dollars. This gives us the same answer: income 73 billion, consumption 62 billion, and saving (and investment) 11 billion dollars.[6]

In the same way as an increase in investment has repercussions on consumption, so there will be repercussions of consumption on investment. An increase in income, due perhaps to an increase in the propensity to consume, will make businessmen more optimistic and increase the volume of investment. An increase in output, in certain conditions, may lead to a large increase in investment to bring about a needed expansion of equipment. And all these repercussions will react on each other in ways which we shall analyze a little more fully below. The reactions may be very complex, but the first and most important rule in all such analyses is to remember all the time that, whatever happens, total income is always the sum of investment and of consumption and that any departure from this truism can be checked indirectly by seeing whether there is anywhere implied a difference between saving and investment.

The line between investment and consumption is somewhat arbitrary.

We spoke above of "investment" by the government that was not really investment because it did not produce goods or services in the future but only had the same immediate money-income-creating effect that investment has. The quotation marks around the word were an indication of something strange about calling the activity investment. All the effects that we were interested in would come about just as much if the government were to spend the same amount of money on consumption. What is important for the effects on current income is the *spending of money,* irrespective of whether it is for consumption or for investment. If the government were to spend an additional 1 billion dollars per

[6] See appendix to Chap. 6, sec. 3.

annum on anything whatever, it would create an additional 1 billion dollars of income directly and this would lead to exactly the same repercussion when the extra income led to extra spending and the extra spending led to still more extra income. With the same propensity to consume, income would increase by 3 billion dollars, 2 billion dollars being created by the additional spending out of the extra 3 billion and 1 billion dollars being created by the government spending.

With the additional 3 billion dollars of income, saving by the public will have increased by 1 billion dollars, and it might seem that there is a discrepancy of a kind that cannot be allowed since there is no corresponding increase in investment and we know that saving must be equal to investment just as 2 and 2 must be equal to 4.

There is no need for alarm here. Saving is still equal to investment. It is true that investment has not increased while saving by the public has increased by a billion dollars. But the increased spending by the government on consumption (which is what it must have been if it was not investment) means that the government has reduced *its* saving (or incurred dissaving) by a billion dollars. Total saving by the government together with the public is therefore no more than before and is still equal to the unchanged investment. The extra saving by the public is exactly offset by the reduction in saving by the government.

Sometimes it is difficult to say whether any particular expenditure is more properly considered consumption or investment. It may depend on what one thinks of the expected future return. But it does not matter which name we give to the spending in question. It does of course matter, or rather it will matter in the future, whether the expenditure was directed to something that will be useful in the future. But the immediate effects on income and on employment are exactly the same whether the investment is highly efficient or not efficient at all or even if it is destructive of future income.

The distinction we have to make is not really between consumption and investment but between spending which is governed by our formula for the propensity to consume and other spending which is not so governed. Other spending is, in the main, investment; but consumption by the government, just like investment by the government, may not be governed by our formula for the propensity to consume and if so it can be handled just like investment.

We may illustrate this by supposing that our formula for the propensity to consume, $C = 40 + \frac{2}{3}(Y - 40)$, referred to consumption by the government of 10 billion dollars and consumption by the public of 30 billion dollars plus two-thirds of the excess of national income over 40 billion dollars. We might say that the 10 billion dollars spent by the government was consumption by the beneficiaries of the government expenditures, the children who went to school, the inmates of hospitals, the users of the roads, and so on. In that case we would proceed exactly as in the last chapter and conclude that if investment is zero income would be 40 billion dollars and that if investment is 10 billion dollars income would be 70 billion.

But we could just as well call the government expenditures "investment" in the future of the nation, in its education and health and earning power and what not. The propensity to consume is now different. $C = 30 - \frac{2}{3}(Y + 40)$. Consumption is now only 30 billion dollars plus two-thirds of the excess of national income over 40 billion dollars. With the government "investment" of 10 billion dollars, income would be 40 billion, consumption by the public would be 30 billion, and saving 10 billion dollars, equal to the "investment." If there were a further investment of another 10 billion dollars, this would lead to an income of 70 billion dollars out of which consumption by the public would be 50 billion, "investment" by the government 10 billion, and other investment 10 billion, with saving 20 billion dollars. These different figures would only be another way of describing the identical situation with the nominal difference that the spending by the government is called "investment" instead of consumption. Where the line is drawn between consumption and investment makes no real difference as long as it is not shifted in the middle of the argument. The important thing in this analysis is the *sum* of the investment and the consumption and this is unaffected by moving the dividing line between the two.

Summary.

There are many determinants of investment. These can be divided into future benefits and present costs. The future benefits depend on technical and on economic elements and they are dependent on estimates in the making of which the optimism and pessimism of potential investors can play an important part. Parallel considerations affect the cost side in the calculations of the profitability of investments.

A more positive consideration resulting from the time element is the necessity for calculating interest. This is so even if the investor invests his own money. Given all the other determinants of investment we can draw up a schedule showing the volume of investment that would take place at each rate of interest. (This *investment curve* is sometimes called the schedule of the marginal efficiency of investment, the efficiency of any investment being that rate of interest which is just sufficient to render it unattractive.) The investment curve, together with the rate of interest, gives us the volume of investment and so the level of income and of employment. What we need now is the determination of the rate of interest.

Investment by the government may take into account benefits for which it is impossible or inexpedient to make the beneficiary pay sufficient to cover the cost of the investment. Governments can also take into account the immediate income-creating effects of investment. These may make an investment socially desirable in time of depression even if the future benefits should not materialize and even if no future benefits were to be expected from it. Even harmful "investments" may then be worth while because of the indirect income-creating effects, although neutral or useful investments would of course be better still.

An increase in investment, by increasing income, brings about further increases in consumption and in income and so on. There results a level of income at which the gap between the extra income and the extra consumption appropriate to that level of income (the extra saving) is equal to the extra investment. Similarly, increased consumption leads to increased investment. But the important thing to remember is that total investment plus total consumption are equal to total income. The same identity is shown in the equality of saving to investment.

"Investment" by the government can be treated as consumption and consumption by the government can be treated as "investment" without disturbing the account of the actual events as long as the propensity to consume is properly adjusted to the definition. It does not matter where the arbitrary line is drawn between consumption and investment as long as the line is not shifted in the middle of the argument. The important distinction is between that spending which follows the formula for the propensity to consume and that spending which does not.

Appendix to Chapter 6

1. Figure 10 shows an *investment curve* indicating the relationship between the rate of interest and the volume of investment. If we measure the rate of interest on the vertical axis and investment on the horizontal axis, we shall get a curve which slopes down from left to right. This indicates that at a lower rate of interest more investment would be undertaken than at a higher rate of interest. Taking any rate of interest we shall be able to read off how many billions of dollars' worth of investment per annum will result from having that particular rate of interest, given all the other conditions that affect the volume of investment.

This same curve is often called the schedule of the marginal efficiency of investment. (J. M. Keynes, who first defined it clearly, called it the schedule of the marginal efficiency of capital.) This is because it is possible to measure the efficiency of an investment by seeing how high the rate of interest has to be to render it unprofitable. If an investment shows a very large return in the future for a very small cost incurred now, it will take a very high rate of interest to stop it from being undertaken. On the other hand, if the future return from an investment is hardly greater than the cost incurred in the present, it will be undertaken only if the rate of interest is very low. For every potential investment there is a rate of interest that exactly offsets the attractiveness of the investment so that the investor

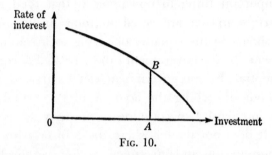

FIG. 10.

is quite indifferent whether he undertakes the investment or not. At any higher rate of interest than this the investment will definitely not be undertaken and at any lower rate of interest it definitely will be undertaken. This critical rate of interest is the measure of the *efficiency* of the investment.

The investment curve may be interpreted as representing an arrangement of all the investment opportunities, as seen by the potential investors at any time, in order of their efficiency. If we take any point A on the horizontal axis and draw a vertical line AB joining this point to the curve, we can say that OA represents a certain volume of investment that is being undertaken. The part of the curve that lies to the left of AB represents all the investments that have a higher efficiency than the investment opportunity at A. The rest of the curve, which lies to the right, represents other potential investments that have a lower efficiency and are not undertaken just because their efficiency is less. AB, which measures the efficiency of the investment opportunity at A, represents the *marginal* efficiency of investment corresponding to the given volume of investment. It is the efficiency of the unit of investment which is the least efficient of all the investments that *are* undertaken but which is *more* efficient than any of those which are not undertaken. The curve thus shows the marginal efficiency of investment for each volume of investment, a lower marginal efficiency having to be accepted with every increase in the volume of investment.

This interpretation of the investment curve as a curve of the marginal efficiency of investment has the disadvantage of seeming to suggest that one could arrange the different investments in such an order without first knowing what the rate of interest is. But the efficiencies of the different investments depend so much on what goes on in the minds of the potential investors, on their guesses as to the probabilities of gain, that the only way to find out anything about efficiencies of investments is to establish a rate of interest and see whether any particular investment is undertaken or not, and even this only tells us whether the marginal efficiency of the investment is greater or smaller than the rate of interest established. Furthermore, it seems to suggest that the different potential investments are independent of each other in their efficiencies, whereas it is certain that the efficiency of any investment depends very much indeed on what other investments are being undertaken at the same time. It is therefore best to consider our curve not as a schedule of the marginal efficiency of investment, but merely as a curve telling us how much investment will take place at each rate of interest—as an *investment curve*.

2. Figure 8 (page 82) shows how an increase of investment from zero to 10 billion dollars moves the equilibrium position from P to Q, indicating an increase in income of three times the increase in investment. There is the same relationship between the increase in investment and the resulting increase in income because there is the same assumption that the marginal propensity to consume is $\frac{2}{3}$.

3. The lower part of Fig. 8 (page 82) shows how an increase in investment from zero to 10 billion dollars shifts the equilibrium level from T, where saving and investment are equal to each other at zero, to U, where saving and investment are equal to each other at 10 billion dollars. With the same marginal propensity to save of $\frac{1}{3}$ a 1-billion-dollar increase in investment would cause income to increase by 3 billion dollars as may be seen on Fig. 8 by supposing the I curve to be raised by 1 billion dollars. This may also be seen in Fig. 9 (page 83) where raising the I curve from the 10-billion- to the 11-billion-dollar level would cause it to intersect the $S(Y)$ curve at B.

CHAPTER 7

Interest[1]

IN THE last chapter we saw that we needed to know the rate of interest to be able to read off on the investment curve what would be the volume of investment. This volume of investment, together with the propensity to consume, would give us the income level and from there we could get to the volume of employment. But right at the beginning of this chain of influence was the rate of interest, which we have not explained at all. What determines the rate of interest?

The rate of interest is the charge for borrowing money.

The rate of interest has in recent years come to mean in economics something a little more like what it means in ordinary English. It is the payment made for the privilege of borrowing money and shows itself in the repayment being greater than the sum borrowed. If I borrow $100 for a year at a rate of interest of 6 per cent per annum, I have to give back $106 at the end of the year. Of this, $100 is the return of the money borrowed and the other $6 is the interest paid for the privilege of borrowing the $100 for a year.

There is still some difference, however, between this meaning of the rate of interest and its meaning in ordinary English. We shall use the phrase to refer to the "pure" rate of interest that is paid merely for the difference in time between the receipt of the money and its repayment. Any recompense for possible dangers that the repayment may not be made when due is left out and considered separately as a risk premium, even though the most convenient way of charging for it may be by simply asking for

[1] See the note at the beginning of Chap. 4.

a larger number of dollars per cent per annum for the loan. This makes the higher charge look like a higher rate of interest, but we would say that only a part of this payment is interest and the rest is payment for risk. In the same way we would exclude any other considerations that might make the charge for a loan greater (or smaller) other than that due purely to the time interval between the borrowing and the repayment.

It is possible to borrow money indefinitely without specifying any date of repayment or even considering any repayment at all. The borrowing may take the form of a permanent loan, yielding a permanent interest, like some government loans in perpetuity or *rentes*. These can easily be fitted into the above definition, which has many conveniences, by supposing the loan to be for a definite period, say a year, with provision for reborrowing the sum again each year, only the interest being actually paid to the lender.

Interest is determined on the market for loans.

The rate of interest being what is paid by a borrower to a lender for the privilege of borrowing money, it must depend on the conditions in the market for borrowing and lending. If there should be an increase in the willingness (and ability) of lenders to lend money, without there being a corresponding increase in the eagerness to borrow, the rate of interest would have to fall sufficiently to reduce the willingness to lend and to increase the eagerness to borrow until the amount demanded by borrowers is equal to the amount offered by lenders so that the market is cleared. Conversely if there should be an increase in the eagerness to borrow without a corresponding increase in the willingness to lend, the rate of interest would have to rise sufficiently to reduce the eagerness to borrow and to increase the willingness to lend until the demand for loans is again equal to the supply.[2]

[2] We speak of borrowers as "eager" to borrow and of lenders as "willing" to lend. This is done merely for convenience of exposition and not to indicate that borrowers must necessarily be more anxious than lenders for

If we knew all the determinants of the eagerness of borrowers to borrow money and of the willingness of lenders to lend money we would be able to figure out the rate of interest at which the loan market would be cleared and could go back at once to the story of the determination of investment and so to employment. But we have to go into a few complications here.

Interest may seem to be determined by the readiness to save and the opportunity to invest.

Most borrowing is by investors who borrow money in order to invest, and most lending is done by individuals who save and lend part of their income. (Lending by businesses of a part of their earnings instead of distributing them as dividends can be considered as involuntary saving and lending by the individuals whose dividend receipts are reduced by this practice.) This tempts one to say that the primary force behind the eagerness to borrow is the opportunity to invest and that the primary force behind the willingness to lend is the readiness to save, so that one can say, going direct to the primary forces, that the rate of interest is determined by the interaction between the opportunity to invest and the readiness to save. At some equilibrium rate of interest the amount that investors want to borrow will be just equal to the amount that savers are willing to lend. At a higher rate of interest savers might be induced to save (and lend) more (although this is not insisted on) while investors would certainly be discouraged since some of the investment would be rendered unprofitable. This would mean a supply of (loaned) savings greater than the demand for them and so a reduction of the rate of interest to the equilibrium level. In the same way a lower rate of interest could not be maintained but would rise toward the equilibrium level at which investment is equal to saving.[3]

the transaction. It is perfectly possible for a lender to be more willing to lend his money than a borrower is eager to borrow it.

[3] See appendix to Chap. 7, sec. 1.

This explanation fails to consider the effects of investment and of savings decisions on income.

This saving-investment explanation of the rate of interest is very widely held and it seems to fit in with our insistence in previous chapters that saving and investment must be equal to each other. Nevertheless, the explanation is unacceptable. It would be useful to look into the errors in the theory because nothing can better help one to understand the relationships actually involved.

The primary objection to this saving-investment explanation of the rate of interest is that it fails to consider the effect of changes in investment on the readiness to save. An increase of investment increases income. An increase in income increases the readiness to save and therefore also the willingness to lend. But the saving-investment explanation leaves this out of the picture entirely, just as if someone were somehow offsetting all these effects and keeping income constant at a given level, apparently at the level of full employment.

If someone were really offsetting any changes in investment and in consumption and so keeping income at some given level, it would be perfectly proper to keep to the silent assumption that when an increase or decrease in the opportunity to invest increases or decreases the eagerness to borrow, this leaves the willingness to lend unchanged and that when an increase or decrease in the readiness to save increases or decreases the willingness to lend, this leaves the eagerness to borrow unchanged. But it is clear that there is nobody keeping income constant, either at the level of full employment or at any other level, and it is most peculiar, to say the least, to assume that income is being kept constant when we are trying to discover what are the determinants of the level of income and of employment. We must therefore reject entirely this frustrating assumption and look very carefully at just these repercussions of the eagerness to borrow on the willingness to lend and of the willingness to lend on the eagerness to borrow. Only by doing this will we be able to find the answer to our question: What determines the rate of interest?

Each dollar of borrowing for investment creates a dollar of lending.

Whenever an increase in the opportunity to invest causes anyone to borrow an extra dollar and invest it, the act of investment creates an extra dollar of income for someone else. If the person who earns this dollar decides to spend none of it but to lend all of it, there is an induced increase in the willingness to lend just equal to the increased eagerness to borrow. The increased opportunity to invest thus fails to have any effect whatsoever on the rate of interest.

It is, of course, most unlikely that the extra income earned would all be loaned and none of it spent, but we can give up this unrealistic assumption without affecting the conclusion. If, say, two-thirds of the dollar is spent and only one-third of the dollar is loaned out, the two-thirds of the dollar that is spent increases a second person's income by just two-thirds of a dollar. If the second person loans out this two-thirds of a dollar, we again have an increase in willingness to lend equal to the increase in eagerness to borrow. If, as is more likely, the second person does not lend the whole of the increase in his income but spends part of it, that merely prolongs the story. Another person then receives more income, and if he lends this out, there is then available a total increase of lending of one dollar —equal to the original increase in the borrowing that was caused by the increased opportunity to invest.

Although nobody may ever be found who decides to save and lend out the whole of any increase in his income, we can see that as this series goes on we get closer and closer to having the increase in lending equal to the increase in borrowing. If we make the simplifying assumption that everybody whose income increases decides to consume two-thirds and to save and lend the remaining third, we get a simple series. The first man who earns the dollar adds to lending one-third of the dollar, spending the remaining two-thirds. The next man saves and lends one-third of this remainder and spends the rest. The next man lends one-third of this rest and spends the remainder, and so on. But one-third of a dollar, plus one-third of the rest, plus one-third of the remainder, and so on, means in effect the whole dollar. For the remainder gets smaller and smaller until it reaches the vanishing point.

If we make more complicated assumptions about the proportions in which the different men along the line divide their added income between spending and lending, we get a more complicated series, but the result is always the same. At every stage a larger or smaller fraction of the remaining part of the dollar is added to the willingness to lend and the process goes on until the whole of the dollar has been added to the willingness to lend. Different propensities to consume will have very important effects on the extent to which the additional investment increases the incomes of the people all along the line, but the increase in willingness to lend generated by the increase in investment is exactly equal to the increase in investment and so to the increase in the eagerness to borrow. A change in the opportunity to invest does not by itself have any effect on the rate of interest. It increases the willingness to lend just as much as it increases the eagerness to borrow.[4]

Each dollar of saving (and lending) creates a dollar of borrowing.

Exactly the same kind of complication comes to light if we examine the effects of a change in the readiness to save. If any individual decides to cut a dollar from his consumption and to lend it, this is an increase of a dollar in the willingness to lend, but we must not forget that the shopkeeper who fails to get the

[4] See appendix to Chap. 7, sec. 2.

dollar (because it is his customer who has become more thrifty) will be a dollar short. If he is to absorb the full effects he will have to borrow an additional dollar to be able to meet all his obligations. On the other hand, if he does not absorb the whole effect but reduces some of his outlays because of the decrease in his sales, somebody else will have his income reduced by the degree to which a shopkeeper passes on reduction in his income (or perhaps one should say "fails to pass on the income he does not get"). The second victim will have to borrow the part of the dollar that the shopkeeper does not borrow. If he decides to pass on some of the reduction in his income in a reduction of his outlays, a third victim is created. A series of income reductions develops, similar in every respect to the series of increases in income following the increase in investment. The amount by which aggregate income is decreased depends on how much each member of the chain cuts his spending and thereby reduces the income of the next man. But the increase in the eagerness to borrow in order to fill the deficiencies always adds up exactly to the original increase in willingness to lend. At each step some fraction of the missing dollar is absorbed and this fraction has to be borrowed. The series goes on until the successive parts of the missing dollar that are made good by borrowing amount to the whole dollar, the remaining fraction shrinking to insignificance.[5]

Thus we see that neither borrowing for investment nor lending out of saving has any net effect on the rate of interest. The investment brings about an increase in the supply of loans that offsets the borrowing, and the saving brings about an increase in the demand for loans that offsets the lending.

The analysis does not depend in any way on the distinction between investment and consumption. Spending the borrowed money on consumption instead of investment would make no difference to the effect or lack of effect on the rate of interest, because it has exactly the same effects as investment on the income

[5] See appendix to Chap. 7, sec. 3.

of the recipients of the spending. In the same way, if the lender set free his money not by being thrifty and reducing his consumption but by being frightened and reducing his investment, this would make no difference for the rate of interest. Whether it is consumption or investment that is affected does not matter for our purpose. All that matters is the effect on spending of either kind and thus on the income created by spending. Borrowing money and *spending* it leaves the rate of interest unchanged. Cutting expenditures and lending the money saved leaves the rate of interest unchanged. In the first case the increase in spending brings about an increase in lending that offsets the initial increase in borrowing. In the second case the reduction in spending brings about an increase in borrowing that offsets the initial increase in lending.

Sometimes the increase in income generated by an increase in investment, instead of increasing the willingness to lend, may decrease the eagerness to borrow. This is true when an individual who would have been borrowing does not need to borrow so much because his earnings have increased. Such a decrease in the eagerness to borrow is equivalent to an increase in the willingness to lend in canceling any effect on the rate of interest. In the same way an increase in thrift, instead of causing every victim whose income is cut to resort to borrowing, may merely decrease the amount which he would otherwise be lending. Again, such a decrease in the willingness to lend is just as effective as an increase in the eagerness to borrow in canceling any effects on the rate of interest.

The argument cannot be saved by bringing in time lags.

At this point of the argument the reader is likely to feel a little uneasy—to sense that something is being put over on him. And there is some justification to this suspicion, as we shall see later in this chapter. Our conclusion was that, although investment is the main reason for borrowing and saving is the main source of lending, neither the opportunity to invest nor the readiness to save has any effect on the rate of interest. This conclusion seems so preposterous that heroic efforts are made to escape it.

A handy way out of almost any difficulty in economic theory is to bring in *time lags* a little loosely. One is tempted to argue here that it may take a long time for the repercussions of the original investment or saving to work themselves out. Meanwhile the increased opportunity to invest does create a net increase in the eagerness to borrow not completely offset by the increased willingness to lend, or the increase in thrift does create an increased willingness to lend which, for the time being at least, keeps ahead of the increases in the eagerness to borrow which would offset it.

This way out is not permissible. The argument cannot be saved by bringing in a time lag because the investment curve is supposed to show the effect not of a *change* in the rate of interest but the results of *having* a certain rate of interest to which the necessary adjustments have been made. If some of the effects of today's increased borrowing and investing have not yet reached the individuals whose saving and lending out of increased income would offset the initial effects, we must not forget that we shall now be reaping some of these effects from a higher investment that took place some time ago. These delays in the repercussions therefore cancel themselves out and cannot dispel our disturbing conclusion.

Borrowing without spending and lending without saving do have an effect on the rate of interest.

We must now confess to a sort of holding back which may have been causing the reader some uneasiness. We have consistently left out of account another possibility of adjustment that is available to all the people involved in our repercussions. We have been assuming that the borrower invests (or otherwise spends) every penny he borrows, that everyone whose income increases either spends or lends out every additional penny he receives, and conversely, that everyone whose income is reduced either reduces his spending or increases his borrowing (or reduces his lending) by a penny for every penny by which his income is re-duced. But this is not necessarily so. And if this is not the case, the exact neutralization of effects on the rate of interest will no longer be necessary either.

If the borrower does *not* invest (or otherwise spend) all the money he borrows but only part of it, the additional lending by those whose incomes are increased by the repercussions of the additional spending will amount to less than the original borrow-ing. There then remains a net effect, *raising* the rate of interest. Similarly, if a lender does *not* reduce his spending by as much as he lends, the repercussions will be insufficient to undo the effect of his lending and the rate of interest will fall.

But this always means increasing or decreasing one's cash balances.

All this is possible because the borrower may add some of the borrowed money to his *cash balances* instead of investing it, and the lender may be lending some money that comes out of his cash balances instead of out of reduced spending. The same kind of thing is possible for the others involved in the repercussions. The lucky people whose incomes are increased by the increase in investment (or other spending) do not have to lend out every penny of their increased income that they do not spend. They can add some of it to their cash balances. Similarly the unfor-tunates who are caught in the reductions of income that result from the thrift of the original lender may not have to borrow (or decrease their lending) even if they do not want to reduce the spending by quite as much as their income has fallen. They may be able to take some of the difference out of *their* cash balances.

This does not save but rather destroys the saving-investment theory of interest.

By bringing in the cash balances we may seem to have saved the original theory that said that the rate of interest is determined by the demand for loans which are mainly for investment and the supply of loans which come mainly out of saving. A change in demand no longer brings about an exactly equal change in supply, and a change in supply no longer brings about an exactly equal change in demand. There is now one rate of interest at which the demand for loans is equal to the supply of loans—an equilibrium rate of interest. At a lower rate of interest there will be more borrowing for investment, but since some of the increased income will be diverted into increasing some people's cash balances, the increase in lending will be less than the increase in borrowing. Demand for loans will be greater than supply and the rate of interest will move up again to the equilibrium position. In the same way a higher rate of interest would make the supply of loans greater than the demand and so cause the rate of interest to fall back again to the equilibrium level. We have a determinate equilibrium rate of interest explained in terms of borrowing mainly for investment and of lending mainly out of saving.

One might think it merely necessary to concede that not all the borrowing is invested—some of it may be "hoarded"—and that not all of the lending must come out of saving—some of it may come out of cash balances or consist of "dishoarding."

But it must be recognized that such a concession really abandons the whole theory. For the rate of interest is raised by borrowing only to the extent that the borrowers fail to invest all the money they borrow but add some of it to their cash balances and to the extent that the other people affected do not spend or lend all their increased income but add some of it to *their* cash balances. We have also seen that the rate of interest is lowered by an increased willingness to lend only to the extent that the lenders lend more money than they save, taking the difference out of their cash balances, and to the extent that the other people affected reduce their spending or lending (or increase their borrowing) by less than the amount by which their income is reduced, taking the difference out of *their* cash balances.

In fact we may say that the concession turns the theory into something very much like its opposite. The rate of interest is raised by borrowing only when it is borrowing that is *not invested* or otherwise spent, and it is lowered by lending only when the lending is *not out of saving* or out of other reductions in spending. But it is much more satisfactory to put the matter positively. The rate of interest is raised whenever people try to increase their cash balances and is reduced whenever they try to reduce their cash balances. The saving and the investment are not directly relevant at all. What matters is what people try to do to their cash balances.

We have spoken as if the only two sources of obtaining money to lend out are one's saving and one's cash balances. This is not strictly true for any individual, but it is a legitimate simplification because we were considering the matter from the point of view of the economy as a whole. We have seen that any *net* addition to lending cannot come out of one's saving but only out of a reduction either of one's own cash balances or of somebody else's cash balances. The alternative we have neglected is that of selling something to get the cash to make the loan. But that cannot lead to a *net* increase in lending unless the buyer of the asset is prepared to let his cash balance be reduced. If he tries to replenish it he will offset the effect of the lending. Again it is only the willingness of someone to let his cash balance diminish which makes possible a net increase in the willingness to lend which reduces the rate of interest. Indeed the selling of an asset can be treated as equivalent to borrowing the money and handing over the asset as a security for the loan. We can thus consider our lender as borrowing the money that he lends, and so there is no net increase in the willingness to lend relatively to the eagerness to borrow.

There remains only the case where the lender begs, borrows, or steals the money that he lends. In this last case, it is obvious that the lending comes out of somebody else's cash balances. There will be a net increase in the willingness to lend relatively to the eagerness to borrow only to the degree that those who have lost cash will acquiesce in the reduction and will not try to replenish their cash balances. If those who have lost the cash do not acquiesce in the reduction but try to replenish their cash balances completely and those who get hold of the cash want to keep some of it in their cash balances, the effect will be just the opposite—a net increase in the eagerness to borrow. From the point of view of the economy as a whole, it is strictly true that a *net* increase in willingness to lend or a *net* decrease in the eagerness to borrow can come only out of *someone's* agreeing to allow his cash balances to diminish.

What we have in its place is a liquidity-preference *and* cash-balances *theory of interest.*

We can now see that the rate of interest is determined by the available supply of money and the amount of money that the public want to keep in their cash balances. The amount of money that a person wants to keep in cash depends on the rate of interest, since that is what it costs him to keep his money in cash—what he loses by failing to lend it out or to repay his debts. The lower the rate of interest, the less it costs to hold money "idle," and the more one can indulge in the convenience of having idle cash in hand for meeting emergencies or for being prepared to take advantage of special opportunities for getting bargains that might crop up at any time. The higher the rate of interest the more it costs to hold cash idle and the less will anyone indulge in this luxury.[6]

[6] See appendix to Chap. 7, sec. 4.

Of course the total amount of money held by everybody in the community cannot be different from the total amount of money in existence. A general increase in the desire to hold cash— to be *liquid*—cannot result in everybody's holding more cash. There can be no increase in the total cash held as long as there is no increase in the amount of money in existence. That is why we had to speak of *trying* to increase or decrease cash balances instead of simply increasing or decreasing them. What happens when there is a general increase in the desire to be liquid—in *liquidity preference*—is that a general increase in the eagerness to borrow and a general decrease in the willingness to lend raises the rate of interest. The rate of interest rises until it has so discouraged those who wanted to borrow to add to their cash and so much encouraged others to lend out some of their cash in order to earn the higher rate of interest that the supply of loans is once more equal to the demand for them. This will happen only when the public is satisfied with the amount of cash they have, considering the high cost of holding it idle.

It is true that the rate of interest must be at a level where the supply of loans is equal to the demand for them, but it is more enlightening to say that the rate of interest is determined at the level where the demand for holding cash is equal to the amount of cash available to be held.

If there is no change in the amount of money in existence, a change in liquidity preference does not change the amount of money the public holds. That is impossible. What it does is to change the rate of interest as much as is necessary to reconcile the public to holding the same amount of money in spite of the change in the desire to hold money.

On the other hand, if there is an increase in the amount of money in existence the public *has to* increase its holding of cash. Again it has to be reconciled to doing this by a change in the rate of interest. If the amount of money in the hands of the public is increased by the monetary authorities, the public will find themselves with more cash than seems reasonable and will try to lend it out or otherwise exchange it for interest-earning forms of wealth. This reduces the rate of interest until the reduction in the cost of holding money—the cheapening of the convenience and luxury of liquidity—persuades the public that it is not really unreasonable to hold the larger amount of money in cash balances.[7]

The supply of money in existence is decided by the monetary authorities. The demand for money to hold, or the liquidity preference, is provided by the public. These two forces between them determine the rate of interest.

Summary.

By the rate of interest is meant the payment made for the privilege of borrowing money. The "pure" rate of interest is what is paid for a loan apart from any considerations other than the difference in time between the date of borrowing and the date of repayment. Risk is another such consideration, and the recompense for it is not a part of the pure interest. The rate of interest depends on the conditions in the market for loans. Since most borrowing is for investment and most lending comes out of saving, one may be tempted to say that the rate of interest is determined by the interaction of the opportunity to invest and the readiness to save.

This explanation is unacceptable because it leaves out of account (1) the effect of increased investment in increasing the level of income and therefore the willingness to lend and (2) the effect of attempts to increase saving in diminishing income and therefore the willingness of others to lend (or their need to borrow). If we take these repercussions into account we find that it is only when borrowing is *not invested* or otherwise spent that it tends to increase the rate of interest and it is only when lending is *not out of saving* that it tends to lower the rate of interest. This conclusion cannot be evaded by loosely referring to time lags.

[7] See appendix to Chap. 7, sec. 5.

Borrowing money without spending it means increasing one's cash balances, and lending money without saving it means reducing one's cash balances. It is only when borrowers or lenders or some of the other people affected by the change want to increase or decrease their cash balances that there is any net effect on the rate of interest. We can therefore simply say that the rate of interest is determined at that level at which the public is satisfied to hold the amount of money in existence. A change in the amount of money in existence also results in a change in the rate of interest since the public must be persuaded (by a higher rate of interest) to be satisfied with a smaller amount of money in their possession or must be induced (by a lower rate of interest) to be willing to hold "idle" a larger stock of money in their possession. The rate of interest is therefore determined by the interaction between the *stock of money*, as decided by the monetary authorities, and the *liquidity preference* of the public—their desire to hold various amounts of money depending on how expensive this is made by the rate of interest.

Appendix to Chapter 7

1. Figure 11 shows an investment curve, marked *I*, that indicates how much would be invested at different rates of interest and a saving curve, marked *S*, which indicates how much would be saved at different rates of interest. At a rate of interest of 4 per cent the supply of saving is equal to the demand of saving for investment at *P*, both saving and investment being 10 billion dollars per annum. At 5 per cent there is shown an excess of saving over investment measured by the distance *AB*. According to the saving-investment theory, this would make the rate of interest fall until it reached 4 per cent at *P* where the excess of saving over investment would disappear. At 3 per cent there is shown an excess of investment over saving of *CD*. This would make the rate of interest rise to 4 per cent with equality between saving and investment at *P*.

2. Figure 12 shows what happens when we bring in the effects of a change on investment on income and, through the change in income,

on the willingness and ability to save. If the rate of interest is reduced from 4 to 3 per cent, investment increases by ED (the amount that D lies to the right of P). But this increase in investment increases income and this shifts the S curve to the right. As long as the entire increase in income is saved, the new S curve must pass through D to show the amount saved in the new situation is greater than the initial saving by ED. It is unlikely that the entire increase in income resulting from the increase in investment at the lower rate of interest is all saved, but that makes no difference because the moment any of the additional income is consumed it creates still more income for somebody else who saves it. The moment he stops saving it he spends it and somebody else is saving it. This is another way of showing that saving cannot be either greater or smaller than investment.

The original S curve is here marked $S_{(4)}$ because it is only the S curve which corresponds to the level of income which corresponds to the level of investment which corresponds to the rate of interest of 4 per cent. $S_{(3)}$ is the S curve corresponding to 3 per cent. If the rate of interest were raised to 5 per cent the reduction in investment would reduce income, and the resulting S curve would be $S_{(5)}$ which is the supply curve of saving corresponding to 5 per cent. For every rate of interest there is a different saving curve which shows S equal to I for that rate of interest. *Every* rate of interest equates S to I. This means that the saving-investment theory of interest does not work. It does not explain why there should be one rate of interest rather than any other.

3. An increase in the propensity to save would mean that an S curve corresponding to a given income would shift to the right, showing the willingness to save (and lend) greater amounts at each rate of interest. But since the decision to save more results in a cut in consumption, there is a decrease in income, which is magnified by the further repercussions on spending. The new $S_{(4)}$ curve will still pass through P, in Fig. 12, and the new $S_{(3)}$ curve will still pass through D because the increased propensity to save (and lend) out of a given income is exactly offset by the resulting decrease in the income out of which to save (and lend). Every additional dollar that someone decides not to consume but to save (and lend) reduces someone else's income by a dollar, so that the amount actually saved does not change at all. Saving still has to be equal to investment. The same

thing happens in reverse if there is a *diminution* in the propensity to save and an increase in the income corresponding to each rate of in-

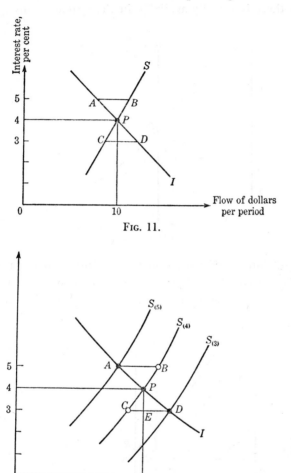

FIG. 11.

FIG. 12.

terest. There is no net change in the saving. Figure 12 is therefore not changed by any shift in the propensity to save. The *incomes* corresponding to the different rates of interest will change, but these are not shown in the figure.

4. In Fig. 13 the $L(i)$ curve indicates the liquidity-preference curve. This curve shows the willingness to hold cash, a willingness that de-

pends on the rate of interest, which is what it costs to hold non-interest-earning cash. The vertical line *AM* indicates the amount of cash that there is actually available in the system at any given time.

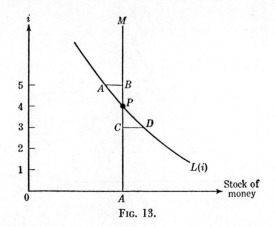

FIG. 13.

At a rate of interest of 4 per cent the amount of money people want to hold is just equal to the amount of money available for them to hold and we have the equilibrium rate of interest indicated by the

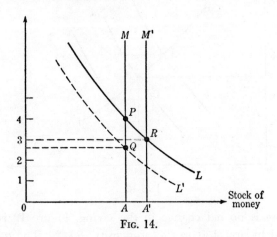

FIG. 14.

intersection of the two curves at *P*. At 5 per cent there would be an excess of the amount of money available over the amount that people wanted to hold—an excess of *AB*. The people who held this excess of money would try to lend it out and this would push the rate of interest down to the equilibrium level at *P*. At 3 per cent there would be a scarcity of cash of *CD* since people would like to hold this much more money than there is in existence. This would drive the interest rate up to the equilibrium level of 4 per cent at *P*.

5. Figure 14 shows how a shift of the liquidity-preference curve from *L* to *L'*, indicating a diminution in the willingness to hold idle cash, would result in a fall in the rate of interest from *P* to *Q* (from 4 to 2½ per cent) if there is no change in the amount of money in existence. The figure also shows how an increase in the amount of money in existence would lower the rate of interest from *P* to *R* (from 4 to 3 per cent) if there is no change in the liquidity preference.

CHAPTER 8

Functional Finance

NOW THAT we have found an explanation of the determination of the rate of interest, we have completed the framework of the theory of employment. Employment depends on the total money spent on the output of goods and services as a whole. Total spending consists of five elements. Two of these consist of consumption, namely, consumption by individuals and consumption by the government. The other three consist of investment—investment by individuals, investment by the government, and investment by businesses. Consumption depends mainly on income, the relationship between income and consumption being expressed by a formula which we call the propensity to consume. Investment depends on the general outlook for an excess of future benefits from investment over the present cost of undertaking it—the opportunity to invest on the one hand and the rate of interest on the other hand. Finally, the rate of interest is determined by its interaction between the stock of money available for the public to hold and the degree to which the public wants to hold its wealth in the form of liquid cash balances—its liquidity preference.

With these series of relationships we can start at the other end and build up the explanation of the determination of the volume of employment. The amount of money in existence together with the liquidity preference gives us the rate of interest, namely, that rate of interest at which the public wants to hold the amount of money in existence. The rate of interest, together with the opportunity to invest (as shown by the investment curve), gives us the volume of investment, namely, that rate of investment which brings the marginal efficiency of investment into equality

122

with the rate of interest. The volume of investment, together with the propensity to consume, gives us the level of income (and of consumption), namely, that level at which the public wants to save just as much as is being invested. Total income, which consists of total investment plus total consumption, is the same thing as total spending, and this gives us the level of employment, namely, that level which is necessary for the production of all the goods and services that this money outlay will buy.[1]

The issue is the prevention of both deflation and inflation.

With this understanding of the mechanism through which the level of employment is determined, we can see what can be done to influence the level of employment. If there is too little employment because of too little spending in the economy, the thing to do is to get an increase in total spending. This may take the form of increasing any one or more of the five elements which make up total spending by working on their determinants. An increase in the propensity to consume (which is the same thing as a decrease in the propensity to save) would serve the purpose. So would an increase in the opportunity to invest. With the same opportunity to invest we could get more investment if the rate of interest were reduced, and we have seen that this could be brought about if we could either reduce the public's liquidity preference or increase the available stock of money.

If there is too much spending so that there is inflation, exactly the opposite changes are desirable. It would then be necessary to decrease one or more of the five elements in total spending. It would help if there could be arranged a decrease in the propensity to consume (which is the same thing as an increase in the propensity to save) or a decrease in the opportunity to invest. With the same opportunity to invest we could still get a decrease in investment by having a higher rate of interest, which could be brought about by a higher liquidity preference or by a de-

[1] See appendix to Chap. 8, p. 137.

crease in the amount of money available for the public to hold in their cash balances.

Inadequate total spending is called "deflation" and its cure lies, of course, in increasing one or more of the elements in total spending. The opposite—excessive total spending—is called "inflation," and *its* cure lies in *diminishing* one or more of the elements in total spending. Inflation is fairly easy to recognize. It is seen in rising prices. Deflation is not quite so obvious. If there are falling prices, then it is clear that we have deflation. But if prices are stationary we still may have quite a considerable deficiency in total spending. It may be possible to increase employment and national income and output without coming up against inflation for quite a while. In such cases too, an increase in spending is desirable even though prices are not falling. Total spending in such a case should be increased until the beginnings of inflation are reached in the form of rising prices. The process must then be called to a halt.

Individual understanding is not enough because individual responses are perverse.

Economic understanding is, of course, always a desirable thing. But a mere understanding of all this by members of the public at large is not of much use in the prevention and cure of inflation and deflation. Even if everybody in the economy were completely well educated in these principles and knew that the economic need of the moment was an increase or a decrease of spending, this would do no good. It might even do a great deal of harm.

This is because it is not always in the interest of individuals to do that which is good for the community as a whole. If individuals learn, for instance, that there is going to be too much spending which will lead to inflation, they may know that this is a bad thing for the economy as a whole and that the evil would be avoided if everybody reduced his spending. But each individual would nevertheless be tempted to hurry to the stores and buy immediately various things that he might be thinking of buying in the future. He will want to buy them now before the price rises. If he were sure that the inflation depended only on his own action, he might be deterred, but he does not think that his own spending amounts to much in the total effect. His own refraining from buying will not prevent the inflation from taking place. Most people would therefore *increase* their spending if they understood that an inflation was threatening, and this increase in spending would increase the inflationary pressure.

In the same way, if there is insufficient spending with heavy unemployment and falling prices, even a universal knowledge and understanding that this could be corrected by everybody's increasing his spending will not help. Most individuals will succumb to the temptation to postpone expenditures in order to benefit from the expected lower prices in the future. And quite apart from any bargain hunting, the expectation of depression and unemployment will make people reduce their spending because they will be concerned with maintaining or increasing their reserves for the difficult times ahead. The result is that spending will be less and the deflation and the unemployment worse than if the public had been ignorant.

What all this means is that the reactions of individuals are *perverse*. Instead of correcting an excess or an insufficiency in total spending, they rather tend to aggravate the situation. A knowledge and an understanding of a situation in which spending is already excessive induce individuals to *increase* their spending, while a situation in which spending is already inadequate induces individuals who know what is happening to *reduce* their spending still more.

Perversity of private action makes social action necessary.

Whenever the *individual* reactions in any situation are perverse, what is needed is *social* action. This is the basic principle of social organization. The members of the society recognize that certain modes of behavior are in the general interest but would not be undertaken voluntarily. Yet if everyone were forced to undertake them, all would be better off. They can, therefore, come to a voluntary agreement that everybody should be forced to behave socially. That is why we are willing to be forced to keep to the right when driving as long as everybody else is also forced to keep the rule or why we agree to compulsory vaccination against smallpox even though each one of us would be safe, though un-vaccinated, as long as everyone else was vaccinated. If there were no compulsion, legal or moral, each of us would be tempted to avoid vaccination because the benefits we get from our own vaccination when everybody else is vaccinated are not worth the inconvenience entailed. But we agree to be compelled for the sake of securing that collective action from which we all gain.

The government has three pairs of fiscal instruments for dealing with inflation and deflation.

If total spending is inadequate there are three ways in which the government can increase it, and there are three corresponding ways in which the government can decrease total spending when it is excessive: (1) The government can increase total spending directly by increasing its own purchases (or offset the insuffi-ciency of demand in relation to supply by reducing its own sales of goods and services). (2) The government can increase total spending indirectly by inducing individuals to spend more. This is done most effectively either by giving more money away (in pensions, subsidies, social-security benefits, and even "social divi-dends") to people who will spend it (or a part of it) or by taking less money away from people in taxes so that they will have more money left to spend. (3) The government can increase total spend-ing even more indirectly by going into the loan market and lend-ing money or (what amounts to the same thing but is less astonish-ing) repaying some of its existing debt with newly issued money. This will have the effect of lowering the rate of interest. The lower rate of interest will induce investors to undertake some additional investment which is now worth while but which was not worth while at the previous higher rate of interest. This additional investment is the indirect addition to total spending.

In exactly the same way the government has three different ways in which it can reduce total spending when it is excessive: (1) It can reduce total spending directly by spending less itself (or offset the excessive demand by selling more goods itself). (2) It can decrease total spending indirectly, inducing individuals to spend less, by reducing its payments to them (in pensions, subsidies, social-security payments, and social dividends) or by taking more money away from them (in taxes). (3) It can go into the loan market and borrow money. This raises the rate of interest and thus discourages certain investments which are no longer profitable at the higher rate of interest. This reduction in investment is the indirect subtraction from total spending.

There are thus three pairs of *fiscal* instruments at the disposal of the government:

1. Buying and selling.
2. Giving and taking (money to or from citizens).
3. Lending and borrowing.

The first item in each pair is appropriate when total spending is too low; the second item in each pair, which is the opposite of the corresponding first item, is appropriate when total spending is excessive. Another way of expressing this is to say that all three first items are inflationary and so are appropriate to correct a deflationary situation while all three second items are deflationary and therefore appropriate to correct an inflationary situation.

These six fiscal instruments are exhaustive.

Each of the six fiscal instruments that constitute the three pairs has many other repercussions on the economy, and we shall have to examine some of these more carefully. But the six instruments are *exhaustive*. They include everything that the government can

do to influence or offset the level of total spending. Every possible action by the government to affect total spending either
is simply the use of one of these instruments or consists of a
combination of two or more of them. Taxation means *taking*
money away from people. Public works means *buying* the bridges
or whatever is produced by the public works. Even requisitioning
of goods can be considered as *buying* the goods and also *taking*
(taxing) away the money paid for them. Selling goods may seem
a little strange for the government, but not quite so strange now
that we have seen the government selling excess war materials in
great volume. Many schemes for the government to buy up goods
in the depression when there is insufficient demand and to sell
them again in boom times when demand is excessive fit into the
category of governmental acting on the economy by buying and
selling.

*A habit of considering fiscal instruments in combinations is
confusing.*

Some difficulties may be experienced by the reader because of
a very strong habit which most of us have been forced to acquire
of considering some of these governmental instruments only in
certain customary combinations. The habit is so strong that it
is almost impossible to think of one of these instruments except
in combination with another instrument even though the other is
not mentioned and often even in spite of its being explicitly
denied. Thus one often hears the argument that total spending
is not reduced by taxation (*i.e.*, by the government's taking money
away from people) because the government spends the money it
takes away. It has even been said that taxation *increases* total
spending because the taxpayers reduce their spending by only
a part of the taxes while the government increases *its* spending
by the whole amount of the tax revenues.

Such arguments rest on the supposition that when one says
taxing one means not simply taxing but taxing-and-spending.

The argument is then correct, but it is very confusing and makes it difficult to consider what would be the effect of, say, increasing taxes without increasing spending. It seems much clearer to keep to the principle, which ought to be self-evident but which is apparently quite revolutionary, of using words to mean no more than they say—of saying "taxing" when one means simply taxing and not when one means "taxing-and-spending." If one does mean taxing-and-spending, one could say "taxing and spending." One could thus deal with the combined effect as a combined effect without seeming to attribute to taxing not only its own effects but also the effects of the spending which is considered together with it.

The same kind of difficulty is also found in reverse, when it is said that government spending does not increase total spending because the taxes the government has to impose to get the money for its spending makes other people reduce *their* spending. This can easily be very misleading. It is possible for the government to increase its spending *without* imposing any extra taxes—it can spend money which it happened to have in stock, or it can cause money to be created, or it may borrow money, or it may buy on credit, and so on. And even if it does increase its taxes, and moreover even if it increases them by the same amount as it increases its spending, it is still far from certain and even far from likely that the people who pay the extra taxes will reduce their spending by exactly as much as the government increases its spending. It is therefore best, and we shall try to keep to this rule in the present book, to make all concomitants of any action explicit and to assume that if they are not mentioned they are not intended. When we speak of the effects of any of the governmental instruments, we shall mean simply the effects of applying that instrument alone. When we speak of the effects of government borrowing, for example, we shall not mean, as is frequently supposed, the combined effects of government borrowing-and-spending, but merely the effects of borrowing when there is no change in government spending or in any of the other instruments or other conditions of the situation.

Functional Finance rules out "sound finance."

Closely related to the implicit association of different instruments is the idea that the purpose of using one of the instruments is to make possible the use of another instrument, usually one which tends to neutralize the inflationary or deflationary effect of the first. Thus it is supposed that taxing is undertaken only in order to make available for the government the money which for some reason or other it wishes to spend. This is indeed why it is so difficult to separate taxing from spending even for the purpose of observing the effects of either one of the two actions. Some writers on public finance go so far as to say that the only legitimate purpose of taxation is to raise money for the government to spend and that taxation for any other purpose is some sort of perversion or improper use of the tax instrument, stigmatized as "nonfiscal."

If we recognize it as a prime responsibility of the government to prevent inflation and deflation and we see in the six fiscal instruments the means by which it can achieve this objective, we have no room left for the traditional idea that the government must collect in taxes all the money that it spends or that it must keep its spending within the range of its tax revenues. The idea that the government must equate its expenditure and its tax revenues—that it must balance its budget—can hardly be fitted in. For if the government undertakes to exercise its economic powers for the prevention of inflation and deflation, that determines its spending, its taxing, and the other economic actions which it undertakes. If this happens to result in government's spending being equal to its tax revenues, then the budget is balanced anyway and there is no need for any principle of balancing the budget. On the other hand, if the application of the six fiscal instruments for the prevention of inflation and deflation results in an unbalancing of the budget, *i.e.,* if it results in government spending being either greater or smaller than tax revenues, one would have to choose between the two different policies. One could leave the budget unbalanced and continue to prevent inflation and deflation, or one could give up the task of preventing inflation and deflation in order to be able to balance the budget. Since the balancing of the budget, when challenged, is usually defended on the ground that it is a way of preventing inflation, there does not seem to be very much sense in this procedure; it would be sacrificing the objective for the sake of an alleged means of achieving it.

In accepting the objective of preventing inflation and deflation through the use of the six fiscal instruments as the proper responsibility of the government, we are abandoning "sound finance," which makes the balancing of the budget the main criterion of fiscal policy, in favor of "Functional Finance," which says that each instrument in the hands of the government should be judged not by any traditional rule, such as that the budget should be balanced, but by the way it functions in the general interest and in the first place in contributing to the prevention of inflation and deflation.

The balancing of the budget is not the only idol that falls when the rational or functional approach is applied to fiscal policy. We may here mention some of the other unorthodox implications of Functional Finance.

One such implication is that taxes should *never* be imposed for the sake of the tax revenues. It is true that taxation makes money available to the government, but this is not an effect of any importance because money can be made available to the government so much more easily by having some created by the Treasury or by the banking system. The important effect of taxation is the effect on the *public* in influencing their economic behavior—in making them spend less because, for one thing, they have less money to spend. It is these effects which should be considered seriously and not the availability of money for the government. If these effects are not desired, if, for instance, there is insufficient total spending which a tax increase would make worse, it would not be wise to suffer this deflation just because the government needs some money which could be provided by an appropriate printing job. The common apprehension that the printing of money is inflationary (which we shall have to examine in detail in a later chapter) is especially inappropriate, since a little inflation in the sense of an increase in spending is exactly what the economy needs when it is suffering from insufficient total spending.

Another result of the functional approach is that government borrowing is seen to be not inflationary but deflationary. It has the effect of raising the rate of interest and discouraging investment and thus reducing total spending. The notion that government borrowing is inflationary, which is very common, derives from a coupling of government borrowing with government spending. The combination usually is inflationary because, if the government borrows *and spends* a million dollars, the reduction in spending by the lenders is probably less than the million extra spending by the government. But the effect of borrowing, taken as borrowing and not as borrowing-and-spending, is deflationary.

The creation of money is completely subsidiary to the six fiscal instruments.

It is important to note that the creation of money does not figure at all in the six instruments. This is because the creation of money has no effects on the economy as long as the printed money stays in the print shop. It is only when the money gets out into the economy that any effects come about. Money which is newly created and kept locked up might as well never have been created.

The six instruments cover all possible ways in which the printed money may get out to have some influence on the economy. The government may use the money to buy things or to give away to people or to repay debt (or make loans to the public).

But these effects are already counted in the buying, the giving, or the lending (or debt repayment). To count the creation of the money in addition would amount to counting the same effects twice. All the decisions of any importance are made when it is decided to apply the fiscal instruments for Functional Finance. This may involve putting some money into the government treasury or taking some money out of the treasury. If any of the instruments involves the paying out of money (*i.e.,* the three first items of each pair), the effects are just the same whether the money paid out was previously resting in the treasury or whether it had to be printed because there was not enough available in the treasury to permit them to be carried out on the scale that was considered necessary to prevent deflation. The use of the instrument should never be hampered just because there may not be enough money stock in the treasury at the moment. To sacrifice the prevention of deflation because of shortage of money which could be printed is no more sensible than to refrain from carrying out any other important government action because the necessary paper forms or stationery would have to be printed.

The size of the national debt is subsidiary to Functional Finance.

If the program of preventing inflation and deflation calls for *borrowing,* it of course entails an increase in the national debt. But this should not be a serious consideration any more than the printing of money, since all the effects on inflation and deflation have already been considered in the application of the program in the first place. And if the program calls for *lending* money and there happens to be no money around, then more money will have to be printed. The size of the stock of money as well as the size of the national debt are results of the actions that will have to be undertaken to prevent inflation and deflation and are never considerations that should prevent the government buying and selling, giving and taking, and borrowing and lending that are indicated by the objective of functional finance—the prevention of inflation and of deflation.

Functional Finance does not interfere with other governmental objectives.

The prevention of inflation and deflation, important as that is, does not constitute the only objective of good government. There are many other things that the government has to do in the general interest. It might be thought that Functional Finance, by governing all the buying and selling, giving and taking, and borrowing and lending by the government, would prevent it from doing anything at all about anything else. This view, however, comes only from a misunderstanding of the nature of Functional Finance.

Functional Finance is in one sense the *last* thing for the government to think about. The government must first of all decide on all the other reasons for buying various things or for taxing certain activities or for applying any of the other instruments of fiscal policy. Only when it has applied itself to all the other problems and tasks does Functional Finance come in. When these other decisions have all been made there results a total of spending by the government as well as by individuals and by businesses, on consumption as well as on investment. All of these are influenced in different degrees by the actions undertaken by the government for reasons not directly connected with the prevention of inflation and deflation. Then we consider whether the total spending resulting from all these forces is deficient or excessive, whether it would result in deflation or in inflation, or whether perhaps it turns out to be just the right amount of total spending that will give us neither inflation nor deflation.

If this last is the case there is nothing for Functional Finance to do. Everything is just fine. But if, as is much more likely, the resulting total spending is *not* exactly at the level which avoids inflation on the one hand and deflation on the other so as to give us full employment, the government has to apply Functional Finance to raise or lower total spending to the requisite level.

In doing this there immediately arises a dilemma from the multiplicity of ways in which the six instruments can be used for this purpose. First of all, if there is a deficiency in spending, this can be put right by increasing any one of the first of each pair of instruments or by diminishing any one of the second in any of the three pairs of fiscal instruments. This gives us six possibilities to begin with. Then there is the possibility of combining any number of the instruments and even of moving some of them in the wrong direction (*i.e.*, in a deflationary manner which tends to *decrease* spending still more), providing the others more than offset this so that the effect is to raise total spending to the desired level. But much more important than this is the latitude which each one of the instruments offers when one comes to apply it. The first instrument is *buying*, but it is left entirely open to the government to decide what it will buy, where and from whom and on what conditions. The same is true in different degrees of all the other instruments. There is abundant scope for choosing many different ways of applying each single instrument in addition to the possibility of choosing among different instruments and the possibilities of relying on several instruments in varying degrees.

This means that Functional Finance is not a policy. It is only a framework within which all sorts of different policies may be applied. It merely indicates how the government, in addition to doing whatever it may want to do on all other matters, can also prevent inflation and deflation and thus give us full employment. Although Functional Finance is in one sense considered last, in another sense it does not have to be considered last. It is not the only interest of government, but neither is it the *least* important of governmental responsibilities. It is considered neither first nor last, but *together with* all the other objectives in arriving at a general policy.

The other elements in the general policy are in no way circumscribed by such an integration. Functional Finance is compatible with conservatism or with communism, with liberalism or with dictatorship, with every conceivable policy other than one which directly contradicts Functional Finance in insisting on having deflation or inflation. Everything else is left alone to be decided in whatever way it was decided before, wisely or foolishly, or perhaps merely being left to chance. Functional Finance is merely the conscious adoption by the government of responsibility for the prevention of inflation and of deflation.

Summary.

The explanation of the rate of interest completes the story of the determination of the volume of employment. The determinants of the total rate of spending are the propensity to consume, the opportunity to invest, the public's liquidity preference, and the supply of money. By working on these determinants we can prevent total spending from going too high or too low, *i.e.,* from causing inflation or deflation and unemployment.

Fiscal policy must therefore be directed toward elimination of inflation and deflation. Deflation can be cured by increasing total spending until the barrier of rising prices is reached. At that point spending should not be increased any further until the barrier has been moved.

Economic understanding by individuals is of little use by itself, because the individual reacts perversely. *Social action* is therefore necessary to prevent inflation and deflation and must be undertaken by the government. There are three pairs of fiscal instruments available for such social action by the government. These are (1) *buying* and *selling* goods itself, (2) *giving* away money (in subsidies) and *taking* away money (in taxes) from members of society, and (3) *lending* (which includes repayment of debt) and *borrowing.* The six fiscal instruments include everything that the government can do about inflation and deflation.

It is necessary to guard against a strong tendency to attribute to some of these instruments what are really the effects of others not clearly separated from them. The substitution of Functional Finance for "sound finance" means the full acceptance by the government of responsibility for preventing inflation and deflation and leaves no room for the principle of balancing the budget or for very much concern about the national debt. The creation or destruction of money does not figure in the six instruments because it is wholly subsidiary to them—just like the printing of other kinds of office stationery.

The government has, of course, many other objectives besides the prevention of inflation and deflation. Functional Finance is merely the balancing item. After all the other uses of the instruments have been decided upon, Functional Finance prevents the total effect from resulting in inflation or deflation.

APPENDIX TO CHAPTER 8

The fundamental relationships are summarized in Fig. 15. M stands for money, i for interest, I for investment, C for consumption, Y for

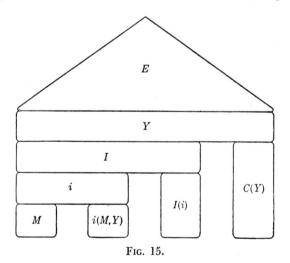

FIG. 15.

income, E for employment, $i(M,Y)$ for the liquidity preference (the willingness to hold cash, measured by the rate of interest necessary to induce the public to hold any given amount of money at various income levels), $I(i)$ for the opportunity to invest (the way in which the decisions to invest depend on the rate of interest), and $C(Y)$ for the propensity to consume (the way the decisions to consume depend on the level of income).

Right on top we have the volume of employment, which rests upon (or is determined by) the level of income. The level of income rests on the propensity to consume and the investment. The investment rests on the opportunity to invest and the rate of interest. The rate of interest, finally, rests on the liquidity preference and the amount of money.

It should be noted that in this house of bricks of the four members which touch the ground only one is represented by a single letter. That one is M, the amount of money which is here considered to be determined from outside by the monetary authority. The other three supporting members which touch the ground—$i(M,Y)$, $I(i)$, and $C(Y)$—are not independent amounts given by some outside authority but represent functions or relationships between the other elements in the structure, all of which intimately depend on each other.

Part III

The Resistances

CHAPTER 9

The Upside-down Economy

or Topsy-turvy Economics

THE CLEAR statement of a problem often brings us more than half of the way to its solution, but this is not true of the present problem. In the preceding chapters we have not only stated the problem of full employment but outlined the method of obtaining it. Yet we are still far from halfway through. This is because understanding the economics of employment is not enough. Far more important is the political problem of getting the solution applied in practice. In a democratic society this means overcoming some very powerful resistances in the minds of the majority of our citizens. Such psychological resistances can be overcome only if they are understood. We must therefore examine them with some care.

We have seen that depression is due to too little spending and that inflation is due to too much spending. Private individuals and businesses cannot be expected to be of much help in checking inflationary or deflationary pressures because their private interests impel them, in general, to do just the opposite of what is needed. It is the government, therefore, that must accept the responsibility for keeping total spending at the level that gives us full employment without inflation. By making use of the fiscal instruments at its disposal it can practice Functional Finance, keeping spending from going either too high or too low and thus assuring permanent prosperity and stability.

Functional Finance seems very plausible but contrary to basic economic principles.

The commonest immediate reaction of anyone who for the first time grasps the principles of Functional Finance is to ask how it is that the government does not carry out such an obviously intelligent policy which is in the interests of everybody. Immediately following this question, however, comes the attempt to answer it by saying that the argument must be wrong although it sounds plausible and no flaw is apparent. The matter cannot be so simple. If it were, all governments would have been practicing Functional Finance for a long time and we would not have suffered from depressions or from inflations.

With further study the conviction that there must be something wrong with Functional Finance is apt to become more and more firmly established. In more and more ways Functional Finance is seen to run counter to basic economic principles. Its declaration that real poverty—the lack of real goods and services—can be remedied by merely printing money smacks of magic or, perhaps, of a failure to understand the elementary lesson of economics: that money is not real wealth but only claims to wealth—that real wealth cannot be created by the printing press. The idea that thrift can be responsible for poverty seems to many not only unsound but immoral. The notion that the economy can be made richer by wasteful activities and by unproductive investments seems too absurd to merit serious examination. The whole theory seems to be quite topsy-turvy and leaves many with nothing but a sort of embarrassment at having been seduced even for a moment by its superficial plausibility.

Topsy-turvy economics is appropriate for an upside-down economy.

In truth it cannot be denied that the economics of Functional Finance, in its application to a condition of unemployment, *is* topsy-turvy. But this is no objection at all. Topsy-turvy economics is just what is appropriate for an economy that is suffering from unemployment. An economy suffering from unemployment is an upside-down economy for which *only* a topsy-turvy economic theory is of any use.

Ordinary or right-side-up economics is concerned with the economical use of resources. The resources are scarce. There is not enough of them to go round for all the purposes for which they are desired. It is important to *economize*—to use less of any resource for the performance of any task, wherever this can be done without too much difficulty—and thereby to set free some of the resources for other uses.

Where there is unemployment, efficiency is uneconomic.

But when there is unemployment this is no longer the case. In such circumstances it is not important or even useful to use less resources in any task. Any other uses could be served by the unemployed resources. There is no point, for instance, in managing to carry out some task with less labor if there are un-employed workers available, because the workers set free would not be utilized for other tasks any more than the workers who are already unemployed. They would merely be added to the unem-ployed. Where there is unemployment, an increase in efficiency in any particular productive process does not result in any increase in the efficiency in the economy as a whole.

Given the determinants of the level of income (the rate of in-vestment and the propensity to consume), the level of real in-come (which is the same as the real output) is determined. Any increase in technical efficiency cannot increase total output. It merely reduces the number of workers who can find employment in producing it. The technical improvement reduces the number of men needed to produce the same output. Technically, of course, employment could be maintained by having the same number of men continue to work and having them produce a larger output, but economically this would not do because a larger output cannot be sold. A larger output would mean a larger income just equal to the larger output. But since the public would want to save *some* of the addition to their income, they would not spend enough to buy the additional supply. Output would, therefore, be reduced to the level ruling before the increase in technical efficiency. Economizing resources by the use of more efficient methods is like pouring more water into a broken vessel with a large hole in it that is already holding as much as it can hold. No matter how much more is poured into it there will remain no more than in the beginning. The savings due to greater technical efficiency merely go to waste in further unemployment just as any additional water merely goes to waste through the hole.

From what has been said so far it might be thought that an increase in efficiency at least does no harm. While it does not serve, in the upside-down economy of unemployment, to increase output, it does not reduce it either, the number of man-hours of employment being reduced in just the same proportion in which the output per man-hour is increased. It might even be thought that there is some benefit in the economizing of effort because more leisure could then be enjoyed. But such suppositions would be quite erroneous. It is not leisure that is provided by the increase of efficiency, but unemployment. What we get is not the tranquillity of refraining from effort but the frustration of failing to find work. In every socially significant sense the increase in efficiency brings not greater happiness but greater misery.

Still further suffering can be brought about by increased efficiency where it adversely affects the determinants of employment. If the technical improvement removes workers from the payroll without directly reducing the amount of work done, the employers are not likely to increase their spending out of the ensuing profits by as much as the displaced workers are forced to reduce *their* spending. The employers' *marginal propensity to consume* is less than that of the displaced workers. The shift in the distribution of income brings with it a reduction in the propensity to consume of the society as a whole, and this change in one of the determinants of the level of income reduces the equilibrium level of output. Not only employment but even *output* will in this case be less as a result of the technical improvement. There is a double reduction in employment. The increase in output per man-hour reduces the amount of work needed to produce the same output, and the reduction in the output causes a further reduction in the man-hours of employment.

Not every increase in efficiency results in a redistribution of income from people with a higher marginal propensity to consume to those with a lower marginal propensity to consume. An increase in efficiency may cause a redistribution of income in the opposite direction so that there is an increase in the over-all propensity to consume. In that case there will be an increase in the level of output and this may partly or even entirely offset the reduction in the amount of employment needed to produce each unit of output. But there are other actions, also called "economizing," which *always* have harmful effects on output and on employment in the upside-down economy of depression.

In the upside-down economy thrift is wasteful.

The simplest of these is thrift. An increase in thrift is a reduction in the propensity to consume—one of the determinants of the level of income. It results in a reduction of both income and employment. In a right-side-up economy, thrift is a virtue. It sets free productive resources from the manufacture of consumption goods to make them available for the manufacture of instruments of production. These permit income in the future to be greater than before. It is a fundamental condition for the rapid growth of the wealth of the economy. But in our upside-down economy which suffers from unemployment, thrift merely reduces demand for products and the resources which might have gone into making them are merely left unused and are wasted.

But this is only a part of the evil wrought by thrift. The workers who lose their employment because of the decrease in demand for their product and the employers who lose their profits on these unwanted goods that are no longer produced themselves have to reduce their demand for other goods and services that they can no longer afford to buy. This reduces other people's income and the repercussions result in a reduction in total income several times greater than the direct reduction in spending from the increase in thrift. Only a fraction of the total reduction in spending (and therefore in income) is a direct reflection of the increase in thrift. The greater part of it is due to the reduction in the income out of which the spending is to be made. Income in fact will fall to the level where the greater desire to save (the greater thrift) is frustrated by the greater difficulty of saving out of a smaller income. The more obstinate the thrift and the greater the insistence on trying to maintain the volume of saving in the face of income reduction, the greater will be the further reductions in spending and in income, and the greater will be the resulting impoverishment.

In the upside-down economy prodigality is beneficial and wastefulness enriches.

The same considerations apply in reverse too. Just as efficiency and thrift lead to suffering and impoverishment, so do inefficiency and prodigality bring relief and enrichment. Monopolistic restrictions, wasteful work rules, tariffs that hinder the international division of labor—everything that reduces productive efficiency—lead to an increase in employment. Since the level of (income and) output is determined by the rate of investment and the propensity to consume, the reduced efficiency means that more work is needed—more employment is available—for the production of the same output. And if furthermore the reduction in efficiency should cause a shift in the distribution of wealth from those with a lower marginal propensity to consume to those with a higher marginal propensity to consume, the increased over-all propensity to consume would permit not only employment but actual output and income to increase. Employment would then increase more than enough to offset the decrease in output per man-hour.

A decrease in thrift, a decision not to be economical but to spend more, is not at all bad for society in the upside-down economy of unemployment. The increased demand for goods and their consumption does not mean impoverishment, for the additional goods are produced by resources that otherwise would have been wasted in involuntary idleness. The increase in economic activity by making business better may induce some people to invest in adding to society's stock of productive equipment. In that case the profligacy of the spenders not only increases the current real income in the enjoyment of goods and services but enriches the economy by raising its future productive power.

In the upside-down economy money and work are scarce rather than goods.

Another peculiarity of the upside-down economy is the reversal of the normal significance of goods, of money, and of work. In the right-side-up economy, goods are scarce, so that it is important to economize in their use. Money is not of basic importance because it is merely the representative of goods and services, and work is something of which we have more than we would like to have. In the upside-down economy of unemployment, goods are not scarce, from the social point of view. It is possible to get more of them by setting some of the unemployed resources to work to make more of them. What is scarce is *money*. The lack of money to spend on the goods is what keeps the unemployed resources from producing more goods. Work, moreover, instead of being a curse, is desired more than almost anything else because the alternative is not the enjoyment of leisure but the suffering of unemployment and deprivation. Of course if people could get income without having to work they would not object too much (although their self-respect in feeling that they are useful members of society who are earning their income is too easily underestimated). But it is only by finding work that they can obtain the income they need.

The paradoxes of the upside-down economy of depression can be followed out indefinitely into all the ramifications of an economics with the plusses all turned into minuses and the minuses all turned into plusses. Everything is upside down. Within very wide limits the wealthier a society the more it will suffer from poverty, for the richer it is in productive equipment the less will be the opportunity of investing in making additions to the stock of productive equipment and the lower will be the level of employment. The productivity of investment is a nuisance, for it means that when the factories or houses have been built, there is no longer so great a need for still more of them, so that investment is checked. On the other hand, if investments do not turn out to be useful, if they are destroyed before they are completed, or if they are badly designed so that they are not of any use when they are completed, they can be started all over again and meanwhile increase employment, income, and the output of consumption goods. It is the understanding of these peculiar characteristics of the upside-down economy that constitutes topsy-turvy economics.

One of the finest attacks on topsy-turvy economics is to be found in Henry Hazlitt's book *Economics in One Lesson.* Mr. Hazlitt is able to tear to little pieces a large number of propositions of the kind put forward in this chapter because all his argument is based on the assumption, mostly unconscious, of a state of full employment in which topsy-turvy economics is completely out of place. Perhaps he will one day consider the possibility of an economy suffering from unemployment and write the second lesson.

Functional Finance is not "depression economics."

The "new economics" that developed from the writings of Lord Keynes has so much impressed both economists and the public at large by its recognition of the possibility of a continuing state of unemployment and its ability to apply economic analysis to such a state that it is sometimes supposed to be applicable *only* to states of unemployment and so is sometimes called "depression economics." This is an error. Lord Keynes vainly sought to forestall it by calling his book the *General Theory of Employment,* etc., to indicate that full employment and unemployment were both special cases falling within the general theory. The false idea that Keynesian economics is somehow more valid or only valid for depression and unemployment arises from an exaggerated concentration on the application of the theory to the problem of unemployment that was on everybody's mind when the book came out. This exaggerated preoccupation with its application to unemployment obscures the fact that Functional Finance and Keynes' general theory of employment not only enable us to deal with unemployment but make possible a more effective approach to the opposite problems of excess demand and inflation.

The moral is to put the economy right side up.

Perhaps one warning is necessary. All the propositions of topsy-turvy economics indicate that efficiency and thrift have bad effects and that inefficiency and extravagance have good effects. But the moral is not that we should wage war against efficiency and everywhere encourage wastefulness and prodigality. The moral is that we should get out of the situation in which everything is upside down—that we should, by the application of Functional Finance, reach the position of full employment. Only as long as we are suffering from serious unemployment is it better to be wasteful and inefficient in detail because that somewhat moderates our inefficiency in total. Only as long as we remain in the unemployment situation where every particular economy merely results in a still greater loss from the chronic waste of unemployment is economizing harmful and wastefulness economic. Every instance of topsy-turvy economics should remind us that

what we really need to do is to put the economy on its feet so
that there would be no need for economics to stand on its head.

Summary.

A general understanding of Functional Finance is not enough
to get it applied in practice. Important resistances remain to be
overcome. Functional Finance seems to many on second thoughts
to be too good to be true and is observed to run contrary to firmly
established economic principles.

This view comes from observing the new analysis of the condition of the economy during a depression. When there is general
unemployment, economizing does not make sense. All economics
has to be reversed because the whole economy is being run contrary to reason. Efficiency in detail only leads to larger waste in
general through more unemployment. Thrift causes impoverishment and prodigality results in increases in wealth. Goods are
not really scarce, money is more important than goods, work becomes an object of desire instead of a curse to be minimized, and
everything is upside down. All these paradoxes arise from the
existence of unemployment and cannot be understood until we
can rid ourselves of the assumption, which is very difficult to
discard, that we have full employment all the time.

The idea that Functional Finance or Keynesian economics is
"depression economics" is unfounded, and the lesson of topsy-
turvy economics is not that waste should be accepted in the place
of economy but that topsy-turvy economics should be eliminated
by putting an end, through Functional Finance, to the upside-
down economy of unemployment for which it is appropriate.

CHAPTER 10

Resistance by Capitalists

THE TOPSY-TURVY nature of the economics of Functional Finance and of the full-employment policies associated with it calls forth resistance not only from economic theorists who find the concepts and ideas disturbing but also from businessmen. Many of the resistances by businessmen are basically of the same nature as the resistance by economic theorists to the unorthodox notions of topsy-turvy economics. But perhaps much more important than this in the resistance by businessmen to Functional Finance is their tendency to apply to society rules of behavior which are eminently applicable to individual businessmen but which may not be at all applicable to society as a whole.

Businessmen fear Functional Finance would cause bankruptcy.

First among these are the concern for solvency and the maxim that an individual should keep his expenditures within his income in order to avoid bankruptcy. If a man spends more than his income, he gets into trouble. An excellent example of this is Mr. Micawber's well-known warning to David Copperfield that if he spends more—ever so little more though it be—than his income, life will be miserable; he will be pursued by creditors and he will not have a moment's peace. But if he keeps his expenditures within his income, he will be happy, honored, and respected.

But what is bankruptcy? A man may be bankrupted if he is unable to meet his obligations. His bankruptcy protects him from further claims by his creditors after his assets have been seized, so that he can go to work and continue to earn a living. He is prohibited, under penalty of a jail sentence, from incurring fur-

151

ther debts without first telling the new creditor that he is bankrupt.

It is clearly nonsense to apply the concept of bankruptcy to the United States of America or to its government in the literal sense. The government of the United States can always meet its obligations to any creditor by giving him money which, if necessary, it can quite legally print for the purpose. There is no court in which the United States can file a bankruptcy petition, and nobody can put the United States in jail for incurring debts improperly while in a condition of undischarged bankruptcy.

Of course bankruptcy is not meant in the literal sense. But if we try to go behind the word and find out what is really feared, we discover that there is concern either for the possibility of inflation or for the possibility of depression and sometimes for both at the same time. The illogicality of the objection is evident. The rules of Functional Finance are expressly designed to prevent inflation and depression. Yet the argument begins by saying that although Functional Finance would prevent inflation and depression, it is a dangerous instrument because it opens the door to the dangers of bankruptcy. It seems safe to assume that inflation and depression are dragged in only to fill the vacuum that appears when the meaninglessness of national bankruptcy is made evident. The fear of national bankruptcy is based on nothing but the simple if illegitimate analogy with the principles of individual prudence.

Logic does not easily overcome habit.

Pointing out the irrelevance or irrationality of the argument is not very effective in removing the discomfort of those who are worried about national bankruptcy. The tendency to apply to others and to society at large concepts which are developed in one's own experience is too strong to be overcome by a simple indication of a logical fallacy. The new theories must become familiar, and until they become familiar the emotional resistance is still able to overcome any intellectual clarification. Even when every one of the possible dangers has been shown to be illusory, the businessman is likely to say that he doesn't know what is wrong but he can feel in his bones that there is something wrong.

One should not be surprised at this effect. The same thing happens whenever any new habits or ways of behaving or reacting have to be acquired. When a man is learning how to skate, for example, he has to learn some relatively simple movements. But these are in conflict with the kinds of movements he habitually makes when walking. He has to become familiar with the new movements by practice and cannot be taught to behave in the appropriate manner by any number of the clearest kind of indications of the differences between skating and walking. Habit is stronger than reason. And so the only way by which reason can prevail is by continual repetition until it has got habit on its side. Unfortunately, by the time this has happened the new theory is very often no longer applicable and our problem arises all over again.

The false belief that capitalism is completely automatic is another source of resistance.

Closely related to the idea that there must be something wrong in disregarding the principle of solvency or of balancing the budget is the idea that our economy does not need any guidance; that it is a complete, self-sufficient, and self-regulating system which would automatically give us full employment if we would only refrain from interfering with it; and that this can be doubted only by those who do not understand it or who wish to destroy it. Adam Smith has spoken of the invisible hand which guides so many of our economic activities. As a matter of fact, he said only that things move *as if* guided by an invisible hand—and he did not really believe that this invisible hand never needed any conscious guidance by social philosophers developing appropriate institutions. But the idea has grown beyond the bounds which Adam Smith set to it. There is a common feeling that there is foolishness and perhaps even impiety in trying to improve upon what is done by the invisible hand.

There is, of course, a very great wisdom in Adam Smith's notion of the invisible hand. But the idea is *not* applicable to the regulation of the level of activity in the society as a whole. It applies rather to the price mechanism and the enterprise system in organizing the allocation of those resources of society which are actually employed. The invisible hand refers to the way in which these institutions bring together the myriad kinds of factors of production toward making the things that people want to consume. The price mechanism harnesses for this purpose the energy and ingenuity of thousands or millions of independent citizens.

The idea of the invisible hand does very great service if it is applied whenever necessary to draw the attention of economic planners to the manner in which the price mechanism operates under a capitalist society and could operate under other forms of society too. But when it comes to the level of employment as a whole, the invisible hand just isn't there. The fact that we have had many and very severe depressions and inflations should by itself be evidence that the invisible hand, for all its usefulness, does not maintain full employment and prevent inflation. Nevertheless, the idea that our society is completely automatic and that anybody who wants to regulate it can only destroy the mechanism is a very powerful source of resistance to Functional Finance.

This resistance makes use of Say's law.

In the hands of some economic theorists—in fact in the hands of most economic theorists of some time ago—this automaticity led to a rather strange development of the principle of classical economics known as "Say's law." Some of the "mercantilist" precursors of classical economics seem to have been guilty of confusing money with wealth, believing that money was wealth in itself and not merely a claim to wealth or an instrument which might possibly play some part in facilitating the creation of wealth. The classical economists were therefore rather concerned with stressing the difference between money on the one hand and the real goods and production of services which lay behind money on the other hand.

They pointed out that while it is possible for any particular commodity to be produced in excess relatively to commodities as a whole, it is not possible for *all* commodities to be produced in relative excess. This now seems fairly obvious, and part of its obviousness is the result of the use of Say's law for a long time. Say's law was very useful in pointing out that while the producers of a particular commodity might sometimes gain by "correcting an oversupply," restricting the output of that commodity and exchanging a smaller amount of it for other commodities on much better terms, it was impossible for society to gain by restricting the output of goods in general. This proposition was called the impossibility of a *general* oversupply. While a relative oversupply of a particular commodity is perfectly possible, its generalization so as to apply to all goods is quite impossible.

But the sound idea of the impossibility of a general oversupply acquired another meaning which is not so sound. As long as we were looking behind money at real goods and services and were not paying attention to money, a general oversupply of everything would mean that too much of everything was being produced relatively to everything else, and this is an obviously impossible and indeed nonsensical statement, as Say's law points out. There is no "everything else" with which the excess of everything can be compared. A general oversupply is impossible.

But when Say's law was applied to a monetary economy, it had to be translated to mean something else, and in the translation a serious error crept in. An oversupply of a particular commodity relative to others means that there is an undersupply of the other commodity relative to it. The supply of the other commodity relatively to it or in exchange for it represented the demand for this commodity. An oversupply of one commodity is therefore the same thing as an underdemand for it on the part of those producing other commodities to exchange for it.

In a monetary society, the oversupply of a particular commodity appears as an insufficient money demand for it. A general oversupply should therefore mean an insufficiency of money demand for goods in general. A general oversupply having been seen to be impossible and indeed meaningless, it seems to follow that a general insufficiency of money demand is also impossible. Say's law was thus supposed to prove that while there can be insufficient money demand for a particular commodity, it is impossible for total money demand—the demand for goods in general—to be inadequate.

Such a conclusion not only does not follow from the argument; it is demonstrably false. The experience we have had of a depression should be a sufficient demonstration of this. The error lies in slipping, without noticing it, from the proposition in real terms, which is sound, to the proposition in money terms, which is different and which is false. While general oversupply is impossible, a general insufficiency of money demand is perfectly possible because it does not have to be caused by any general oversupply. It may come about simply because the individuals, the businesses, and the government do not spend enough money in the aggregate to buy all the goods and services that the economy is capable of producing.

Resistance often takes the form of assuming that we always have full employment.

In the more recent technical economic literature on the subject, much of this confusion has been cleared up and new interpretations have been given to Say's law in attempts to rescue it from the shambles. Nevertheless, resistances by businessmen and others who may roughly be called capitalists often take the form of assuming that we always and naturally have full employment.

One of the best examples of this is the book by Henry Hazlitt, mentioned previously, called *Economics in One Lesson*. Apart from one thing, this is a very good book. It very clearly draws attention to a number of fallacies which can do harm and have done harm to our society. But the one thing that is wrong is that Mr. Hazlitt continually uses arguments which assume that our economy is right side up. For example, he continually takes it for granted that every time some resources are set free, they will in fact be used somewhere else in the economy, and this is why it is important to economize in their use, using as little as possible for any purpose so as to make them available for other uses. He takes it for granted, to take another example, that any increase in spending must raise prices and lower the value of money, just as would indeed be the case if there were full employment and it was impossible to produce any more goods to be bought with the additional money expenditure. In the absence of this possibility it would indeed be true that any increase in spending on money demand would lead to higher prices, but the existence of this possibility is the core of the problem of unemployment. There are very many ways in which full employment is implicitly assumed, but it is hardly necessary to mention more than these two here; many others are mentioned in other parts of this book and it is an excellent exercise, in reading newspaper editorials and columnists on economic matters, to note how many of them start with the unconscious and implicit assumption that there is full employment. Given this habitual assumption, it is not surprising that they so often reach the conclusion that any steps toward maintaining full employment are unnecessary or can only do harm.

An important element is the feeling that money is sacred.

Another source of resistance by capitalists is to be found in a feeling that money is something too holy to be touched by human hands. Thought on this subject is inhibited by the declaration that Functional Finance might involve the creation of money without any increase in the gold or other "backing." Such "unbacked" money is called "fiat money," and the phrase is uttered with accents of horror and condemnation as if nobody could doubt that it would mean the end of the world or at least an inflation of the dimensions experienced in Germany in 1923.

Very often this objection seems to be based on the idea that in the normal course of events money is provided not by human action but by Nature with a capital "N." The idea of money being made (and destroyed) by mere man seems to be a shocking thought. It is as if all the "sound" money which is in existence always has been in existence and always will be in existence—a theory of the immaculate conception of money,[1] original and indestructible.

The idea that the value of money depends on its backing by gold or silver is closely related to the idea that the value of money is based on precious metal which is supposed to be intrinsically valuable. Such a view seems emotionally much more satisfying than the pedestrian explanation offered by modern economics. It is boring to look at particular markets and particular commodities to see what causes particular prices of goods and services to be raised or lowered by sordid bargaining between the buyers and sellers. It is unromantic to recognize that when we have the prices of the items in our market basket we have what there is of real content in the value of money. It is so much easier to accept the theory that an "unbacked" change in the quantity of money "*must*" effect the value of money—especially for "practical" men who like to display their contempt for theory. Ancient myth and discarded theory thus buttress the common notion that money is too sacred to be created by mere considerations of expediency. The creation of money where this may be necessary for carrying out the rules of Functional Finance thus appears as a violation of "natural laws" which govern the "soundness" of money.

All of these resistances, although very strong in their emotional

---

[1] I am indebted for this expression to my friend Ernest Van den Haag.

content, are extremely weak in their logic. This is their nature, and it makes it rather difficult to deal with them in any analytical manner.

Summary.

Practical businessmen tend to resist Functional Finance partly because of their unconscious attachment to the theoretical principles of classical economics and partly because of their tendency to apply to society as a whole the principles of solvency that are appropriate only for private business probity. When it is pointed out that the nation cannot go bankrupt in the literal sense, an attempt is made to save the position by declaring that by bankruptcy is meant inflation or depression. But demonstrating the illogicality of this defense is not very helpful as long as businessmen feel that there is something wrong with Functional Finance. The only thing to do is to keep repeating the tenets of Functional Finance until the novelty wears off.

Another source of resistance is the feeling that the capitalist society is completely self-regulating—that it is impious as well as dangerous to interfere with the "invisible hand." To point out that Adam Smith's invisible hand is fully occupied in guiding the proper utilization of those resources which are in fact employed and does not concern itself with the problem of the level of employment does not help very much, for in this case, too, it is feelings rather than logic that are at the bottom of the difficulty.

Closely related to this is the assumption that we always do have full employment and the use of Say's law to prove that a general insufficiency of demand is impossible. This argument is based on a fallacious translation to a money economy of the perfectly sound proposition that a general oversupply is impossible.

Finally there is resistance by those who seem to believe that money is too sacred to be tampered with in terms of expediency but that there are some "natural" laws which govern money.

Phrases like "fiat money" are used to induce terror of the dangers involved in subjecting money to human control in the social interest. It is almost as if it were not believed that money is in fact made by human hands—a theory of the immaculate conception of money.

CHAPTER 11

Resistance by Anticapitalists

THE RESISTANCE to Functional Finance by anticapitalists is even more violent and even more irrational than the resistance by capitalists.

Underconsumptionists claim that adequate money demand is impossible under capitalism.

The simplest of these objections are those of the underconsumptionists. The underconsumptionists declare that it is impossible for the money demand for goods and services to be adequate in a capitalist economy. Their argument corresponds almost exactly, although in reverse, to that of the capitalists who state the direct opposite, namely, that it is impossible for the money demand for goods and services to be *inadequate* in a capitalist economy, *i.e.*, that unemployment is impossible. As usual, the truth is to be found in the middle. Adequate demand is neither inevitable nor impossible. But just as the capitalists who parade under the banner of Say's law have a feeling that a capitalist society is self-sufficient and does not need any monkeying around by mere human beings, so the underconsumptionist feels that, unless the "flaw in the capitalist system" is corrected, it cannot work at all. The result is that the underconsumptionists, instead of saying that steps should be taken to increase spending whenever it is insufficient—and consequently also having to say the opposite, namely, that steps should be taken to decrease spending in situations where it is excessive—assume that it is *always* insufficient and that it is always necessary to add to the flow of spending in order to keep the economy working.

If the underconsumptionists' theories were correct, one would expect to see our societies rapidly reduce their economic activities because of insufficient demand, to find that the reduction in economic activity would not alleviate the insufficiency of demand, and so to see the economy rapidly fall into complete inactivity.

Perhaps the best developed of the underconsumptionist theories are those associated with the social credit movement and Major Douglas in England. Their argument consists of four parts. The first part consists of the statement that some of the costs incurred in producing commodities for the market do not constitute income for the recipients. Some of the costs are payments for raw materials or machinery, and only a small part of these payments is earned by the people who sell the raw materials or machinery. Consequently, the underconsumptionists argue, there is not enough money distributed as income in the capitalist system to pay for the whole of the product at prices which cover all the costs of production.

The economist arguing with the underconsumptionists points out that this is not necessary since it is not true that the whole product has to be sold to consumers. It is true that some of the money cost of making consumption goods is paid out to people to whom it does not constitute income, but this is balanced by the fact that some of the product consists not of consumption goods but of intermediate goods—of machinery and raw materials— which do not have to be bought out of income but come out of other business funds. While it is true that the people directly engaged in making consumption goods do not earn enough to be able to buy all the consumption goods at prices that cover the whole cost, the other people who are employed in making inter- mediate goods—the machinery and the raw materials—and who do not buy these goods out of their incomes can buy the con- sumption goods that are not bought by those directly employed in producing them. Indirectly, counting all those engaged in making the intermediate goods, enough income is received in the economy as a whole to permit all the product to be sold. The consumption goods can be sold to the consumers and the intermediate goods can be sold to the manufacturers, who buy them to convert them into other products.

This ends the first act of the underconsumptionist play.

Act Two begins with the underconsumptionist's agreeing with the economist, complimenting him on his acuteness in observing the fact that the money paid out for machinery and raw materials ultimately becomes income to other people not directly employed in making consumption goods, so that these in turn can buy the consumption goods left over by those employed directly in making them. But he then goes on to argue that the money paid out for machinery and raw materials becomes available as income only at later stages when the workers employed in making the machinery and materials receive some of this money as their wages and salaries, etc. Their demand, therefore, the underconsumptionist now argues, will arrive too late to be of any use. The economy will again suffer from underconsumption although now there is a different reason given for this.

The economist points out that, while it is true that money paid out for equipment and materials does not become income in the hands of workers and others until much later, this does not matter because those workers and others will at any time be receiving the corresponding incomes flowing from the payments made for materials and machinery at previous points in time. There will be a continuous flow of income which could be sufficient to buy the current output of consumption goods.

Thus ends Act Two.

In Act Three the underconsumptionist again agrees with the economist's view but points out that when a businessman who has borrowed money from the bank repays a loan, the money is extinguished; and he looks with alarm at the continuous extinction of all the money in existence so that the economy will not be able to carry on.

The economist points out that, although this is true of the money paid back to the bank, the banks keep in business by creating and lending out again more money to others and frequently to the very same people. This creation of money cancels the destruction of money going on at the same time so that the amount of money can be maintained and no catastrophe threatens from this angle. Historically, in fact, the stock of money has been continually increasing over the long run.

This is the end of Act Three.

In Act Four the underconsumptionist begins as usual by agreeing with all the previous criticisms and bringing forth a new argument. This time he says that there is really enough income created to buy all the product and cover all the costs—that total income is indeed equal to and created by the total cost. Nevertheless people will be saving part of their income and not spending all of it, so that there will not be enough money spent to buy the total output of industry.

The economist points out that, although consumption (which is what remains of income after you have subtracted the saving) is insufficient to buy the whole product of industry, there is also going on a demand for the product of industry which we call investment, and it is perfectly possible for the investment to take the place of the gap caused by saving so that there can be an adequate demand for the total product of industry.

The curtain goes down on Act Four, rises once more, and the economist expects to hear a fifth argument. To his surprise, he hears the first one all over again as if it had never been proposed before. The economist in the same way goes through Acts Six, Seven, and Eight which are repetitions of Acts Two, Three, and Four, but when Act Nine appears and is again exactly the same as Act One, the economist loses patience and gives up the argument, and the social creditors are able to claim with apparent sincerity that nobody has been able to rebut their arguments.

Marxists sometimes postulate a reserve army of unemployed.

Much more definitely anticapitalistic are the Marxist socialists. They are even more violent opponents of Functional Finance for a number of reasons which must be considered separately because they definitely do not mix.

First of all is the Marxist dogma that capitalist society must have a reserve army of unemployed in order to be able to operate. There is a sense in which this is true, as we shall see below, but this is not the sense which the Marxists have in mind. Their argument is based upon a continual shifting in the middle of the argument from what individual capitalists do to what the capitalist class as a whole does. They say that competition between capitalists trying to make profits tends to bid up wages and bid down the prices of products and so to diminish their profits. In order to maintain their profits the capitalists, now acting not as individuals competing with each other but like a well-organized and integrated army, are said to maintain a reserve army of unemployed workers who bid against each other and thereby keep the wages down. The logic is not very strong but the feelings about this seem to be extremely strong so that it is not improper to call it a dogma that capitalist society must have a reserve army of unemployed. Consequently, any attempts to remove the reserve army of unemployed by a policy which would establish and maintain prosperity are claimed by the Marxist to be destined to failure.

Sometimes Marxists argue that curing depressions is immoral rather than impossible.

The second argument, which would seem to be quite unnecessary and irrelevant if the first argument were true, is that it is wrong rather than impossible to get rid of unemployment under capitalism. It is against the true interests of the people, according to Marxist revolutionaries, to do anything which would stabilize economic prosperity. This argument seems to be based not upon the acceptance of the impossibility of curing capitalist unemployment, but rather on the fear that it may be successfully cured. Any attempt to improve the working of a capitalist society is denounced as partaking of the sin of "reformism." Reformism, by making capitalism work better, prevents the continual worsening of conditions which is necessary for laying the groundwork for the final successful revolution leading to the dictatorship of the proletariat and the socialist and later communist society.

This same principle of allowing or indeed encouraging things to get worse so they ultimately may become better through the communist proletarian revolution is indeed a basic principle of Marxist theory and cannot be illustrated more clearly than in the opposition by communists to the Marshall Plan, because the Marshall Plan, by helping to reestablish prosperity in Europe, prevents the breakdown which is a necessary step in the social revolution.

A good communist or Marxist is able to combine these two arguments and apparently to think at the same time (1) that reforms cannot be accomplished and (2) that the accomplishment of the reforms constitutes the most grievous sins of our sinful times. This kind of thinking, sometimes called dialectical, has been satirized by George Orwell in his fascinating book *Nineteen Eighty-four,* where he gives it the perfect name of "double-think."

Sometimes Marxists dismiss the issue by definition.

The third objection to Functional Finance by communists is a kind of reinsurance in case the first two arguments do not work. This is an argument not of morals, saying it is wicked, or of science, saying it is impossible, but of semantics, changing the meaning of the word. It is claimed that if something were done to cure unemployment, then what we would have should no longer be called capitalism. Against this device for magicking away a fact by giving it a new name, there is nothing to be done.

The three Marxist arguments we have considered refer to the application of Functional Finance to a capitalist society. But Functional Finance is applicable not only to capitalist society but to any society which makes use of money, and socialist societies make use of money too. How do the Marxists react to the idea of the application of Functional Finance to socialist societies?

Marxists also object to Functional Finance under socialism.

There is first of all the well-established doctrine among Marxists that it is improper to consider in any detail the method of operation of a socialist society—at least until the social revolution has been achieved. To do so is to be guilty of the sin of utopianism. Utopians are people who draw pictures of societies the way they would like them to be. Utopians were criticized, and with some justification, by Marx and by later Marxists for paying insufficient attention to the means of implementing their programs. They did not indicate how one is to get to these better societies. It is necessary to develop a means of moving toward the good society from the actually existing situation, of showing how to get there from here.

This excellent advice has been carried to the illogical extreme of saying nothing at all about where we are moving to but considering only where we are moving from. Any attempt to indicate what the new society would be like is denounced as utopianism or, for good measure, as "bourgeois utopianism." The Marxist is even worse off than the hillbilly who, when asked whether he could read, said, "Well, I can read on the signpost how far but I can't read where to." The Marxist cannot read how far, and he refuses to read where to.

This attitude was largely responsible for the chaos which followed the Russian revolution when for the first time the Marxists had to pay some attention to the problem of how to run an economy. They had until then concentrated all their energies on developing means of overthrowing the existing order, seizing power, and then waiting to see what it would seem obvious to do. They had no understanding of the nature of the working of a society, and the tremendous sufferings of the Russian people, especially in the first few years after the revolution, are largely due to the recklessness of the revolutionaries in seizing power without knowing at all what they would do once they had it.

Marxist anticapitalism, therefore, while denying that any society which uses Functional Finance is capitalist, simply refuses to speak about socialist societies, saying that all those interested in socialist societies must not use up any energy in doing anything except seizing power, handing it to the specified organization, and trusting it to bring about the society of the future.

But when the communists were in power they could no longer avoid thinking about these problems and dismiss them by calling their consideration utopian; they had to consider whether they would use these instruments as means of making their society work. And here we find a very powerful resistance to using instruments which are capitalistic. Most conspicuous among these is the use of the rate of interest, a fundamental part of Functional Finance.

The irrational objection to "bourgeois" instruments is slow to fade.

Olaf Stapledon, in his book *Last and First Men*, which is probably the most imaginative, the most ingenious, and the most interesting of all the books about the future, describes the colonization of the earth by the inhabitants of Mars. The Martians consist of elementary particles of life which are in telepathic communication with each other and which combine to perform any tasks they have in common, but which have no individuality. Their concept of life, therefore, is based upon their own experience, and when they see men and animals moving about on the face of the earth, they believe they can test whether they are alive or not by seeing whether they continue to function when they are taken apart in the way in which any Martian organization of life units would continue to function. When they take these animals apart and find that they cease to function, this is considered proof that there is no life on earth, but merely some kind of machinery. The Martian colonizers of the earth, however, when they have lived here for a long time, come to the conclusion that there is some kind of life on earth. This thought is so repugnant to the parent Martian body—and they are aware of this thought because of the telepathic communication—that it becomes necessary to liquidate the Martian colonists on earth because of their entertaining this heresy. Each time a new colony is sent down, it is contaminated by the same heresy and has to be liquidated.

A similar development has been taking place in Russia where engineers, economists, and others keep on discovering the rate of interest as a useful device. They have to disguise it so that it does not look like that capitalist instrument which should not be touched by the socialist society, but occasionally this subterfuge is discovered and they are liquidated or ignored and their suggestions not applied. Others discover the rate of interest again, and we here have a similar series of events where we can see the Russians slowly and painfully discovering the elements of "bourgeois" economics that go toward the development of a theory of Functional Finance. In this the Russians are repeating a cycle similar to the one that led to their making use of money and prices although they had originally intended to abolish money and prices at the time of the revolution.

So we see that the Marxists oppose Functional Finance both for capitalist and for socialist societies, giving reasons which purport to be scientific, moral, and semantic.

There are not very many complete Marxists in the United States, but many Marxist ideas have been very widely spread so that they are quite important in constituting elements of resistance to Functional Finance by vaguely anticapitalist "liberals" in American society. These resistances are not very much less powerful than the capitalist resistances to a policy for maintaining full employment via Functional Finance.

Summary.

Resistance to Functional Finance by anticapitalists is even more violent than by capitalists. Underconsumptionists have a series of arguments purporting to prove that money demand is inevitably inadequate under capitalism unless continually supported by social credit of one kind or another. This does not stand up to examination any more than the capitalist argument that money demand is inevitable and automatically adequate.

Marxian socialists tend to maintain the dogma that capitalism naturally and inevitably maintains a reserve army of unemployed. From this it is supposed to follow that it is impossible to prevent depressions and crises in capitalist economies. It is further argued, with complete contempt for consistency, that to cure depression under capitalism is "counterrevolutionary," which means that it is contrary to the true interest of the people, because it prevents the inevitable course of history as revealed by dialectics. The prevention of depressions would stop things from getting worse and worse and thereby remove the main reason for the proletarian revolution—to make them better again. Finally it is argued that if depressions were prevented, the resulting state of society should not be called capitalism.

Marxists also object to the use of Functional Finance in socialist societies. Where power has not been achieved by the dictatorship of the proletariat, any attention to how socialist societies would operate is denounced as "utopian," and where power has been achieved by the Marxists, they have a most powerful and irrational prejudice against the use of "bourgeois" instruments like money, prices, markets, and the rate of interest.

CHAPTER 12

Other Resistances

IN THE last two chapters we have considered resistances to Functional Finance by "capitalists" who believe that positive action for the maintenance of full employment is *unnecessary* under capitalism and resistances by anticapitalists who believe that succcssful action for maintaining full employment is *impossible* under capitalism. There are many other resistances, some of which we shall consider in the present chapter.

These remaining objections are made by people who would agree that it is both necessary and possible to do something to prevent depressions under capitalism.

Some resistances are based on remnants of classical doctrine.

We have already considered some of the resistances that arise from an indoctrination in "classical" economics with its unconscious assumption that full employment is always and automatically in existence. We considered this among the resistances by "capitalists," but the position is also held very strongly by many who would never think of calling themselves capitalists—by people who are neither very wealthy nor particularly addicted to the outlook of the businessman. Even though they may have been emancipated from certain capitalistic prejudices they are unable to complete the process and accept the logical conclusions of the new position they have been convinced is right.

An example of this is the attitude to the proposition in Functional Finance that taxation should be undertaken only if it is desirable to reduce the income or the expenditure of the taxpayer. When it is applied to the issue of interest payments on

171

the national debt the resistance comes to the fore. The semi-convert to Functional Finance will agree that the national debt is no more a national impoverishment than it is a national enrichment. But he will balk at the suggestion that the interest payments on the national debt are just as neutral with respect to the national income as the national debt is neutral with respect to the national wealth. The idea of borrowing the money with which to make the interest payments on the existing debt, and thereby getting still further into debt, is too shocking. It causes him to forget that he has just recognized the relative innocuousness of the national debt which would be slightly increased by this procedure.

Many resistances are due in a similar manner to a method of presenting Functional Finance that is too sudden or too extreme or in some other way too shocking to the reader. In the article in which I first introduced the phrase "Functional Finance" [1] I used a very large number for a hypothetical size of national debt. I did not want to go into the question of how large the national debt would be. I wanted to show that no matter how large it was supposed to be there still would not result the kind of evil that people were most worried about. The experiment was a failure. The very large number that I put down as the imaginary national debt, instead of stopping the argument about the size, so shocked many readers that they were unable to pay attention to the rest of the article. (The national debt and some complications connected with it will be discussed in a later chapter.)

Resistance often shifts from economic to political grounds.

One of the resistances arises from a queer combination of arrogance and timidity. Quite frequently, when a man who has been objecting on economic grounds is convinced that he was wrong—when he has been persuaded that the policies which he

[1] "Functional Finance and the Federal Debt," *Social Research*, February, 1943.

was saying would not work would in fact work quite satisfactorily—he shifts his ground from economics to politics. He will stop arguing that Functional Finance would not work or that it would do harm instead of good but will instead argue that there is no chance of its being applied and therefore it is not worth spending time in discussing it. He will say: "I agree that Functional Finance would indeed work if it were applied, but there is no chance of its being applied." He declares that the "public" is unalterably opposed to Functional Finance so that only a dictator who could ignore public opinion would be able to apply it.

As a matter of fact the public is much more easily able to understand Functional Finance than the economists, who resist it for a long time before they accept it. The propositions of Functional Finance and the arguments necessary to explain them are not really so very subtle or so very complicated. The basic difficulty is the economist's strong attachment to the dogmas of "sound finance" with which Functional Finance comes into conflict. But he mistakes his emotional resistance for an intellectual difficulty. If the difficulties in the way of accepting Functional Finance were intellectual, the economist would be right in supposing that the public would not be able to do better than himself. The public would indeed not be prepared to devote as much effort as he had to devote before accepting the economic principles of Functional Finance. But the difficulty is not intellectual; it is emotional—and the public is much freer from an emotional attachment to "sound finance" and "classical economics" and Say's law than is the professional classical economist.

Unsophisticated members of the public, of average intelligence, find it very easy to understand the principles of Functional Finance. They are usually quite willing to accept it tentatively as very plausible, while waiting for a check on it by their specialist economist friends. What we have then is the public waiting for economists to give the OK signal, while economists turned amateur politicians declare that it is no use giving any such OK because the public would never accept it.

Of course, as long as there are some economists who are opposed to Functional Finance on economic grounds, these are easily able to bring in enough complications to make the ordinary man in the street decide that he had better retire from the fight until the economists have come to a substantially unanimous agreement. In such a situation the economists who have been persuaded that the economics of Functional Finance is all right but are silent because they are afraid it will not get sufficient political support to be put into effect by their silence are themselves holding back the application of Functional Finance until such time as the very last die-hard economic opponent of Functional Finance is persuaded or dies of old age. It is extremely discouraging for one who thinks that economists could and should be among the most forward leaders of society to find that the most frequently heard objection to Functional Finance is that it is "economically all right but politically impossible." The economist who says this is too arrogant in contrasting his superior understanding with the alleged inability of the public to understand Functional Finance and too timid in his estimate of his ability to help the public to understand it. In this way Functional Finance can be stalled for a long time while the intimidated public and the frightened economist wait for each other to cross the bridge first.

Remaining problems are considered as objections.

Functional Finance will not solve all human problems or even all social problems. This permits resistances to Functional Finance to take the form of stating all such unresolved and strictly ir-relevant problems as if they were objections to Functional Finance.

Here the proponent of Functional Finance is really caught in a dilemma. Whether he can indicate solutions to these remaining problems or not, he always appears to get the worse of the argu-ment. This is because he has to guess what are the kind of solu-tions to these other problems that the questioner has in mind. If he should suggest a solution to one of these other problems which is not acceptable to the questioner, he is of course lost. On the other hand, if he tries to avoid guessing the questioner's particular preferences and says that there are many different ways of dealing with these other problems that are not solved by Functional Finance or by full employment, he is dismissed as unpractical and vague and not giving a clear notion of how, in fact, Functional Finance will work.

An extreme case of this is where the questioner has got himself completely concentrated on a particular problem and thinks that other problems are unimportant. Thus many will say: "Well, what does Functional Finance do to destroy monopoly?" And when the answer is given that it does not do anything directly at all about that other problem, he is likely to shrug his shoulders and dismiss Functional Finance as unimportant even if correct. Those who see all our social evils as primarily psychological and who think that what is necessary is to psychoanalyze everybody naturally also dismiss Functional Finance and indeed almost all of economics as irrelevant to the important problems of the world.

It must be admitted that Functional Finance would not cure all problems. The course of true love would not begin to run smooth, and those who are unhappy for hidden psychological reasons would undoubtedly find new excuses for being unhappy even in a world in which there were no inflations, no depressions, and no unemployment.

Higher employment may reduce real wages.

One of the problems raised as an objection is the possibility that with higher employment the real wages of workers will be lower. This is a distinct possibility. If there are sharply diminishing returns to labor so that when the unemployed men are put to work they add relatively little to the product, then they cannot be profitably employed unless prices are raised sharply in relation to wages. In other words there would have to be a sharp reduction in real wages.

If there are such sharply diminishing returns to labor that an increase in employment involves a reduction in the real wage, the amount each worker would get per unit of work in the form of wages would be less, and it is even possible that the total amount going to all the workers together in wages would be less than before, the increase in the number of workers getting wages being more than offset by the reduction in the amount of real wages obtained by each worker.

But even in this case (unlikely as it is) there would be no real objection to the increase in employment, whether this increase was due to Functional Finance or to anything else. As long as the newly employed have any marginal product at all—as long as they contribute anything at all to production—there will be a larger national income—a larger cake—to be divided among the whole population.

The increase in the cake would in this case all go into larger incomes for the owners of capital and land and for the receivers of profits. They would be receiving not merely a larger absolute amount but a larger proportion of a larger total national income now that a smaller proportion would be going to labor in the form of wages. But it would then be possible, by social-security measures, by changing the progressiveness of taxation, and in other ways, to shift some of this concentrated wealth from the rich to the poor. The poor would not be exactly those whose pay envelopes, in their real purchasing power, had been reduced as a result of the increase in employment. But it would naturally include those of the workers who most needed to be recompensed for their misfortune. Since the total income is increased by the increase in employment it would be possible to recompense everybody who had suffered from the reduction in real wages and still leave more to the rest of the population out of the larger cake than they had before the increase in employment. This is not to say that it would be practical to try to arrange the compensatory redistribution of income so that no single person was damaged by the increase in employment or even so that no significant group of people would be worse off in the full-employment situation than in the previous depression. Such nice adjustments of social policy probably will never be possible. But it is sufficient if the general level of income is raised while everybody is protected from severe hardship arising out of a policy which is in the general interest.

A gradual approach to full employment is therefore sometimes recommended.

Some economists who believe that the case we have been considering is normal, namely, that real wages would normally fall very much with full employment, do not reject Functional Finance outright but rather say that it should be adopted gradually. They say that the level of employment should be permitted to increase only slowly while the general efficiency of the economy increases as a result of accumulation of more useful productive capital or as a result of improved methods of production. In this way employment could be increased without any reduction in the real wage. When the general increase in efficiency has offset the effect of the diminishing returns to additional employed workers, it would be possible to have full employment without a lower real wage than in the beginning. The objection to Functional Finance would then no longer be valid.

The first and most important answer to this is that there is no need to forego the benefits even in this interim period. Compensation to all those who are damaged would take up only a part of the benefits resulting from the high level instead of the lower level of economic activity. And it should be noted that this kind of argument really accepts the necessity and the feasibility of Functional Finance and only suggests that it should not be applied too rapidly.

The evidence that an increase in employment would in fact

result in a reduction of real wages is rather weak. During the war we had a great increase in employment and output increased so much more than proportionately that real wages in the United States were much greater than in the prewar depression even though a large part of the resources of society were being devoted toward producing war materials and services.

Lord Keynes, the originator of the basic ideas of Functional Finance, himself believed, when he first developed the theory, that increased employment would indeed bring with it a (slight) reduction in real wages. At least one Marxian opponent denounced Keynesian economics as an attack on the working class. He charged Keynesian economics with attempting, in the jargon of communist theology, "to solve capitalist crisis at the expense of the workers." But further clarification of the theory has shown that the increase in employment does not necessarily involve any reduction in the real wage. The basic operation is not a lowering of the real wage but an increase in money demand for goods and services. It is possible that the increase in money demand would raise prices relatively to wages and thus lead to a fall in real wages. But it is also possible that the increase in money demand will permit firms to reduce their rate of markup per unit because they will be producing in a larger volume, and such a reduction in the effective degree of monopoly would have the opposite effect and *raise* the real wage. This seems to have happened to a very large degree in the increase in economic activity associated with World War II.

If the application of Functional Finance should result not merely in the achievement of full employment but in the expectation that full employment is going to be maintained indefinitely, these positive effects on the real wage would be much more important. The very large profits made by corporations and by business in general for several years now after World War II are the result of a pricing policy based on the expectation that the full employment will not last. Businessmen feel they must have a rate of markup which would enable them to cover their overhead even when working at much less than capacity. Such rates of markup naturally result in extraordinarily high profits as long as very high employment persists. For a while this is regarded as only right, since the firms must make enough in good times to be able to last out the bad times. But if the bad times should not be expected to come, the continued, high, boom-time profits being made would tempt more competition to come in and participate. This increase in competition would result in lower rates of price markup or profit margins, more moderate profits, and prices *lower* in relation to wages. Real wages would thus *rise* rather than fall as a result of Functional Finance. But this, it must be remembered, is to be expected only when Functional Finance has been demonstrated in practice to such general satisfaction that there is no longer much fear of a return to the pre-Functional Finance world of good times and bad times.

The argument that increasing the level of employment must reduce the real wage because of the diminishing returns to labor derives much of its plausibility from one of the backwashes of the "classical" assumption of the normality of full employment. In an equilibrium of full employment one would expect to have the equipment of society adjusted to the currently available number of workers. A sudden increase in the number of workers would mean that there was no really suitable equipment or tools available for the new workers to use, and this would indeed probably reduce the marginal productivity of labor quite considerably.

But in a condition of underemployment the picture is normally quite different. There is lots of unused capacity. Firms are operating at a low degree of utilization of their equipment just because they are adjusted to a world of ups and downs, of good times and bad times, and the marks of bad times are just as much the underutilization of capacity as the underemployment of men. All business is feverishly trying to get more orders and is looking forward to an improvement in business which they visualize not so much as a time when they will be able to charge a higher price as a time when they will be able to produce and sell a larger output. They would even settle for a reduction in price if there were a sufficient increase in the orders the salesmen brought in. More men can therefore be absorbed without any sharply diminishing returns and there is a distinct possibility of what genuine diminished returns there are being offset by an increase in the degree of competition (or decrease in the degree of monopoly) coming with the increase in employment.

These opposing tendencies may cause prices to rise relatively to wages or may cause prices to fall relatively to wages. The most probable result is that the opposing tendencies will largely cancel out so that an increase in employment would have very little effect on the real wage. One must look for the force behind the kind of objection we have just considered not in the economic analysis but rather in the psychological causes for resistance to Functional Finance and to new ideas in general.

Many objections to Functional Finance are really objections to prosperity.

Another objection to Functional Finance is that it would result in inflationary pressure. Sometimes this is due to a misunderstanding of the whole nature of Functional Finance—a failure to recognize that the policy is just as much directed toward preventing inflation or too great a money demand as it is directed against deflation or too little money demand. But there is another element in it which is much more serious and much more worth taking into account. When there is a high level of employment, no matter how it comes about, there will be pressure for higher money wages. The higher money wages have the effect of raising prices so that there is no increase in real wages. When workers discover that their higher money wages are all lost in buying goods at higher prices so that they cannot get any more goods with their higher money wages, they will press for wages to rise again. This could result in inflation. Here we have a really serious problem and one which we shall have to discuss more fully in a later chapter.[2]

Yet another resistance to Functional Finance, which again is really an objection to full employment, takes the form of complaints about the loss of certain incentives. Efficiency, punctuality, attention to work, and effort by workers are much reduced when there is no longer such a great fear by the workers that they will lose their jobs. The basis for this objection is to be found in such phenomena as absenteeism, the difficulty of finding servants, the demand for what look like extremely high wages compared with what there had been before in certain parts of the economy, the lack of discipline, and sometimes the lack of respect and maybe even of gratitude by workers to employers for having given them jobs.

In one sense this kind of objection is much more genuine than the others, because these phenomena do indeed result from full employment. And yet they are arguments which are less respectable than any of the others. When examined very closely they can be recognized as an attempt by privileged groups to maintain their privileges at the expense of less fortunate members of society.

There are resistances that are basically illiberal.

What is really claimed here is that workers, or at least certain kinds of underpaid workers, are inferior creatures and should recognize it as their duty to retain this status. They should be in continual fear of the grave risk of severe and prolonged unemployment; they should be subservient to their betters and should be satisfied to continue to work for very low wages in those areas in which they find themselves caught by accident of fate or of birth. They should be prevented by conditions of depression from escaping to the better opportunities which would

[2] Chapter 13, "High Full Employment and Low Full Employment."

be opened for them by general economic prosperity. These implied claims are illiberal in the truest sense of the word. When their implications are spelled out in the light such objections rapidly vanish in the American atmosphere.

The charge that Functional Finance (or full employment brought about in any other way) is bad for industrial discipline is occasionally made by managers of large corporations. Many people therefore consider the demand for servility by workers (to be extorted by a fear of prolonged unemployment) to be a *capitalistic* objection. But it is not really capitalism that should be blamed for such claims. It is really illiberalism. It is not the belief that capitalism is better than other forms of economic organization which lies behind this kind of objection but rather a belief, very much older than capitalism, that some people ought to be on top and other people ought to be underneath. Actually, capitalism and the liberalism which made it possible for capitalism to develop out of precapitalistic forms of society did a great deal to weaken this hierarchical view of the proper relations between men. It is only a mystical Marxian identification of all the good things in the good society with the destruction of capitalism that permits capitalism to be saddled with all the evils that have developed in the long and bloody course of human history.

There are resistances by liberals.

There are also objections by liberals, but a word of warning is perhaps necessary here. The word "liberal" is used in the original sense of the great liberals like Adam Smith who wished to liberate men from the precapitalist societies of status and who wanted to see a society in which all men were treated equally and given equal opportunities for expressing their personalities and living their fullest lives. This warning is most necessary because the word liberal is frequently used nowadays to indicate anybody who has any criticisms to make of existing society (unless he is merely crying for some imaginary good old times before capitalism developed). But many anticapitalists are not at all liberal. Communists or Stalinists are just the reverse of liberal. They are working toward the establishment of a society in which status and subservience to authority are much more definitely a guiding principle than in any capitalist society.

Liberals in the true sense are men who wish to liberate men from any kind of oppression whether by feudal lords or by capitalist barons or by tyrants who call themselves (or maybe even consider themselves to be) socialists working in the interest of the people in some redefined form of "democracy."

The objections by liberals are not economic but political. They rest upon the fear that the extension of governmental activities or even merely the extension of governmental responsibilities by Functional Finance is dangerous for the maintenance of individual liberty. They are mainly based upon an imaginary administrative or political difference between Functional Finance and sound finance. The objecting liberals seem to have the notion that sound finance gives the government a definite rule, namely, to balance the budget, whereas Functional Finance leaves the government free to exercise discretion. It is this governmental discretion or power which is feared.

In fact, there is no such administrative or political contrast between sound finance and Functional Finance. What Functional Finance does is not to replace a rule by govermental discretion, but rather to replace one rule by another rule. Functional Finance tells the authorities, instead of keeping expenditures equal to revenues, to follow a different rule and keep the total rate of spending at the level which gives full employment and avoids inflation. In both cases there is a rule; in both cases there is the possibility of departure from the rule; in both cases there are opportunities for discretion on the part of the authorities in choosing between different ways of following the rule. Functional Finance only brings about the substitution of a more reasonable new rule for the old rule. It does not increase the power of the government.

It merely asks for the recognition by the government of responsibility for the power which it already has.

Liberals are sometimes inclined to object to Functional Finance because of the association of it in their minds with certain anti-liberal ideas. One of these is the notion that Functional Finance would encourage economic nationalism because from the point of view of any country an excess of exports over imports counts as investment. An export surplus can therefore serve, like any other investment, to increase the level of employment. But to suppose that Functional Finance needs any such narrowly national activities for its functioning is a misunderstanding. It is only in topsy-turvy economics that many foolish things are advisable because the alternative of doing nothing in a depression is still more foolish. In the upside-down economy of unemployment an excess of exports over imports can benefit society in the same way that any destruction of resources or any diminution in efficiency can benefit society. Functional Finance does not say that these bad things become good things without qualification, what it says is that we should remove the conditions under which these bad things are relatively good.

In England, at a time when a domestic full-employment policy was prevented by a depression in the rest of the world and an unwillingness to permit the pound sterling to adjust itself, a proposal was made by Keynes that England impose a revenue tariff which would permit an increase in employment in England without this causing a shortage of foreign currency. But it is really because Functional Finance could *not* be practiced that this apparent [3] departure from liberal free-trade economics was made,

---

[3] The revenue tariff was only *apparently* a departure from the liberal principles of free trade because it was proposed together with a policy for increasing the spending level in Britain. There would have been no net decrease in the demand for imports and no diminution in the level of foreign trade. The revenue tariff was necessary only in order to prevent the increased level of spending in Britain from resulting in a greater demand for imports (at the rate of exchange which was taken as unalterable) than England would have foreign currency to pay for. In the absence of the revenue tariff

and as soon as the pound was permitted to fall to a more realistic value in 1931, the arguments put forward by Keynes for a revenue tariff entirely disappeared. This did not prevent those who wanted tariffs for other nonliberal ideas from making use of the argument, but that is another story.

There is reason for believing that the resistances can be overcome by education.

All the resistances discussed in the last three chapters turn out to be almost entirely based upon misunderstandings of the nature of the disease and of the nature of the remedies proposed. This makes it possible to believe that they may be overcome by education. If there were important resistances which were genuine in the sense that it was really in the interests of large and influential parts of the economy to have and maintain conditions of unemployment, instability, fear of depressions, and so on, then it would be difficult to suppose that mere education would be able to overcome these resistances. But there are no real, basic economic objections. There are only misunderstandings due to the confusion of means such as capitalism or anticapitalism with the ends of building a good and free society or the other more mixed confusions discussed in this chapter. There is therefore reason to hope that enlightenment and education will in time cause Functional Finance to be accepted not as the line of a particular party but as simple common sense.

In fact, it seems that to a considerable extent this has already

---

it would not be possible for England to have the increase in domestic spending because the concomitant increase in demand for imports would have caused England to lose its reserves of gold and foreign investments and foreign credits in paying for the additional imports. Keynes' policy would not have interfered with or reduced the amount of foreign trade. It would merely have used the proposed revenue tariff to limit imports by just as much as imports were being limited by the depression in Britain. There would then have been no need for maintaining the depression. These matters are discussed further in Chaps. 21 and 22 below.

become the case and that in the United States we will not have any severe depressions from now on. This is because every party understands that it *is* possible to alleviate depression by government deficits. Our political leaders are far from convinced that such deficits are satisfactory or desirable. But there has developed a general understanding that depressions *can* be mitigated by spending by the government or by spending by people whose taxes are reduced by the government. This knowledge can no longer be hidden. No matter what party is in power, whether liberal or conservative, whether Democrats or Republicans, the pressure to prevent a recession from turning into a severe depression will be irresistible. It will call into being public works, government spending, and tax reductions sufficient to prevent any really severe depression. To prevent depressions altogether and to have a high level of full employment all the time is another matter and one for which a great deal more education is still necessary.

Summary.

Even people who agree that it is both possible and necessary to do something to prevent depressions and inflations under capitalism show resistance to Functional Finance. People who are half convinced that Functional Finance is good and necessary are easily frightened by unexpected implications into dropping what they have already grasped. In this way people who have been convinced that the national debt is not a subtraction from the national wealth are disturbed by the idea of meeting an interest obligation by letting the debt grow larger or are frightened by examples in which fantastic figures for the national debt are used to emphasize logical points.

Resistance often takes the form of a shift from economic to political arguments when the economic ground has disappeared from beneath the objector's feet. The public is then charged with being unable or unwilling to understand Functional Finance so that "although it is perfectly sound economically it is politically impossible." Such amateur "political realism" by economists who accept the economics of Functional Finance constitutes a sad flight from their political responsibilities as potential leaders of public opinion.

Resistance often takes the form of stating irrelevant problems that are not solved by Functional Finance as if they were objections to Functional Finance. This puts the proponents of Functional Finance in the dilemma of picking one of many methods of attacking a problem, which may not be favored by the objector, or pointing out that there are many different ways of dealing with them and being dismissed as "vague." Sometimes the objector has fallen in love with a particular problem and thinks everything else is unimportant.

The possibility that high employment may result in lower real wage rates is sometimes stated as an objection but more often as a reason for introducing Functional Finance slowly. The arguments for this objection are stated in terms of diminishing returns to labor and rest on an unrealistic picture of a depression with equipment fully employed. They can be met by pointing out that there will always be a larger cake to distribute to everybody including the wage earners. The probable practical insignificance suggests that the psychological resistance is here more important than the economic analysis.

Objections to Functional Finance as inflationary may be due to confusion or to the recognition of a serious full-employment problem. There are many problems that arise only when there is full employment and many of the objections to Functional Finance turn out to be resistances to full employment. Some of these arise from an illiberal desire for the maintenance of differential status between different classes of the population and are precapitalistic rather than capitalistic. Other resistances are provided by liberals who are afraid that Functional Finance might endanger personal liberty by increasing the power of government. Such objections are based either on a misunderstanding of the difference between sound finance and Functional Finance in their administrative or political operation or on an association between Functional Finance and certain antiliberal foolishnesses of the upside-down economy which Functional Finance wants to abolish rather than to nourish.

Because almost all of the resistances to Functional Finance are due to confusion rather than to real sectional interest it is possible to hope that education can succeed in overcoming them. The more rudimentary lesson, of how to prevent very serious depressions, seems already to have been learnt albeit reluctantly.

Part IV

Full Employment and Inflation

CHAPTER 13

High Full Employment and Low Full Employment

FUNCTIONAL FINANCE is directed not only at preventing depression but also at preventing inflation. It aims to keep total spending from going too high just as much as it aims at preventing total spending from going too low. But more attention is usually paid to the prevention of depression and unemployment because this is probably a more important problem than the prevention of inflation. This concentration has led many people to suppose that Functional Finance is directed entirely or almost entirely toward depression, and they have, in fact, called it "depression economics," meaning perhaps thereby to imply that as soon as there is no longer a depression Functional Finance becomes inapplicable and we have to go back again to "sound finance."

Functional Finance is not the same as "depression economics."

Now it is true that when the upside-down economy of depression no longer exists, we have something like the world of classical economics, in which there is always full employment. But this is only a superficial similarity. The recognition of the current existence of full employment, whether the full employment is accidental or the result of policy, is not the same thing as the classical assumption that we always and naturally have full employment so that we do not have to worry about the possibility of too little spending or of too much spending. Even if there is full employment we still have to think about the danger of spending becoming too small or becoming too great. The principles of Functional Finance are just as applicable and just as necessary in preventing spending from being too great as in preventing spending from being too small. Functional Finance may be more important for the prevention of depression because the prevention of depression is more important than the prevention of inflation, but it is not merely depression economics.

The distinction between deflationary and functional unemployment is inadequate.

Avoiding both inflation and depression means achieving full employment. But we have already seen that full employment is not as clear a concept as might be wished. A preliminary attempt was made near the beginning of this book (in Chapter 2) to diminish the ambiguity or elusiveness of the concept of full employment. There we made the distinction between deflationary unemployment and frictional unemployment and said that Functional Finance could be directed only at removing deflationary unemployment. In other words, deflationary unemployment is that unemployment which can be cured by simply increasing total money demand for goods and services. Frictional unemployment is the unemployment which remains and which cannot be removed by merely increasing total money spending still more. It can be reduced only by the removal of the particular frictions which prevent unemployed men and unfilled vacancies from getting together. When all the remaining unemployment is frictional unemployment we have "full employment."

But when we look at this more closely we find that there is no such simple line between frictional unemployment and deflationary unemployment. There is a large volume of unemployment which we cannot dismiss from consideration by merely saying that it is frictional and can be cured only by the removal of particular frictions.

One way in which this problem is often expressed—usually by critics of Functional Finance—is to say that there is a region (between depression and inflation) where we have *both* depression and inflation. If in a condition of depression the rate of money spending is increased, a point is reached at which further increases in money spending would not bring about any permanent increase in employment but would only cause inflation. Yet at this point the number of unemployed will be much greater than that made necessary by the real technical frictions.

In the United States of America it is technically possible for the number of unemployed to be reduced below 2 million. This is proved by the fact that in 1946 and 1947 the number of unemployed *was* less than 2 million while the economy was working very satisfactorily. The number of *frictionally* unemployed in the strict technical sense must have been less than 2 million. Yet if the number of unemployed is reduced below 6 million or thereabouts, wages and prices begin to rise and we have some inflation. This is what is meant by saying that there is a range—namely, between 6 million unemployed and 2 million unemployed—when we have both depression and inflation. The lower extreme of this range, at which there are 6 million unemployed but at which wages and prices begin to rise, we shall call "low full employment." The upper extreme of the range, where all the unemployment is truly frictional in the technical sense, we shall call "high full employment." [1]

The disturbing influence is the bargaining power of labor.

The special influence that causes wages and prices to rise even though the number of unemployed is much greater than what is

---

[1] These two numbers, 2 million and 6 million, are merely guesses. It may be that more accurate numbers would be 1½ million and 4½ million. Considerable investigation would be necessary to get more reliable estimates, and the numbers themselves may change with changing conditions. But there are two such numbers that correspond to high full employment and to low full employment, and the two numbers will be used throughout this book as shorthand expressions for whatever the true numbers might be of those that would be unemployed in the conditions of high full employment and low full employment.

made necessary by real frictions is the excessive bargaining power of the workers. If there are less than about 6 million unemployed in the United States of America, the bargaining power of the workers is excessive. The pressure for higher wages by workers is greater than the resistance to wage increases by employers, and wage rates tend to rise more rapidly than the over-all increase in labor productivity. Employers are unwilling to suffer interruptions in production because business is pretty good. Other workers are not easy to find. Employers may even bid up wages in attempts to expand rapidly to take advantage of relatively good business. And so wages rise.

As wages rise, costs rise and the prices of the products rise. The possibility of raising the prices of the products is a most important consideration in persuading employers to pay the higher wages. The increase in prices destroys the expected benefit for the workers from the increase in wages. They can buy no more goods now with their higher money wages than they were able to buy before with their lower money wages. This leads to a demand for another wage increase to give the workers the expected increase in their real wage, of which they consider themselves to have been cheated by the price rise, and the next round of wage increases leads to another price increase, another disappointment, and another demand for wage increases; in this way we get the spiral of inflation.

It is not impossible for a wage increase to start off a depression rather than an inflation. This could happen if the wage increase took place at a time when conditions of demand, or perhaps some sort of price control, prevented the increase in cost from being passed on in higher prices. But these are rather special cases. In the former case the impossibility of passing on the increased wages in higher prices would indicate that we were on the verge of falling below even the low full employment into a condition of depression. The increase in wages would not bring about the depression; the depression was about to descend on the economy anyway. The wage increase would rather have the opposite effect of preventing the fall in prices and the expectations of further falls in prices which would have aggravated the depression. In the second case the stabilization of the price level by price control changes the whole picture and makes it necessary for the wage level to adjust itself to the price level. As we shall see below, this would interfere with the possibility of achieving high full employment.

If we are to keep to the formulation of Chapter 2, according to which all unemployment that cannot be cured by more spending is called "frictional unemployment" and is compatible with full employment, we shall have to say that we have full employment even when there are 6 million unemployed in the United States. Any increase in spending has the effect not of increasing the level of employment but merely of raising wages and prices. The 6 million would therefore have to be classified as frictionally unemployed. But only 2 million of the 6 million are unemployed for reasons that are really frictions in the normal sense of the word. It is the bargaining power of workers that causes wages to rise as soon as the number of unemployed is reduced below 6 million. Excessive bargaining power can therefore be considered a kind of friction. It is not a technical friction. We may call it an economic friction. If something could be done to remove this economic friction we would be able to reach the much higher level of employment with only 2 million unemployed. But as long as the economic friction remains and the reduction of unemployment below 6 million causes inflation, we have to say that full employment means having 6 million people unemployed. This is the low level of full employment. The elimination of the economic friction would permit us to reach the high level of full employment with only 2 million unemployed.

Overfull employment can only be temporary.

It is of course possible for money demand to raise employment above the low level of full employment so that there are less than

6 million unemployed. The output of goods and services would be increased too. But such "overfull" employment cannot be maintained. Wages and prices will rise. They may at first rise quite moderately, but that is only because workers are being deceived and are not realizing that their higher money wages are being eaten up by higher prices. With, say, 3 million unemployed the bargaining power of workers is able to raise wages by, perhaps, 15 per cent per annum. But this is true only as long as workers are assuming that prices are going to stay constant (or, what is more likely, they have not thought about changing prices at all). The increase in money wages is taken to be an increase in what they can buy with their wages. It will not take the workers long to discover that prices are in fact rising so that a much greater increase in money wages is needed to provide the expected increase in real wages that they have bargained for. But they can never catch up with the rising prices. They are like the proverbial donkey carrying the proverbial carrot in front of his nose. The more rapidly wages are increased the more rapidly prices will increase. In short the rise in prices and wages becomes cumulative and self-accelerating.

It is possible for the inflation to continue for a while, but as it accelerates in the way described, greater and greater increases in money spending are needed to maintain the same level of employment. If the inflation is maintained for some time at an ever-increasing rate, we get the disruptions of the economy that come from the establishment of expectations of the inflation continuing further still and at still faster rates. The rate of spending increases even faster than at the rate needed for maintaining the same level of employment, and we get a still higher level of employment and of course a still greater bargaining power of workers and still greater pressures for higher wages and still more rapidly rising prices. But instead of this leading to more production and higher levels of living, the opposite happens. It is found to be more profitable to buy things quickly, before their prices rise, than to produce things. Production therefore falls. All the nor-

mal criteria for distinguishing relatively more useful from relatively less useful activities break down. Many necessities run
short because the factors of production have been shifted to the
production of much less useful things or to the characteristic
activity of the inflation—running to buy something before someone else gets there or before the price is raised.

This process must come to an end before very long. It may be
stopped soon by a shortage of money. But even if the monetary
authorities cooperate in keeping the inflation going by creating all
the money needed as prices keep on increasing, even to astro-
nomical figures, as in the European hyperinflations after both
world wars, the inflation comes to an end when the inflation is no
longer endurable, and some new kind of money is adopted to
take the place of the old money, which becomes completely worthless.

It is not possible to maintain a level of employment which is
so high that it makes the bargaining power of labor great enough
to make wages rise more rapidly than the productivity of labor.
Such a high level of employment is self-destructive because it
brings about and then depends on the maintenance not merely of
rising prices but of prices that are rising at an ever-increasing
speed. This cannot be maintained and so it is impossible to reduce the level of unemployment permanently below the 6 million
level as long as such a low level of unemployment has the effect
of giving excessive bargaining power to labor.

Greater bargaining power does not help labor as a whole.

In the last few paragraphs there has been much emphasis on the
evils of excessive bargaining power of labor. This emphasis is
easily denounced as showing an antilabor attitude. But such a
denunciation would be based on an assumption that an increase
in labor's bargaining power is good for labor, enabling labor to
make a better bargain in real terms and to get a larger share in

the national income. This assumption, plausible and even "self-evident" as it appears to many, is completely unfounded.

During the inflation that is brought about by an excessive rise in money wages (*i.e.*, the excess of the rise over the increase in the productivity of labor) it is difficult to say what may happen. In the confusion some workers may find that for a time their wages rise more than the prices of the goods they buy. Most workers will find the opposite to be the case. And when the inflation becomes severe enough to disrupt the economy, almost everyone will be worse off. But when the inflation is stopped or if the inflation is prevented from developing cumulatively, the great bargaining power of labor will be found not to have done labor as a whole any good at all.

This is because an over-all change in wages in general without any change in the relation of particular money wage rates to each other has no necessary effect on the real wage rates or on the real situation in the economy as a whole. A general rise in money wage rates (relative to productivity) results in a proportional general rise in prices and in money incomes, so that in real terms everything is just as it was before.

Representatives of workers are prone to believe that a general increase in money wage rates would increase the real wages of workers at the expense of the owners of other factors of production (whom for our present purposes we may call their employers). Representatives of workers therefore tend to favor increases in money wage rates. Representatives of employers are prone to think the same, and for this reason they in turn tend to frown on general increases in wage rates. But in both cases the tendency to believe that to raise money wages will benefit workers and harm employers is the result of thinking of the effects of money wage increases only in a single trade or only in a single firm and then assuming, quite falsely, that the general effect of a general increase in money wages is the same as the local effect of a local increase in money wage rates.

When it is remembered that a *general* increase in wage rates raises the costs of all competitors and increases the incomes of the workers it becomes evident that prices will not stay the same but will rise. And furthermore it can be shown that the rise will be in the same proportion as the general increase in wages, so that the workers are not able to buy any more with their higher money wages and the employers will be able to obtain just as much real profit as before. The workers do not gain from the general increase in money wage rates and the employers do not lose anything from it until there is the inflationary disorganization of production.

Labor's share is determined by more basic social institutions.

Unless there is a fundamental change in the general institutions of society, in the degree of monopoly or the degree of competition, there will remain the same degree of markup between costs and prices—the same range of profits in the different occupations resulting from the existing degree of competition or monopoly. For this reason prices will rise in the same proportion as costs. The difference between costs and prices, or in other words the profits, will also increase in the same proportion as wages and prices, but the higher money profits will not mean higher real profits any more than the higher money wages mean higher real wages.

It might be argued, and it too frequently is argued, that not all costs are wages, so that costs will rise less than wages and therefore prices will rise less than wages. But this objection seems plausible only as long as we forget what these other costs are. The cost of raw materials and other nonwage costs of any firm are nothing but the prices of the products of other firms and consist of the costs plus profit markup in these other firms. If the other firms' costs consisted entirely of wages, their prices, which are the nonwage costs of our first firms, would rise in the same proportion as wages. All costs, including "nonwage costs," would therefore rise in the same proportion as wages, and prices would rise in the same proportion too. To the extent that the other firms also have nonwage costs we have to bring in still other firms whose products constitute *their* nonwage costs. The analysis can be complicated in this way indefinitely, but the result is always the same. When all the effects are taken into account the conclusion is always that prices will rise in the same proportion as money wage rates if there is a general increase in money wage rates in the economy as a whole.

Another way of showing that this is what must occur is to consider the effects on the economy if costs and prices in general did not rise in the same proportion as wages. It would then be profitable for all producers to try, wherever possible, to replace labor by machinery or land or other factors of production whose costs have risen less. This would constitute an increase in demand for all these other factors which would keep on forcing their prices up. Only when their prices had risen as much as money wages in general would this pressure cease and the previous equilibrium relationship between all prices including wages be restored.

The proposition that raising money wages leaves unchanged the real wage and the fraction of the national income going to labor is equally true for all levels of employment. It is just as true for a condition of depression as for a condition of full employment and for exactly the same reasons. It is true that the level of economic activity itself can and does have important effects in determining what share of the national income goes to labor. If there is an increase in the level of economic activity, with no change in the fundamental economic and social institutions that determine the way the national income is shared between labor and the rest of the economy, there will be a smaller *proportion* (but a larger absolute amount) going to labor and a larger proportion going to others. But if the level of economic activity remains constant, an increase in money wages in general results in a corresponding increase in prices which leaves real wages just where they would have been in the absence of the general increase in money wages and prices.

To point out this truth is not the same thing as refusing to be interested in increasing the share of the national income that goes to labor. It is only to point out that raising the general level of wages is not a way of achieving the object. Extremely impatient people, however, are prone to get angry with a signpost, however accurate it may be, that tells them that the way they want to go is not going to lead to the place they want to get to. This chapter is not concerned with policies that really would increase labor's share. It is concerned with pointing out that a general increase in money wages must not be assumed to be the same thing as or even to lead to an increase in real wages.

Bargaining power is effective only for relative wage rates.

An increase in the money wages of a *section* of the economy is different. Even though the products made by the workers whose wages are raised may themselves rise, there will be no such rise in the prices of the goods made by the other workers whose wages are left behind. The prices of their products will also stay behind. The worker with the *relatively* higher wages will enjoy an increase in his real wage. He will be able to buy more goods and services with his wages (that is, if he remains in employment— which is much less certain now that his product is dearer relatively to the product of the workers whose wages have not been raised). That is why he wants to raise his money wages whenever he can.

But we have seen that if *all* sections get their wage rates increased they find that the prices of what they buy rises in the same proportion as their wages so that their expected gains turn out to be empty. Their disappointment only causes them to ask for another and bigger money wage increase. They will of course be disappointed again and as many times as they try this trick.

In time they may learn that they cannot win at this game, but unfortunately this discovery does not stop the inflationary process.

Understanding is not enough to prevent inflationary pressures.

It does not help very much for the workers or their representatives to understand that the increases in money wages must turn out to be merely nominal—that price increases will inevitably take away all that seems to be gained by the money wage increases. Such understanding by workers and their leaders cannot by itself stop the process of rising wages and prices and inflation because no group of workers will want to be left behind in the race. Even though this is a race in which however fast you run you stay where you are, it is also a race in which if you do not run as fast as the rest you will be moving backward—you will find that the prices of what you buy rise faster than your wages—and your real income actually falls. And if you should run faster than the others your income will in fact be greater because your wages will have risen faster than the prices of the things you buy that are made by other workers whose wages have not risen as much as yours. In this way the fruitless race to inflation and disaster can go on and on, faster and faster, and cannot be stopped by merely making the runners aware of the general futility of the race. Each dares not stop as long as the others are running, and so the race goes on.

A reserve army of unemployed seems to be necessary for stability.

It is of course possible to put an end to this inflationary race by the simple application of Functional Finance. A restrictive fiscal and monetary policy can reduce effective demand to the level at which the inflationary spiral is stopped by the unwillingness of employers to grant wage increases and by the reduction of the workers' pressure for them. But this way of preventing inflation would mean giving up the benefits of a high level of employment and introducing a reserve army of some 6 million unemployed men in order to reduce the excessive bargaining power of the workers. This sounds very much like the Marxian doctrine that a reserve army is necessary for the maintenance of capitalist society. Keeping 6 million unemployed instead of the 2 million made necessary by real technical frictions means a cut in the national income of some 15 billion dollars per annum. Clearly it would be most desirable to have a more economical and a socially less objectionable way of preventing inflation.

Low full-employment equilibrium depends on wage rigidities which we cannot hope to remove.

In the next chapter we shall consider a plan for eliminating this reserve army of unemployed, but before we go on to that we must consider an apparent theoretical difficulty. How can we have two full-employment equilibria, a low level of full employment with 6 million unemployed which seems to be stable but undesirable, and a high level of full employment with 2 million unemployed? [2]

If we had the perfect flexibility of wages that is sometimes assumed in economic theory, Functional Finance would indeed tend to move the economy to the high level of full employment. As long as there were more than 2 million unemployed there would be a tendency for wages and prices to fall and it would clearly be appropriate for the total level of spending to be increased. In this way the high level of full employment would be reached and maintained.

The wage rigidity that prevents wages and prices from falling and high full employment from being reached by the simple application of Functional Finance does not depend upon the great strength that collective bargaining and trade unions have reached at the present time. Even weak trade unions can cause a great deal of trouble to an employer who attempts to cut wages, and

[2] I am indebted in the following section to discussions with Professor Armen A. Alchian of the University of California at Los Angeles.

this will make him hesitate to do so. Even if there were no trade unions at all, the mere idea that a certain wage rate is reasonable or right or proper or fair—that it is antisocial to reduce wages—is sufficient to establish that degree of wage rigidity downward which can make a low level of full employment a stable position. Employers themselves feel that it is not nice to reduce wages or that they will not be well looked upon if they do. If no wages can fall, wages will rise in those areas where there is a *relative* scarcity of labor. If there are more than 6 million unemployed there is plenty of labor in almost every labor market. But if there are less than 6 million unemployed there will be scarcities of labor in some parts of the economy. Wages will rise in these parts but will not fall elsewhere. There is therefore an increase in the general level of wages and, if the increase is greater than the over-all increase in productivity, an increase in prices, and this starts the inflationary spiral.

The automatic achievement of high full employment through Functional Finance therefore depends on an absence of any conception of fair wages, on an immediate readiness of employers to reduce money wages as soon as there is the slightest excess of supply of labor over the demand in any labor market, and on an immediate readiness of the workers to accept such money wage reductions. The kind of flexibility of wages that is necessary to give a single high full-employment equilibrium is therefore not likely ever to exist and is of no practical significance. We cannot expect Functional Finance alone to give us high full employment.

Without Functional Finance even perfect wage flexibility would not give automatic high full employment.

It is even more difficult to imagine high full employment being reached automatically *without* the application of Functional Finance, no matter what extremes of flexibility of wages are assumed. But it is useful to look into this because there are some neoclassical economists who seem to like to argue that all our employment problems are due to wage and price rigidities. If there were perfect flexibility of wages and prices, anything less than high full employment would result in falling wages and prices. This could lead to the expectation of further declines in wages and prices and to a *reduction* in employment or an accelerated aggravation of the unemployment because an expected further fall in prices makes investment and economic activity in general look much less profitable. There would be an increase in the desire to hold cash (which would be continuously appreciating in purchasing power as prices fell), and this would feed the depression still further. We could in short have a *hyperdeflation* that could be economically much more devastating than any hyperinflation—economic activity could be reduced to near zero, and it is most likely that some violent political upheaval would put an end to the process if it were permitted to continue by a government faithful to the end to the tenets of classical economic theory.

There is a limit to hyperdeflations in that there is a certain amount of money in the economy which does not disappear in the course of the hyperdeflation and which becomes more and more valuable as prices fall. A great deal of money does disappear; much credit money, whether issued by banks or by others, may be destroyed, and therefore you could get wages and prices continuing to fall along with the terrible disruption of the economy. But there is a core of money which does not disappear—gold and the hard money provided by government. As the hyperdeflation proceeds, the value of the stock of money becomes so great and the people who own this money are so rich that this will overcome their tendency to hoard the increasingly valuable money. They will increase their demand for goods and services and this will put an end to the hyperdeflation and to the depression.

It is doubtful whether anybody ever seriously suggested this as a practical way of governing our economy. The large volume of money which we need for the smooth working of a modern economy is already so great in relation to the national income that wages and prices could fall for a long time before the end of this road was reached. We must recognize, however, that the increase in the value of the stock of money when prices fall is a significant item, and it is probably true that modern Keynesian economists and protagonists of Functional Finance have paid insufficient attention to this element.

A less fantastic proposal of anti-Functional Financiers is that the volume of money income should be stabilized by monetary authorities.[3] This would then give the high level of full employment if you could remove all the frictions and rigidities we have spoken about. This is true. The only objection is that there is no feasible way of removing the rigidities. It would not be sufficient to weaken the most powerful trade unions or even to destroy them. It would not be sufficient to destroy all trade unions. Social security would have to be abolished. Workers' savings and credits would have to be taken away. There would have to be removed from the minds of both workers and employers the idea of a fair or decent wage rate. There is no practical possibility of removing the ideas of fairness of wages and of the defenses that workers have against wage reductions and there is very doubtful desirability in doing so. If the rigidities are not removed, stabilizing money income would prevent hyperdeflations, but it would be compatible with quite severe depressions and much more than 6 million unemployed.

Our problem is then: How can we get from low full employment, with 6 million unemployed, to high full employment, with not more than 2 million unemployed? How can we abolish the reserve army of unemployed without falling into inflation and destroying the stability of our economy?

[3] Presumably by the monetary and fiscal instruments of Functional Finance but with the aim of stabilizing the volume of money income instead of with the direct aim of full employment.

Summary.

The more frequent consideration of depression than of inflation in connection with Functional Finance has led to its being called "depression economics." But this is incorrect; Functional Finance is just as applicable to the prevention of inflation as to the prevention of depression. Achieving full employment means avoiding both depression and inflation, but there are serious ambiguities in the concept of full employment. These are insufficiently removed by the distinction between deflationary unemployment and frictional unemployment. There is a range between depression and inflation where wages and prices are rising even though there are more unemployed than can be blamed on frictions in the normal sense. In this range one can see indication both of depression and of inflation.

The influence that causes wages and prices to rise even when there are large numbers of unemployed is the excessive bargaining power of labor. The bargaining power of labor is excessive whenever it causes wages to rise more rapidly than over-all productivity. This causes prices to rise *pari passu* with wage increases so that there is no real wage increase but only inflation. Excessive bargaining power by workers may be called an "economic friction" to distinguish it from real or technical frictions that form a more "genuine" limitation to the attainable level of employment and output. The elimination of economic friction would permit the high level of full employment to be reached.

Even without the elimination of economic friction increased total spending can raise employment above the low full-employment level (*i.e.*, unemployment can be reduced below the 6 million level) but this can only be temporary. This is because "over-full" employment causes inflation, and inflation cannot be continued indefinitely.

To call labor's bargaining power excessive is not to be against the interests of labor. Excessive bargaining power of labor does not increase the real wage or the share of the national income going to labor. An over-all change in the level of wages causes a proportional change in the level of prices. Labor men tend to favor and employers tend to frown on general wage increases because they assume, quite falsely, that a general wage change has the same effect as a local wage change. But the real wage is determined by more basic social institutions, such as the degree of monopoly, which are unaffected by the level of money wages. This is true for all levels of economic activity. To point this out may be disappointing to labor if it removes an illusion.

A *section* of the economy *can* increase its real wage by raising its money wage relatively to the rest of the economy, but if all sections try this we have inflation. The inflation cannot be prevented by mere enlightenment as to the effects of wage increases because nobody can afford to keep out of the inflationary race. And stopping the inflation by Functional Finance means establishing low full employment and maintaining a reserve army of 4 million unnecessarily unemployed people.

The stability of the low level of full employment depends on downward wage rigidities. It is impractical to propose their abolition because that would involve not merely destruction of trade unions but impoverishment of all workers, abolition of social security, and removal of the general feeling, shared by both workers and employers, that there is a "fair wage" which it is undesirable to lower. Furthermore such a complete removal of wage and price rigidities would subject the economy to the danger of hyperdeflations that would be more devastating than hyperinflations. Together with Functional Finance the abolition of all wage and price rigidities would result in high full employment. Together with a policy of stabilizing the level of money income hyperdeflations would be prevented, but there could still be very serious depression. But since the abolition of all wage and price rigidities does not seem feasible, we are left with our problem of how to get high full employment without inflation.

CHAPTER 14

A Wage Policy for Full Employment

THE FULL-EMPLOYMENT situation that would be reached in a modern economy by the simple application of Functional Finance would be one of *low full employment*. Whenever the number of unemployed falls below a fairly high figure—about 6 million for the United States—the bargaining power of labor causes wages to rise and starts an inflationary movement even though there is no technical reason, in terms of real limitations on the mobility of labor, why unemployment should not be reduced to a much lower figure. In the United States it should be possible to reach a *high full-employment* equilibrium with less than 2 million people unemployed. These 2 million would be unemployed because of real frictions that prevent them from being available where they could immediately find work.

For this we need a wage policy which will prevent the inflationary wage increase that results in low full employment instead of high full employment.

The wage policy must be directed at particular money wage rates.

Such a wage policy would have to provide a method of determining or at least influencing what happens to wages. The first thing to note is that the wage policy must be directed not at real wages (the amount of goods and services that can currently be bought with the money wages), but at *money wages* (the rates of payment per hour or per day).

In a fundamental sense real wages are much more important than money wage rates, but it is only the *money* wage rate that policy can directly affect. It is possible to raise (or to lower) a money wage rate and to know that it is in fact raised (or lowered). This is not true for the real wage. An attempt to change the real wage by changing the money wage may be entirely frustrated. If an increase in the money wage rate results in an equal rise in the prices of the goods and services bought by the worker, the real wage will not in fact have been raised at all. And as we have seen, such a frustration is far from abnormal. Raising money wage rates always increases costs, and increased costs naturally result in higher prices. Prices cannot therefore be assumed to stay still when money wage rates are raised, and there can be no assurance that real wages are raised by raising money wage rates. What can be raised or lowered or kept constant, by a fairly simple decision, is not the real wage but the money wage rate.

The second thing to note is that it will not do for the wage policy to be directed at the general level of money wage rates. This is because an over-all change in wages in general without any change in the relation of particular money wage rates to each other brings about a proportional change in prices, leaves the real wage rate unchanged, and has no effect on the volume of employment. If there was a low level of full employment before such a change there will be a low level of full employment after the change in the general level of money wage rates. The wage policy must be directed at the *specific* wage rates in particular industries, trades, and regions—it must refer to the particular wage rates in the particular *labor markets*.

The wage policy must also yield general stability.

But although the wage policy must be directed at particular wage rates in particular labor markets it must be such as to result in desirable *general* effects on the general level of wages and on the general level of prices and incomes.

The most important effect of an increase in the general level of money wages and the concomitant increase in prices is the effect on the relationships between debtors and creditors because of the reduction in the real value of the debts. There is also a monetary effect. At the higher level of money wages, prices, and incomes, a larger quantity of money is needed to carry on, with the same convenience as before, the same level of real economic activity, that is, in employing the same number of men and producing the same quantity of goods and services. But these are matters which although far from unimportant are not as important as the other issues raised (except of course to the individual debtors and creditors).

If the monetary authorities do not increase the stock of money, money will be tight. This tightness of money could result in a curtailment of investment and of other economic activity, with resulting unemployment and a reduction in the real output and income of the economy. Such unemployment would be blamed by many on the increase in the money wage. But others would blame the unemployment on the failure of the monetary authorities to increase the stock of money. It is to be expected that when there had been sufficient discussion as to who is to blame, attention would be shifted to the task of alleviating the unemployment, and it would be considered easier to increase the amount of money than to roll back all wages and prices. (Functional Finance would, of course, have prescribed immediate supply of the additional money needed.) The amount of money would then be increased and we would have the higher wage and price level without any real change in the production and consumption of goods and services or in employment as compared with the situation before the money wages were raised.

Nevertheless, raising or lowering the general level of wages and prices can be very disturbing, not only to the debtors and creditors but to those in charge of monetary policy and to investors and all who are concerned about what wages and prices are going to be in the future. And this is true even if cumulative inflation and cumulative deflation are prevented. Although it is possible to make adjustments to rising and falling price levels (as we shall see in more detail in the next chapter) life is much easier if we have

a stable price level and a constant value of the dollar. We therefore want a wage policy which will have the effect of keeping the
value of the dollar stable.

It is not possible to stabilize both wages and prices.

It is not possible to have a wage policy which would stabilize
both the general level of wages and the general level of prices.
This is because productivity is continually increasing. The accumulation of more and better tools for men to work with and the
continuing process of invention and scientific discovery increase
the output per man and reduce the cost and the prices of products
in relation to the wage rate. The increase of productivity has been
of the order of about 3 per cent per annum. This means that if
the general level of wages is kept constant, prices will fall at about
3 per cent per annum and that if prices are to be kept constant,
wages should rise at about 3 per cent per annum. In choosing between these two possibilities it seems far preferable to stabilize the
price level (and thereby the purchasing power of the dollar) and
let money wage rates rise at 3 per cent per annum. It makes the
financial management of the economy much easier and it is probable that workers like to see their increased real income over time
take the form of more dollars in their pay envelopes (without any
deterioration of the dollars' buying power) rather than the less
tangible form of being able to buy more goods with the same number of dollars.

*Full employment and free mobility of labor are essential
prerequisites.*

There are two more things we must do before we can get to the
actual wage policy. We must consider two prerequisite conditions
without which the policy could not work and we must focus attention on the social function of wages.

The first of the two preconditions is the maintenance of full employment through adequate money demand. This may be effected by the application of Functional Finance, but for the present purpose it would not matter if adequate money demand for full employment were maintained in any other way—by government spending on war or war preparation, say, or by simple accident or good luck, which however continued to operate for a long time and was expected to continue to provide adequate demand for full employment.

The second precondition is the removal as far as possible of all artificial and unnecessary resistances to or restrictions on the movement of workers into any occupation in any part of the economy. The reason for this will become clearer when we consider the social function of wages.

The social function of wages must be recognized.

The function of wages is to induce workers to work and to get them to do the kind of work that is most effective in satisfying the needs of consumers—to get them to make the goods and to provide the services that the consumers prefer. Higher wages are the means of attracting workers by inducing them to come to where they are wanted more. Lower wages are the means of persuading workers to leave the places where they are wanted less. And it is always *relatively* higher wages and *relatively* lower wages that are significant in this context.

Higher wages have to be offered to induce workers to go where there is an increase in the demand for their product or to go where they would otherwise not want to go because the conditions of work are not good enough or the kind of work is not what they like to do. In a free society, the workers can be obtained only by making the conditions of work and the pay sufficiently attractive to induce them to move to the places where they are needed or by making the conditions of work and the pay sufficiently bad where they are not needed to induce the proper number of workers to leave these places and go elsewhere. The final judges in a free society must be the workers themselves, free to move or not to move in accordance with their own judgment of the adequacy of the pay and of the attractiveness of the conditions of work.

The wage policy can then be based on indices of relative attractiveness.

We can now state the criterion we needed, which, it must be remembered, should tell us what each particular wage rate in each particular labor market should do—whether it should rise as fast as general productivity or go ahead of it or lag behind it—and the prescription must be such that it would result in the general level of wages rising as fast as productivity so that we can have a stable dollar, avoiding inflation and depression. With productivity increasing at 3 per cent per annum wages must rise at 3 per cent per annum to give us a constant price level, or in other words a constant value of money.

Such a criterion is provided by the *relative attractiveness* of different occupations as shown by the eagerness of workers to move into or out of any occupation in response to the need for them in the occupation. An *index* of relative attractiveness of any occupation is provided by the ratio between the number of people who are qualified and ready to work in the occupation but have not been able to get a job there and the number of people actually employed in the occupation.

For the economy as a whole the corresponding figure is an average that may be called the "national average index" of attractiveness of all occupations. If, in measuring the relative attractiveness of an occupation, we included in the number seeking work in it only those who were already in the occupation, the index of relative attractiveness would turn out to be the level of unemployment in the occupation. But there is no reason for counting only those who have succeeded in the past in obtaining work in the desired occupation and not counting those who have not been lucky enough to get in. The index of relative attractiveness is therefore obtained by taking the total number of workers who are qualified for and want to work in the occupation at the given wage and conditions but who are not working there now, whether they are working elsewhere or not, then taking the number of workers actually employed in the occupation, and then dividing the first number by the second number.

This then is our wage policy: *Where the index of relative attractiveness is more than twice the national average, the money wage rate should not be raised at all but should be kept constant while other wages move ahead.* By their high preference for employment in such an occupation the workers themselves are showing that they are overprivileged compared with conditions elsewhere and workers elsewhere should be permitted to catch up.

Where the index of relative attractiveness is not too different from the national average, say between half the national average and double the national average, the money wage should be increased at 3 per cent per annum, that being an approximation to the long-run increase in over-all productivity.

And *where the index of relative attractiveness is less than half the national average, the wage rate should be increased at twice the standard rate, i.e., at 6 per cent per annum.* Here the workers are underprivileged relatively to workers elsewhere. They should be helped to a fairer wage which would serve the proper function of getting the supply of workers in a more adequate relation to the demand for them.

The result would be some wages rising at 6 per cent per annum, some rising not at all, and the bulk of wages as well as the general level of wages rising at 3 per cent per annum. Prices would then be stable or, if productivity increased at less than 3 per cent per annum, would be rising very slightly. If productivity increased by only 2 per cent per annum, prices would rise at 1 per cent per annum.

No arbitrary authority is necessary.

There is a danger of our formulation giving the impression that some authority would be given arbitrary power to decide whether it is desirable for a worker to be moved into or out of any particular industry or to decide arbitrarily that wages should be raised or kept down in any particular industry or labor market. That would be directly contrary to the purposes and the philosophy of the plan. Such power in the hands of any individual or group of individuals would be in basic conflict with our ideas of a free society in which workers are free to work where they wish to. But there is no need for the concentration of such arbitrary power in the hands of any officers or officials of any organization, either governmental or nongovernmental. The workers themselves will be making the decisions, and by this is really meant the workers themselves and not any officials of any organization that claims to represent them. There need be no interference with the free preferences either of the workers who make the different products or of the public who desire to have the different products and services made available for their use.

The workers exercise their decision by simply registering their willingness to move from where they consider the wages and the conditions of work and the rates of pay less satisfactory to where they consider these more satisfactory. This is why it is necessary to remove every possible restriction or hindrance in the way of movement from one labor market to another as well as to provide every possible assistance to mobility in the form of information, facilities for training or retraining, loans to remove immobilities for financial reasons, and so on. If workers are prevented from moving into any labor market or from registering as able and willing to move into one, the index of relative attractiveness loses its validity.

If there is an increased desire for any product, more people will be able to find employment in the labor market that produces this product and the index of relative attractiveness will be *reduced.* The index will also be reduced if workers decide that they do not like the work and would rather go elsewhere. In either case the reduction in the index of relative attractiveness of the occupation of the labor market will have a tendency to move the labor market from the category which would have its wages frozen to the category that has its wage rates rising at 3 per cent per annum or from this category to the category which has its wages raised 6 per cent per annum. The increase in wages would be appropriate in increasing the inducement of workers to move to where the product is needed more. Conversely, if there is a decrease in the need for the product of any labor market, or if the workers take a special fancy to a certain occupation so that there is an inordinately large number of people looking for work in the labor market in relation to those who are able to work in it, this is evidence that the conditions and pay are too attractive. The wages there should then be frozen while other wages keep on rising, so that the workers are induced to go elsewhere. The workers themselves determine the number that seek work in each labor market. The consumers of the product, by the extent of their purchases of it, determine the number of workers who are able to find work in the labor market. Between the two the index of relative attractiveness is determined, untouched by the hand of any bureaucrat.

The wage policy can foster stability and social harmony.

Statistics of the number of people working in each labor market will have to be collected quite frequently as well as statistics of the number of people seeking work in each labor market, in order that statisticians may derive from these figures the index of relative attractiveness of working in each labor market. From all these individual indices of relative attractiveness the national average will be computed, comparison with which is necessary for each labor market before it can be told whether the particular money wage rate should be frozen for the time being, whether it should rise at the standard rate of 3 per cent per annum, or whether it should rise at twice the standard rate, namely, at 6 per cent per annum.

A man who registers himself as seeking work in a labor market where he is not currently employed would of course have to satisfy someone that he is suitable for the work, either by virtue of having done the work before or by some other test. There are clearly many difficulties of administration to be worked out before the plan could be applied successfully in practice, but the principle is clear. Everyone who wants to take advantage of good conditions in any occupation in any part of the country and who is able to do the work and willing to take a job when it is available can register and his registration will show itself in the index of relative attractiveness.

With the index of relative attractiveness of each labor market as a general guide, collective or individual bargaining could continue to operate without the compulsion on everyone in a full-employment situation to run the fruitless inflationary race for fear of being left behind the others. The index would provide a reasonable rhythm for the forward march of money wages, keeping time with the increase in over-all productivity, indicating when each particular money wage should rise and by how much, and doing this in a way which would stabilize the value of money and work harmoniously for the efficiency and the prosperity of the economy as a whole.

Summary.

A wage policy is needed to prevent excessive bargaining power of labor from causing inflation as soon as the low level of full employment is reached and thereby preventing the attainment of the high level of full employment. The wage policy would have to indicate what should be done, not to real wages or to the general level of money wages but to particular wage rates in particular labor markets. But it would nevertheless have to bring about stability in the general levels of wages and of prices.

It is not possible to stabilize both wages and prices completely, but it is possible to let wages rise at about 3 per cent per annum (an approximation to the long-run over-all rate of progress in labor productivity) and this would result in stable prices and a stable dollar.

Preconditions for a successful wage policy are the maintenance of full employment and the removal of all unnecessary restrictions on the mobility of labor from one labor market to another. It is also necessary to keep in mind the social function of wages in inducing people to work and to move from the production of things wanted less by consumers to the production of things wanted more by consumers.

The wage policy then consists of rules indicating that wages should in general rise at a rate equal to the rate of increase in productivity (about 3 per cent per annum), that wages should rise faster where the *index of relative attractiveness* is sufficiently less than the national average, and that wages should be frozen where the index of relative attractiveness is sufficiently greater than the national average.

The result would be a general wage level rising at 3 per cent per annum and a constant price level (which means a stable dollar). No arbitrary authority is implied in the wage policy, the index of relative attractiveness being determined automatically by the demand of the consumers for the product and the willingness of workers to work in any occupation at the current pay and conditions of work. Workers would tend to move to where their product is more desired by consumers and to where they prefer to work, so that the resulting constellation of wage rates would be in accordance with the preferences of both workers and consumers.

There are many details of administration yet to be worked out, but the general principles are clear and the policy could work to permit the achievement of a high level of full employment while fostering economic stability and social harmony.

CHAPTER 15

Some Clarifications of the Wage Policy

Unemployment can and should be reduced by increasing labor mobility.

The 2 million or less that are unemployed at the high level of full employment do not constitute an absolute goal beyond which we may not even aim. The real technical frictions *can* be reduced. People may more generally acquire more than one skill so that they can move into another occupation if there is no immediate vacancy in their current occupation. People may learn about possible new jobs while they are still working on the old one, preparing beforehand to leave the old job on a Friday or Saturday and to start the new one on Monday. By such devices for increasing mobility the volume of truly frictional unemployment could be reduced perhaps to a million or perhaps even only half a million. It is only when high full employment has been in existence for some time that we can learn by trial and error in what ways it is feasible to increase labor mobility and reduce the volume of frictional unemployment.

The maximization of mobility is regarded as a very bad thing by some sociologists who seem to be unable to distinguish mobility from movement and who declare that movement causes great harm in breaking up families, creating neuroses, and so on. It seems more plausible to believe that when a family is broken up by a movement of a worker to a new job it is trouble in the family which is the cause of the movement rather than the other way round. All that is proposed is that in accordance with a basic principle of a free democratic society people should be allowed to judge for themselves what is best for them to do. Attempts

220

may be made to educate people so that they may choose with a better understanding of the implications of their choices, but there should never be a higher authority telling people what they want to do or maintaining hindrances to movement on the ground that the people taking advantage of their freedom to move would be acting unwisely.

Genuine unwillingness to move must be respected.

At the other end of the scale a similar tendency to dictate is shown by an undue concern about the immobilities that prevent unemployed men and unfilled jobs from getting together because of the reluctance of people to move. They have comfortably settled themselves and found friends or found an occupation which they like better than the alternatives available and they want to stay even at much poorer pay which has lagged behind while pay elsewhere was rising. The pay is poor because the product is not worth more to the consumer of the product. But as long as the worker instead of going elsewhere prefers to stay and do the work for what the consumer is willing to pay there is no reason to suppose that it would be better for him to move. The preferences of people for living in one place rather than another or for working at one occupation rather than another should not be treated as frictions which it is desirable to overcome. Removing ignorance or providing the money needed to make a move or to obtain the necessary training always permits people to better themselves and is therefore always an improvement. But true preferences of individuals for a place of living or a kind of work are beyond and above the whole of our economic structure. To sacrifice the preferences of the population for the sake of making the economic machine work more smoothly is to commit the basic sin of putting the means above the end.

*Price-level changes are possible without inflation or
deflation.*

In the discussion of the effects of excessive spending or of excessive bargaining power of labor it is difficult to avoid giving
the impression that any increase in prices means inflation. But
that is not the case. It is possible to have prices rise and yet avoid
the basic evils of inflation, the injustices, the frustration of legitimate expectations, the disorganization of the economy, and the
ruin and impoverishment of large sections of the population. It
is also possible, though more difficult, to have falling prices and
yet avoid the evils of deflation.

If money wages in general rise at 3 per cent per annum, prices
and the value of money will be stable. This is because productivity
may be expected to increase at about that rate. If money wages rise
faster than this, the result will be a corresponding increase in
prices. Thus if wages rise at 5 per cent per annum while productivity rises at 3 per cent per annum, prices will rise at about 2
per cent per annum. This is not too serious if the rise in prices
is expected and all contracts and other arrangements are made in
the light of this expectation. As part of this adjustment the rate
of interest must be 2 per cent per annum higher, *i.e.,* 4½ instead
of 2½ per cent per annum if that would have been appropriate
with constant prices. With the higher rate of interest we can
conceive of a perfect adjustment to the rising prices with pensions
being allowed to increase so as to make up for the declining real
value of the dollar and similarly with everything else. We can adjust ourselves to a price level rising at 2 per cent per annum as
completely as we can adjust ourselves to a price level rising at 1
per cent per annum or even at *zero* per cent per annum, or in
other words a constant price level. It would be somewhat more
trouble and involve more complicated bookkeeping, but it is
quite feasible.

If money wages in general do not rise as rapidly as the increase in productivity, prices will have to fall. If productivity, for example, increases at 3 per cent per annum and wages do not rise at all, prices will fall at 3 per cent per annum. There would then have to be a correspondingly *lower* rate of interest to maintain the same real relationship between debtors and creditors and to keep the same investments worth while in spite of the expectation that future products will be sold at a lower price. If the appropriate rate of interest with a stable price level is 2½ per cent, the appropriate rate of interest with prices falling at 3 per cent per annum is *minus* one-half of 1 per cent per annum.

But although it is theoretically possible to adjust the rest of the economy to a rising or falling price level, to attempt to do this would not be practical. For one thing the adjustment is possible only if the direction and the degree to which prices are going to move is correctly anticipated. Correct anticipation of price level changes is feasible, if at all, only if the change is smooth and in one direction. The purpose would *not* be served by having the rate of interest move up and down to offset *fluctuations* in the rate of change of the price level. The rate of interest is only one of the items that would have to be adjusted, together with monetary obligations of all kinds, rents, pensions, relief payments, and so on that would require adjustment for changes in the price level to prevent waste, injustice, and disorder. A special difficulty arises for the case of falling prices in that a negative rate of interest is very difficult to arrange, and if it is not arranged when prices are falling, investment and consumption are discouraged and depression and unemployment emerge. For all these reasons the *practical* policy is to have the general level of money wages rise just sufficiently to offset the increase in productivity. The price level will then be stable and there will be no need for a negative rate of interest in order to prevent depression.

Understanding and responsibility by labor are no substitute for a wage policy.

The tendency for wages to rise at a level of employment considerably below that of high full employment may be due not merely to *collective* bargaining but to the determination of wages by *bargaining,* whether individual or collective. It may be that if there were no collective bargaining but only individual bargaining, employers would be less reluctant to pay higher wages because they would not feel that they were bound. Since they would be offering the higher wages to small groups or even to single individuals, they would know that if conditions worsened they would be able to cut wages. They might therefore be more ready to agree to a raise when bargaining with individuals than when bargaining with a strong union which could enforce a long-term contract.

In Chapter 14 the inflationary race is described as one which it is impossible for the participants to stop even if they realize its fruitlessness for all of them together. This may seem to be contradicted by the fact that in recent times one or two of our most enlightened labor leaders have recognized the connection between wages and prices and have claimed to be interested not only in the workers in their particular occupation but in labor in general. They have declared themselves to be against price rises and have indeed occasionally used phrases like "We are in favor of raising wages only if it is not accompanied by rising prices."

But these statements do not really seem to have been quite serious; at least one does not hear them when the prices are raised, and we do not have workers going on strike because the price of their product has been raised. In general workers and labor leaders believe that raising the price of their product is a fine thing. It gives them more of an opportunity for getting and keeping higher wages. This means that they are really thinking of their sectional interests and not of the interests of labor in general.

In England more thought has been given by labor men to the problems of full employment and many of the thinkers on this subject have spoken of dealing with this problem by having a more responsible organization of labor—a national rather than sectional organization—which would have to consider the interests of labor as a whole. But this does not help very much. For one thing a national labor organization might be even more inflationary in response to political pressures for higher wages, because it would not be deterred, as sectional labor organization might be deterred, by the danger of getting too far ahead of other labor groups. An integrated labor organization would not be afraid of being left behind in the race, but it also would not have to be afraid of getting too far ahead, and the net effect is not certain.

Even if an integrated labor organization fully recognized its responsibility for preventing inflation it would still have to know what to do about particular wage rates in the different parts of the economy. It would itself need to have a wage policy of the kind proposed in Chapter 14.

It is sometimes argued that although raising money wages by itself may not do much good to labor, there is a net gain if this is accompanied by measures for limiting the rise in prices by increasing the degree of competition or reducing the profit margin in one way or another. This is perfectly possible. But such a coupling of the two measures is a rather shameless device for obtaining credit for the wage increase which is really due to the accompanying measures. The accompanying devices would be just as effective in increasing the real wage if there were no wage increase at all to steal the credit.

The spread between low full employment and high full employment was compared above with the Marxian notions of a reserve army of unemployed. The similarity between the two concepts lies in the function of the 4 million unemployed in keeping the bargaining power of the labor from becoming excessive.

But the differences between the two concepts is more important than the similarity. The Marxian reserve army of unemployed is deliberately maintained by the capitalists as a means of increasing their profits. The low level of full employment, in contrast, means smaller profits for capitalists not only in absolute terms but as a percentage of the national income. The Marxian reserve army of unemployed was supposed not merely to keep down the money wage of the workers but to lower their real wage—in fact the Marxian analysis is, in this context, an example of extremely classical economics. The low level of full employment has no important effect on the real wage of the worker; it is merely a way of preventing a parallel increase of wages and prices which would leave the real wage substantially unchanged. And finally the Marxian reserve army was maintained by the capitalists in some collective capacity, although the nature of the organization or the telepathic coordination which performed this function is wrapped in mystery. The low level of full employment is not maintained by any capitalist conspiracy. It is what we would get by the simple application of Functional Finance with our present method of determining wage rates by individual and collective bargaining. Very few capitalists have shown much interest in the application of Functional Finance. They are mostly given to loud but not overconvincing declarations of loyalty to "sound finance."

Wage rate adjustment may be made either frequently or infrequently.

There are many ways of bringing about the appropriate 3 per cent per annum increases in money wages.

We have the three categories of labor markets: those where the index of relative attractiveness is between half and double the national average, those where the index of relative attractiveness is less than half the national average, and those where the index of relative attractiveness is more than double the national average.

The wage increase could take place once a year, the first category getting a 3 per cent increase, the second category getting a 6 per cent increase, and the third category getting no increase. It would also be possible for the wage adjustment to be made every four months. The increases would then be only 1 per cent or 2 per cent or no change for each of the three categories. On the other hand it would also be possible to have the adjustments only once in three years. They would then be very substantial—10 per cent or 20 per cent or no change.

Which method of adjustment is chosen should depend on what is more satisfactory to the workers and to the employers and could very well be one of the matters for collective bargaining. The more continuous adjustment would involve least dislocation once it had been put into operation and would result in a more complete adjustment to the current conditions. It has been declared that workers would not be interested in such unexciting wage increases as 1 per cent three times a year or even in the possible 2 per cent increases every four months.[1] There might be some advantage to annual adjustments which could be considered together with other issues in the course of the collective bargaining agreements.

The index of relative attractiveness of employment in any labor market could reach all the way from zero, when nobody is registered as able and willing to take jobs in the occupation, to several

---

[1] Dr. W. Woytinsky advises very strongly against the small and frequent raise and is in favor of the large raise every three years, not only because of the alleged psychological preference of workers for more tangible if less frequent increases but on the ground that a settlement of the wages for three years would give security and stability to the employers in the industry. This does not seem convincing to me. The expectation of a large change would be more disturbing than the small and continuous adjustment. The large adjustment would also result in undesirable changes in *relative* wages if the different industries had their changes made at different times and would become an unreal monetary change, negated by price increases, if they should all take place at the same time.

hundred per cent if the number of registrants is several times as great as the number of workers actually employed in the occupation. If every employed person in the economy registered himself as seeking a job in an occupation *other than* that in which he was currently employed, the national average index would be the ratio of the labor force to total employment. Since *some* people will be employed in the occupation they most prefer out of all those for which they are adequately prepared, the national average index would probably be considerably less than 100 per cent.

If 30 per cent of the labor force register themselves as seeking work in markets where they have not been able to find jobs, the national average index would be 30 per cent, or simply 30. This would mean that in every labor market where the index of relative attractiveness was between 15 and 60, wages would rise at 3 per cent per annum (or 1 per cent every four months). Where the index was less than 15, wages would rise twice as fast as this. And where the index was over 60, the wages would be frozen.

It does not matter if productivity does not increase uniformly or at 3 per cent per annum.

Productivity may not increase at 3 per cent per annum and it may not increase at any constant rate. This is not of importance for the plan. It would be possible to adjust the general money wage rise to the rate of increase of productivity. But it would be much better to adopt some figure like our 3 per cent and to stick to it no matter what happened to productivity within quite a wide range. This might result in a mildly rising, mildly falling, or mildly fluctuating general price level, but it is not important to have absolute constancy of the price level. The important thing is that *cumulative* price movements are prevented.

Since it does not matter if prices rise or fall by a couple of percentage points per annum as long as no cumulative movements can develop, it cannot matter very much what index number is used for measuring what is happening to the price level. It would probably be best to have stabilized the index number that measures the cost of living corresponding to the income level at which there is the greatest concentration of population (the modal income group). More people would then find their dollar constant than if any other index number were stabilized. But perfect stabilization for every group is not really possible and concern for this matter betrays an inappropriate and impossible perfectionism.

High full employment requires a wage policy rather than a price policy.

The wage policy may seem to some to be unfair to labor in that it seeks to check the inflationary spiral of wages and prices by checking the increase in wages. It might be asked: Why not stop the inflation by checking price increases instead? Why pick on wages to hold down?

There are two reasons why it is better to stabilize wages than to stabilize prices. The first is that our policy of stabilizing wages does not destroy the effectiveness which the price mechanism has in our modern economy. It does not fix the different wage rates in relation to each other. Stabilizing prices is less desirable because it usually means price controls which prevent the operation of the market system and of the price mechanism which have contributed so much toward making the modern standard of living possible.

The price level can be stabilized without fixing individual prices if it is done by rationing spending in general or by limiting total spending in some other way. But this brings us to the second reason why stabilizing wages is preferable. If we stabilize prices by limiting spending, we are in fact keeping prices from rising by keeping demand down to the level where the bargaining power of the workers is no longer excessive. We are then back at the low level of full employment with the reserve army of unemployed that we want to avoid. It is only by checking the inflation via wages instead of via prices that we can get high full employment instead of low full employment.

Summary.

The 2 million or so unemployed with high full employment can be further reduced in number by measures for increasing labor mobility. Mobility must not be confused with movement, and in a democratic society the people themselves should be the judges whether it is better for them to move or to stay where they are.

It is possible for prices to rise without causing the evils of inflation and it is possible, though more difficult, for prices to fall without causing the evils of deflation, provided the price changes are clearly foreseen and appropriate adjustments are made in the rate of interest and in long-term contracts and other obligations.

It is *bargaining* about wages that is responsible for inflationary pressure at less than full employment, not necessarily *collective* bargaining. Declarations by labor leaders against inflation do not seem to be very serious. A unified labor policy might be even more inflationary than the present labor policy unless it included a wage policy like the one here proposed. An increase in money wages is sometimes given the credit for an increase in the real wage, when the latter is really caused by some other accompanying change such as a reduction in the degree of monopoly. The 4 million additional unemployed in low full employment have more differences from than similarities to the Marxian "reserve army of unemployed."

The adjustments in money wages could be frequent and small or infrequent and large. It does not matter very much if the increase in productivity is more than 3 per cent per annum or if it is less than this or if it fluctuates from time to time. The wage policy would still prevent any *cumulative* inflation. It is possible to prevent inflation by stabilizing prices instead of stabilizing wages. The wage policy for high full employment concentrates on wages not because of an antilabor bias but because a price policy, even if it could be carried out without sabotaging the price mechanism, would give not high but low full employment.

CHAPTER 16

Wage Policy—Effects and Problems

Only in the beginning need there be much adjustment.

The introduction of our wage policy for high full employment would bring about a great deal of movement of labor from some occupations to others and a great change in relative wages in the different occupations. But after a transitional period there would emerge a new and stable situation with a new constellation of wage rates and a different division of labor among the different occupations. There would be more people employed and relatively lower wages in those occupations which had provided privileged positions by keeping outsiders, in one way or another, from sharing in their good fortune. Many would have escaped from the sweated industries and those who remained would be able to command better pay and conditions. The credit for this however should go not to the wage policy but rather to the maximization of mobility that is a condition for its successful operation.

Once the new constellation of wage rates has been established in which the conditions of overprivilege and underprivilege in the old constellation have been corrected there will not be very much movement of labor or very much change in the relative wage rates. Further changes will be necessary only to allow for shifts in the demand for particular products or for changes in the techniques of producing them. The maximization of mobility is not incompatible with a very high degree of stability as soon as adjustment to the new situation has been made.

The new constellation of wages and employments would be stable and optimal.

The new constellation would constitute an optimum set of wage rates and an optimum distribution of the workers among the different occupations. This would be an optimum not from some narrow technical point of view but from a point of view that takes fully into account the preferences of workers for working and for living in the different conditions available in the different parts of the country, as well as the preferences of consumers for the products of the different occupations. It will be an optimum from the point of view of productivity because workers will have moved to where the productivity and therefore the wage is greater unless the disadvantages of the work outweigh the advantages. Productivity thus includes the well-being in the worker in his work— not the least important product of economic activity.

The new constellation will be an optimum from the point of view of freedom because the removal of obstacles to movement and the positive provision of the means and opportunities for movement, including information and training or retraining, would mean that workers are really free to take advantage of all opportunities for improving their own lot while maximizing their contribution to the welfare of others.

It will also be an optimum from the point of view of fairness. Nobody will have just cause for jealousy at conditions elsewhere because if he thought he was not being given as good a deal as anybody else, he would be able to go to the other place and partake of these opportunities. Everybody will then feel that the place where he is in the economy is not worse than any other place for which he is fitted or for which he could make himself fit by training or other preparation.

Some people would be at the margin of indifference and a slight change in conditions would persuade them to move to a new situation. But most people would not be on the margin. They would

positively prefer to be where they are rather than anywhere else—
that is why they have chosen their place. They would be well
within the margin ("intramarginal" is the technical term) and
would be enjoying a "surplus" of benefits over the best available
alternative. This surplus would tend to keep people where they
are. Instead of the evil stability that exists when people want to
move but cannot, we shall have the good stability that exists
when people can move but do not want to.

It may seem extravagant to claim that fairness and justice and
freedom and efficiency (or productivity) would all be brought
about simultaneously by the new constellation of wages and employments. But all these seemingly different ideals are only different facets of the same optimum and all derive from the maximization of freedom. It is the freedom of people to move that results in
their moving to where they produce more (efficiency), in the absence of any discriminatory restrictions (fairness), and in each
worker being paid for his work an amount that corresponds to
his contribution to the social benefit (justice). Of course this does
not solve all problems, such as the problem of satisfying the needs
of people who are unable to earn by their contribution to society
as much as they need and who must be helped in some other
way. But it does offer the benefits that have frequently been
claimed for the perfectly competitive society, and it does this
because it is after all nothing but an artificial piece of machinery
devised to take the place of the perfect labor market which does
not exist, probably cannot exist, and would threaten us with
dangerous instabilities if it should exist.

The share going to labor would be increased indirectly.

The wage policy does nothing directly about the justice of the
share of the national income going to labor as a whole. It affects
directly only the rewards for different kinds of work in the different parts of the economy. We have seen above that one of the
difficulties in the way of acceptance of the wage policy in prac-

tice is the combination of the feeling that justice requires an increase in the share of the national income going to labor, with the belief that this share can be increased by increasing money wages in general.

We have argued that the belief is a mistaken one. Yet the application of our wage policy would in the long run tend to increase the share of the national income going to labor. The higher level of employment and of economic activity made possible by the wage policy would make business easier. The chief headache of businessmen—bad conditions of business or the fear of bad conditions of business—would be removed. Businessmen would be more venturous and enterprising and more people would want to go into business. The possibility of operating industry continuously at high levels of capacity would make it possible for the rate of markup or profit per unit to be reduced. The increased competition would bring this possibility into actuality, reducing the degree of monopoly and thus changing the basic economic relationships that determine real wages and the worker's share in the national income. Indirectly, therefore, the wage policy would also contribute to this aspect of distributive justice.

The wage policy does not allow for any reductions in money wages at all. This may be criticized as involving a departure from the optimum situation by preventing people from working in an occupation which they like even though they would have to work for very little if the product is to be cheap enough to induce the consumer to buy it. This is a genuine deviation from the optimum, but it does not seem sufficiently serious to warrant a change in the policy. The maximization of mobility would give most people the opportunity of finding some other and more useful occupation where they would find similar satisfactions. But this is a case where further study might indicate some modification. Where the index of attractiveness rose to three or four times the national average it might be desirable to lower the wages so as to permit more workers to indulge in such strongly favored occupations. .

The wage policy can be integrated into our collective-bargaining customs.

In an authoritarian society the wage policy could be introduced by a decree simply laying down the policy as rules telling everyone when each wage rate should be raised and by how much. These rules would still be most democratic in maximizing the freedom of workers and of consumers, but the way they were established would be dictatorial. A dictator who always decided on such democratic solutions to particular problems might perhaps qualify to be called a benevolent dictator or perhaps even a democratic dictator. But the trouble with dictatorships is just that they cannot be trusted to be benevolent and democratic. We therefore have to rely on democracy.

In our democracy everybody believes in collective bargaining. Even business leaders nowadays cannot make a speech without declaring a fervent belief in the true Americanism of collective bargaining (with modifications). If it is felt that the wage policy usurps the main function of trade unions and makes collective bargaining impossible or unnecessary it would be impossible to put it into practice. Fortunately it is perfectly possible to incorporate the principles of our wage policy into the machinery of collective bargaining where instead of "rules" imposed by a dictator they become nothing more than the explicit crystallization of the objective conditions of the labor market which always have been and always must be in the background of every collective bargain. Publication of the indices of relative attractiveness of work in the different labor markets would merely help the bargainers to reach the necessary agreements more consciously and therefore more efficiently. Having the different parties to the bargain present in the negotiations would still be of very great value in preventing one side or the other from improperly manipulating the indices by using the many opportunities that there are for statistical finagling in the absence of vigilant inspection.

The wage policy does not prevent exploitation. It only makes it explicit.

A more serious problem lies in the possibility of trade unions in privileged positions wanting to hold on to their privileges or even to increase them further. Such trade unions would object to a scheme which would freeze their wages while others caught up with them in relative attractiveness.

This problem is not solved by the wage policy. If a group of workers demand a rise in pay when the index shows that they are far ahead of the national average, that means that they are asking for the further improvement of an already privileged position. If the group is well enough organized it may go on strike, deprive the community of essential services, and by the use of force or by the exploitation of the strong sentiment among workers that it is disgraceful to cross a picket line, they may be able to enforce their demands.

All that the indices of relative attractiveness can do is to make clear what is happening. It is then a matter of political decision whether to submit to the holdup or to engage in a fight to prevent it.

A group of workers who attempted such an extortion would naturally object very strongly to their demand being put in this language. It is always possible for them to point to other injustices in the society which are worse than the one which they are endeavoring to perpetrate, but the two wrongs do not make a right. The establishment of a new privileged group is not likely to improve the situation. Most of the benefits accruing to the new group will probably come from those who have already been robbed by the other impositions.

The wage policy need not be applied explicitly to conditions of work or to the whole of the economy.

The money wages paid for work are only one of the conditions governing the relative attractiveness of different occupations. We must also consider such things as music while we work, the lighting and heating, the cleanliness and pleasantness of the work, as well as pensions, disability benefits, holidays, etc. To bring these items into the index of relative attractiveness would certainly make it impossibly complicated. Fortunately it is better to leave them out because this permits workers to choose between better conditions and more money. An improvement in conditions would make the labor market more attractive, raise the index of relative attractiveness, and thus keep money wages down. If the workers prefer more money they will not demand the improvements in conditions.

Just as conditions will adjust themselves if the money wages are regulated in accordance with the wage policy, so will wages and conditions adjust themselves in parts of the economy where for one reason or another the wage policy rules are not applied directly.

There are labor markets where, for example, it is too difficult to tell whether people qualify to be counted for the index of attractiveness. But if employment is full and mobility is maximized it is sufficient if the wage policy is applied *directly* to a large part of the economy. It would have its effect *indirectly* on the rest of the economy through the normal operation of supply and demand.

Cheating both by workers and by employers may be expected and can be countered.

Improvements in conditions are adjusted automatically only if they do not cost more than the possible increase in wages. A well-organized group of workers might try to circumvent the wage policy by demanding "conditions" like free housing or free meals or free clothing, making what is really an increase in wages look like an improvement of conditions which is outside the wage policy and not regulated by the index of relative attractiveness.

Such a trick might be countered by ruling out improvements in conditions wherever the index of attractiveness was already, say, three times the national average, but many other ways of cheating could probably be invented, and it would be necessary to figure out ways of preventing such perversions of the purposes of the wage policy.

Employers, as well as workers, might be tempted to evade the wage policy. They might offer wages higher than the wage policy provides in attempts to get workers from each other when labor is scarce. Since the affected workers would readily cooperate in accepting the wage increases such departures from the policy might be thought difficult to prevent. But all that is necessary is to make the excess wage payments nondeductible as legitimate business expenses from the employers' income for income-tax purposes. This would mean that the higher wages would come out of the employers' own pockets and that would be an adequate deterrent.[1]

More research on high full employment should be very rewarding.

The wage policy for high full employment as presented here is not a finished plan ready for adoption by the government of the United States. A great deal of public discussion is necessary before the inevitable attempts by opponents to misrepresent it as un-American or as antilabor are overcome and before it becomes familiar enough for political feasibility. Current experience will be of help in this. The recession of 1949 constitutes a pretty

[1] I am indebted for this suggestion to Professor Fritz Machlup of Johns Hopkins University, who has independently developed a very similar plan for wage determination.

good example of a movement from high full employment (unprotected from inflation and therefore unstable) part of the way to low full employment.

The failure to reach high full employment instead of low full employment is not fatal to the security of our free society. Even low full employment would suffice to make the democratic society far more attractive than any visible alternative. But the difference between high and low full employment, some 15 billion dollars of national income, and the more important social and political effects, such as the effect of the recession on the world dollar shortage, cannot be dismissed as unimportant. The matter is still worth much serious study and research.

Summary.

The introduction of the wage policy would bring about considerable changes in relative wage rates and in the distribution of labor between the different occupations, but after there had been an adjustment relative stability would be reestablished. There would then be a new and optimum constellation of wage rates and of the numbers of workers in the different occupations. The optimum will have taken into account the preferences of workers and of consumers and will be an optimum from the points of view of efficiency, of fairness, and of freedom. Some people will be at the margin of indifference between different occupations, but most people will be "intramarginal." They will be enjoying "surpluses" and we shall have stability because people will no longer wish to move. All the different optima derive from the maximization of freedom and the artificial establishment of the ideals associated with the naturally perfect markets of pure economic theory.

The establishment of stable high full employment through the wage policy would indirectly increase the relative share of labor by making business easier and reducing the rate of markup of prices over costs, or in other words reducing the degree of monopoly. The absence of any provision for reducing particular money wages is not a serious defect and if necessary could be corrected.

In a democratic society the wage policy could not take the form of decrees about wage rates. It would have to take the form of publishing the indices of relative attractiveness and letting them influence the collective wage bargainers. The indices will be a crystallization of the objective conditions which must be in the background of the bargaining in any case. A more serious problem can arise when a privileged group uses its strength to push for further extensions of its privileges. The wage policy does not solve such problems. It can only make clear the nature of the issue—it cannot decide whether it is better to submit to exploitation or to fight it.

Conditions of work other than wages are best left out of wage policy. This permits workers to choose between wage increases and improvements in conditions. It is not necessary for the wage policy to be applied to the whole economy if it is difficult to apply it in some parts. The influences will spread out to such parts of the economy through the normal operations of supply and demand.

Attempts to disguise wage increases and improvements in conditions can be circumvented, and other methods of cheating will no doubt have to be countered. Attempts by employers to circumvent the policy can be prevented by income-tax regulations. The wage policy for high full employment needs much research and discussion before becoming politically feasible.

Part V

A Closer View of Functional Finance

CHAPTER 17

Is Saving Good or Bad?

Or Saving and the Multiplier[1]

THE IDEA that Functional Finance considers saving to be a vice rather than a virtue seems to many people so wicked that it prevents them from examining the matter very carefully.

Thrift is good for reducing expenditure but is bad if there is too little spending.

Functional Finance does not say that saving is bad. It recognizes that more saving means greater building up of the productive equipment of the society and that this makes possible a higher standard of living in the future. What Functional Finance does say is that in certain circumstances (but not in others) *thrift* (which is not the same thing as saving) can do harm to society.

Thrift is the preference *not* to consume income. A more thrifty individual consumes less out of a given income and saves more. A dollar less of consumption means a dollar more of saving. But this argument is valid for an individual only because we can assume that when he cuts his consumption his income remains the same.

When we consider the community as a whole we can no longer assume that if the community consumes less, its income will remain the same and that more will therefore be saved. Every dollar consumed by (a member of) the community is a dollar earned by (another member of) the community, and every dollar

[1] Readers who have skipped Chaps. 4 through 7 should skip this chapter too. See the note at the beginning of Chap. 4.

by which consumption is cut means a dollar cut in the community's income. If income is cut by just as much as consumption, the difference between income and consumption—which is what we call saving—is no greater (and no less) than before. Thrift reduces consumption all right, but because that reduces income too, thrift does not increase the amount saved. And if more is not saved we do not have any of the good effects that go with more saving.

Thrift does have the effect of reducing total spending. Whether this is good or bad must therefore depend on what the rate of spending is to begin with. If there is too much spending, thrift corrects this and is good. If there is too little spending, thrift aggravates this and is bad.

Saving is only the reflection of investment and need not be mentioned.

Investment is the spending of money for things that are *not* currently consumed. (Spending on things that *are* currently consumed is not investment but consumption.) An increase in investment therefore means an increase in income without an increase in consumption. But if income goes up while consumption does not, the excess of income over consumption, which is what we call saving, goes up by the same amount. Any increase in investment therefore increases saving by an exactly equal amount.

If an increase in thrift happens to be accompanied by an equal increase in investment, so that consumption is cut by just as much as investment is increased, income will be unchanged and saving will increase by just as much as consumption is reduced. But it would be wrong to attribute the increased saving to the increased thrift. It is all due to the increased investment. The test is that the investment by itself would have increased saving by just as much (while incidentally also increasing income by that amount). The thrift by itself would have reduced income but would have had no effect on saving. The saving thus depends altogether on the investment. The credit for all the good effects that we see when saving does in fact take place is really all due to the investment which is directly responsible for the increase in productive equipment (the goods bought but not currently consumed) and without which there could not have been any saving. Saving is nothing but the shadow or the reflection of the investment.

It really would be best in all these matters never to mention saving, and this is possible because saving is not a real thing at all. Consumption is real and investment is real, and the two together create the income which is just as real. Thrift, though more psychological, is important in determining how much will be consumed and therefore also how great income will be. But saving is nothing but an arithmetical computation of the difference between two magnitudes—the income and the consumption—and once we know how much is invested we already know how much is saved. Investment is equal to the excess of income over consumption because it creates the income that is not created by consumption. Saving is defined as the excess of income over consumption. In the house we are building saving is superfluous; it needs to be discussed only because it worries people who have not realized that it is only a shadow and nothing to be afraid of.

The answer to the question of this chapter is therefore that saving cannot be said to be either good or bad. There is no point in praising or blaming it because it has no independence and cannot cause any good or any harm. It is only a result.

The income effect only strengthens the liquidity-preference theory of interest.

In Chapter 7 we rejected the supply of saving as a determinant of the rate of interest and replaced it by liquidity preference because the unreality of the supply of saving showed itself in its overdependence on the level of income. It has been objected that liquidity preference is also affected by the level of income and should be subjected to the same test. We can now apply this test and see what happens.

We rejected the saving-investment theory of the determination of the rate of interest because we saw that any rate of interest, whether lower or higher than the alleged equilibrium level, was also an equally good equilibrium level. A lower rate of interest, for example, seemed to show an excess of investment over saving, but if we took into account the effect of the increased investment on income we saw that saving instead of being less would be greater and that it would be greater by just as much as investment is greater. Saving would still be equal to investment and we would again have the same kind of equilibrium as before. Only by leaving out of account the effect of the greater investment on income could we seem to have an independent supply curve of saving that determined an equilibrium rate of interest.

The liquidity-preference theory survives this test. A reduction in the rate of interest increases investment and this increases income. The greater income means an increase in economic activity and a need for more cash to enable the greater volume of transactions to be carried on with the same degree of liquidity convenience. The liquidity-preference curve thus is shifted, as the supply of savings curve was shifted, by taking the income effect into consideration.

But the greater income merely *increases* the excess of demand for liquidity over the amount made available by the monetary authority. The introduction of the income effect into the liquidity-preference theory thus strengthens rather than damages it.[2]

Maturity is important even if only a possibility.

The idea that Functional Finance abhors thrift is further strengthened by the concept of the *mature economy*. This is the idea that we have already accumulated all the productive equip-

---

[2] See appendix to Chap. 17, sec. 1.

ment we need and are so rich that we want to save a large part of our income.

Full employment means an income of, say, 250 billion dollars a year. Out of this people would want to save, say, 30 billion dollars, so they would consume 220 billion dollars. This consumption would create 220 billion dollars of income, and if there were another 30 billion dollars of income created by investment, all would be well and we could have our 250-billion-dollar full-employment income. But in the mature economy there is no need for 30 billion dollars of investment year after year. As a result, the investment required for full employment will not be undertaken and we shall have not full employment but depression. Because of this sad picture, the economists who draw attention to the possibility of "economic maturity" are often denounced as pessimists of a most heinous variety, and books have been written to answer them that draw pictures of unlimited needs for investment.

How probable the mature economy is nobody can really say because it depends on whether inventions which have yet to be made will increase or diminish the need for investment. All that economists who speak about the mature economy want to do is to indicate a possibility that is worth considering. To refuse to consider it because its arrival is not certain is rather like refusing to take out an insurance policy until it is proved that your house is going to take fire within the next twelve months.

Expectation of maturity shows optimism, not pessimism.

Stranger still is the assumption that the economists who expect the mature economy fairly soon are pessimistic. For only if nothing is done about it will the mature economy cause depression. If we are prepared for it the mature economy would be a great blessing. We would not need to build so much additional equipment for the future, and we could use more of our resources for providing a higher standard of living here and now. Only as long as we insist on staying in the upside-down economy where every good is an evil and allow our resources to be wasted by unemployment is the benefit of maturity—the benefit that we no longer need to use resources for investment—also an evil. But if we have a full-employment policy, we need pay no special attention to maturity. Automatically, the need for less investment means more consumption.

The multiplier depends on the degree of thrift.

In a depression an increase in investment not only increases income directly but causes more consumption (because of the increased income) and this additional consumption increases income still more. Because of these repercussions, income increases by several times the increase in investment. The number by which we must multiply the increased investment to obtain the resulting increase in income is called the "multiplier." Some of the confusion about the goodness or badness of thrift is associated with the multiplier.

The size of the multiplier depends on how much people will consume out of an additional dollar of income. This is called the marginal propensity to consume. A marginal propensity to consume of ¾ means that if a person's income is increased by a dollar his consumption will be increased by 75 cents. His marginal propensity to save will then be ¼ since he would be saving 25 cents out of his extra dollar of income. The multiplier is the inverse of the marginal propensity to save, so that if the general marginal propensity to save for the people in the society is ¼, the multiplier will be 4. An increase in investment will result in an increase in income four times as great as the increase in investment.[3]

The reason for this is that, unless income has increased by

[3] In the examples discussed in Chaps. 6 and 7 above it was assumed that marginal propensity to consume was ⅔. The marginal propensity to save was therefore ⅓ and the multiplier 3.

exactly four times the increase in investment, the population will not be satisfied about the relationships between their income, their consumption, and their saving. They want to spend ¾ of the increase in their income and to save ¼ of it. The amount they actually save will always have increased by exactly as much as the investment increased. If investment is increased by $100 and income is increased, as a result of the repercussions, by $400, the marginal propensities to consume and to save would be satisfied. The $400 increase in income could have come about only if consumption had increased by $300 which, together with the $100 of increased investment, increased income by the $400. Consumption has increased by ¾ of the increased income and saving has increased by ¼ of the increased income.[4]

But if income has increased by, say, $300, the propensities would not be satisfied. Consumption would have increased by $200 (otherwise income could not have become $300 greater than before) and saving must have increased by $100 (and is of course, as always, equal to investment which has also increased by $100). This means that the public is consuming not ¾ of their additional income but only ⅔ of it, and that they are saving not ¼ of their additional income but as much as ⅓ of it. They will therefore try to correct this by increasing their consumption. As long as they have increased their consumption by less than $300, income will be less than $400. They will all along be saving exactly $100 because every additional dollar spent creates an additional dollar of income, leaving the difference between them constant at $100. But they will still be saving more than ¼ and consuming less than ¾ of the additional income and will therefore be trying to correct this by increasing their consumption still further.[5]

If they should increase their consumption above $300, income would rise above $400 and the $100 they would be saving would

[4] See appendix to Chap. 17, sec. 2.
[5] See appendix to Chap. 17, sec. 3.

be *less* than ¼ and they would be consuming more than ¾ of their income. They would then correct this by *reducing* consumption and so bringing income again closer to the equilibrium level of $400 about the previous income. At this equilibrium and only at this equilibrium the amounts they consume and save correspond to their propensities, and the increase in income has increased by a factor, called the multiplier, which is the inverse of the marginal propensity to save.[6]

The propensity to save is very closely related to thrift. The more thrifty the population the smaller, in general, will be the marginal propensity to consume, the larger will therefore be the marginal propensity to save, and consequently the smaller will be the multiplier, and the less thrifty the population the greater will be the multiplier.

A large multiplier is not necessarily better than a small one.

In times of depression a large multiplier seems to be desirable because it measures the efficiency of investment by the government as a creator of income. If the multiplier is 4, 1 billion dollars of additional investment would result in increasing income by 4 billion dollars. If the multiplier were 8, ½ billion dollars of additional investment would suffice to bring about the 4-billion-dollar increase in income. Unfortunately the operation also works in reverse: if there is a *decrease* in investment, a large multiplier causes a larger decrease in income. Whether it is good for the multiplier to be large or small now seems to depend on what we think is going to happen to investment. But this too is an illusion.

Even if we want to increase investment in order to bring about an increase in income, the size of the multiplier is not really important. This is because there is no point in reducing the amount of investment expenditure needed to bring about the increase

[6] See appendix to Chap. 17, sec. 4.

in income. Economizing is out of order, for our objective shows that we are in a depression where the economy is upside down.

It is true that if the same increase in income is brought about by a smaller investment, a larger fraction of the increased income will take the form of consumption. If half a billion of investment instead of a billion is sufficient to increase income by 4 billion dollars, we can have $3\frac{1}{2}$ billion dollars of additional consumption instead of only 3 billion. But we cannot say whether it is better to have the $\frac{1}{2}$ billion dollars' worth of consumption or to have the $\frac{1}{2}$ billion dollars' worth of investment goods.

If for some political or other noneconomic reason the government is prevented in a severe depression from increasing investment by more than, say, a billion dollars, then it is better for the multiplier to be large. A multiplier of 8 instead of 4 would result in an 8-billion-dollar increase in income instead of a 4-billion-dollar increase as a result of the government increasing investment by 1 billion dollars. In such a case thrift is bad because it reduces the multiplier. But if the government is not tied but can invest as much as may be necessary to obtain full employment, there is no reason for wanting to have a large multiplier. The required effect on income can be obtained by having twice as much investment instead of twice as great a multiplier. This would mean less additional consumption (6 billion instead of 7 billion dollars), but whether more investment or more consumption is preferable is another question.

Equilibrium analysis explains the multiplier better than process analysis.

It is almost impossible, in explaining the multiplier, to avoid giving the impression that when investment is increased, which increases income, which increases consumption, which increases income again, and so on, the effects on income take the form of a series of repercussions in successive time periods. This is unfortunate because it is much better to think of the multiplier as describing the relationship between an increase in investment and the resulting increase in income when there has been a fairly complete adjustment to the increase in investment. How long it will take for the adjustment to take place will depend on circumstances. If the change is pretty well understood the adjustment may take very little time. It is even possible for most or all of the adjustments to be made in anticipation. If it is known that the government is going to increase investment beginning on January 1 by 1 billion dollars per month and the multiplier is 4, producers of consumption goods may arrange to have an additional 3 billion dollars of consumption goods per month available starting on January 1. Income would be increased simultaneously with investment by a total of 4 billion dollars per month and we have the final effects of the multiplier right at the beginning of the increased rate of investment.

Such excellent anticipations would probably be exceptional, but this example shows that it is not *necessary* for the repercussions to be strung out in time with each successive repercussion one period later than the previous one. Rather it is a matter of the accuracy of foresight and the flexibility of consumers and producers in adjusting to new situations that determine how quickly the new equilibrium will be approximated. Depending on the degree of advance information and the accuracy of anticipations, the new equilibrium should normally be approached in anything from zero up to three or four months. What happens during the period of adjustment has so far not been thoroughly explored. The process of adjustment is such a tremendous complex of individual reactions and probably varies so much from case to case and from moment to moment that economists have been wise to concentrate on the approximation to equilibrium that emerges from it. It is because there are such approximations to equilibria that it is possible for economics to be of some service even while the details of the adjustment to the equilibrium still await microscopic examination, just as it is possible to make use of the principles of mechanics without solving the mysteries of molecules and mesons.

The alternative approach is to assume some period of time elapsing from when a person's income increases to when he increases his consumption.[7] Assuming this period is a month, the marginal propensity to consume is ¾ (the multiplier therefore 4), and the government undertakes an additional stream of investment of $100 (million) per month starting on January 1, we can describe the process of events through time.

In January the total income of the economy is $100 above the original level because of the government investment.

In February income is up from the original level by $100 + $75. The $100 is created by government investment in February and the $75 is created by the consumption in February out of the extra $100 earned in January.

In March income is up by $100 + $75 + $57. The $100 is created by government investment in March, the $75 is created by the consumption out of the income created by government investment in February, and the $57 (¾ of $75) is the consumption out of the income created by the $75 of consumption in February which came out of the $100 of income created by government investment in January.

In April income is up by $100 + $75 + $57 + $42 ($42 being approximately ¾ of $57).

In May income is up by $100 + $75 + $57 + $42 + $31.

And so on. Each month income is greater, but each month there is a smaller increase. Although income keeps on increasing indefinitely, the total increase over the original level will never quite reach $400 although it will get closer and closer to this

[7] There can be no interval between the time one person increases his spending and the time when the next individual's income increases, because these are not two different events that can occur at different times but merely two aspects of the same event: the payment by the one to the other.

amount month after month, and if we wait long enough we can get as close to the $400 as we may wish.[8]

That the sum of our series can never exceed $400 can be seen by noticing that each step takes us ¼ of the way to the goal. The first step of $100 is ¼ of the distance and leaves us $300 short of the goal. The second step ($75) is ¾ the size of the first step. But the remaining distance to the goal is only ¾ of the original distance so that the second step covers ¼ of the remaining distance. The third step is only ¾ of the second, but the remaining distance has once more had ¼ taken off it so that the third step once more covers ¼ of the remaining distance to the goal. The same thing is true no matter how many steps we take. No matter how many steps we take we can never quite reach the goal because every step takes us only a part of the way (namely, ¼ of the way). Although the $400 will never quite be reached, we get close enough to it in about a year for all practical purposes.

Process analysis implies questionable assumptions.

This period approach to the multiplier is very appealing. It can be put in the form of impressive tables and charts, and it has an air of realism because it emphasizes a time lag—the fact that it takes time for people to adjust their consumption to their income. Unfortunately the approach is based on a number of questionable assumptions.

It assumes that the time lag is the same for everybody or that it is satisfactory to use an average time lag instead of the very different time lags that would be appropriate for different people. To bring in differences in the time lags would make the presentation quite messy, but to leave them out makes the realism spurious. The neatness resulting from assuming the period to be a month is also spurious, for the average of the time lags would probably be two or three months. Such simplifying devices are irresistible in exposition but are dangerous for analysis.

[8] See appendix to Chap. 17, sec. 5.

Much more serious is the implied assumption *that all goods are made to order.* Those people who earn the extra $100 in January order $75 worth of goods in February. Just this amount of goods are made and just $75 is earned in making them, and similarly with the other increments in the following months. It would be much more realistic, but not so easy to put into a neat table or chart, to suppose that when there is an increase in income and in consumption businessmen try to anticipate the demand, adjusting their output by trial and error rather than not making anything until a consumer has ordered it. If they do try to anticipate we are back with the equilibrium analysis to which the trials and errors lead. We must admit that we have not any neat account of the microscopic process by which the equilibrium is approximated, but that is better than to delude ourselves with the supposition that the artificial description of our multiplier working month by month is really a successful analysis of a genuine economic process.

Another difficulty about the multiplier is that it sounds too much like magic. How can an expenditure of $100 bring about an increase in income of $400, especially if even the $100 is a costless decision to spend some idle or newly printed money? The answer is, of course, that magic is perfectly appropriate for the upside-down economy where men and resources are unemployed simply because there is a taboo against providing the needed money spending. The removal of a destructive taboo always works miracles.

Outside the upside-down economy of unemployment the multiplier loses its magic power. If we have full employment the multiplier can still operate to increase income by more than the increase in investment, but the increase is only an increase in *money* income and not in real income. Employment and output do not increase—we merely have inflation.

The propensity to consume is an end, not a means.

There has been some discussion among economists as to what is the optimum rate of saving, by which we must presume is meant the optimum degree of thrift or the optimum propensity to consume. If the public is very thrifty (*i.e.,* has a low propensity to consume), there will be so little demand for consumption goods that investment too will be discouraged. There will be little consumption and little investment. There will consequently also be little saving—the high propensity to save will be more than offset by the lowness of the income out of which to save.

In such a situation a decrease in the propensity to save (which is the same thing as an increase in the propensity to consume) would increase consumption as well as investment and would therefore also increase income, which is the sum of these two. It is desirable to increase these and so we again see that thrift is undesirable if we are in a depression.

But as soon as we leave the upside-down economy the matter ceases to be so simple. If we apply Functional Finance and have full employment, a higher propensity to save means less consumption and more investment (and also more saving) and a higher propensity to consume means more consumption and less investment (and also less saving). The whole nature of the problem changes. We can no longer maximize both. If we have more of one we must have less of the other. We no longer have a technical problem of maximization but a political problem of choosing how the limited resources are to be allocated between producing consumption goods and services for present enjoyment and producing investment goods to increase output in the future.

In a purely capitalist society time preference is served by monetary policy.

It is possible for the political decision to be made by some dictator, but it is also possible for the decision to reflect democratically the preferences of the public. A high-investment political party might campaign for votes against a high-consumption political party.

A more subtle and more efficient method of determining the preferences of the public could be provided by the price mechanism. In a purely monetary full-employment policy, the rate of interest is adjusted, by changes in the amount of money, so as to bring about the volume of investment just needed for full employment. The distribution of resources between the production of consumption goods and the production of additions to productive equipment is then in accordance with the choice by the public between consuming their income and saving it. If the public wants to save a quarter of its income, the purely monetary full-employment policy would mean bringing about a volume of investment equal to one-quarter of the full-employment income. The public would spend on consumption three-quarters of their full-employment income. Between the two the full-employment income would just be maintained. The wish of the public to save a quarter of their income is translated by the full-employment policy into the investment of that part of the available productive resources.

This solution may be criticized for accepting as the judgment of the public a propensity to consume that is strongly influenced by the existing distribution of income and wealth among the population. This distribution is not immutable. Society can alter the distribution of wealth and income and has indeed taken quite strong steps in the direction of reducing inequality. All who are dissatisfied with the current distribution are entitled to support legislation for more progressive taxes or for the reduction of monopoly or for the reverse of such measures. But in a democratic society we must at any time take the existing legal and institutional arrangements as the most authoritative expression of the will of the people, and we must accept the results of these arrangements, pending their change by democratic processes, as the results that the people intended to bring about.

Accepting the current propensity to consume and bringing about full employment by purely monetary policy may be called the democratic capitalist solution. There is also a democratic collectivist solution, where although all investment is undertaken by the state, the allocation of resources between consumption and investment is made to reflect the preferences of the public as between provision for present enjoyment and provision for investment for the future.

In a purely collectivist society time preference can be served by fiscal policy.

In a collectivist economy, just as in any other, it is desirable to avoid less productive investment as long as more productive investments are possible. The best way of doing this is to have a rate of interest against which to check the rate of return of investments, proposed investments being accepted if they promise a rate of return at least as high as the rate of interest and being rejected if they are expected to yield less. A higher rate of interest would mean more rejections and less investment and therefore more consumption, while a lower rate of interest would mean more investment and therefore less consumption.

The adjustment of consumption to investment (so that the sum of the two provided the right amount of spending for full employment) could be brought about by increasing or decreasing the net income distributed to the population (after taxes and subsidies).

Part of the machinery for getting the distribution between investment and consumption to correspond to the preferences of the public would be the existence of savings banks where citizens could deposit savings out of income and obtain interest at the same rate as is being used for the regulation of investment, and from which citizens would be able to borrow money, on the security of their future earnings, appropriately insured, also at the same rate of interest. This would seem to provide another means by which consumption could be adjusted to offset changes in investment. The population might vary their consumption in relation to their income (the balance being deposited with or withdrawn from the savings banks). But this kind of adjustment is excluded by the device for obtaining the optimum rate of investment.

The optimum rate of interest which would result in the optimum division of resources between investment and consumption is that rate of interest at which deposits in the savings bank are exactly equal to withdrawals, including borrowing, *i.e.,* the rate of interest at which *net* saving is zero. A rate of net saving other than zero would be an indication that the public, in the aggregate, is dissatisfied with the volume of investment being undertaken by the government.

The public is expecting future distribution of income to show the fruits of current investment. Every citizen who saves some of his current income and deposits it at the savings bank to earn the current rate of interest (which is equal to the marginal return on investment or the marginal efficiency of investment) is showing that he prefers the expected return of some additional investment to the sacrifice in present consumption that it entails. Every citizen who withdraws savings (or who borrows money) for consumption, foregoing (or paying) the same rate of interest, is showing that he prefers the present consumption to the greater future benefits that could be obtained by investment. To the extent that these savings and dissavings cancel out, they may be considered as loans by the savers to the dissavers and no adjustment in the current rate of investment is desirable. But an excess of saving over borrowing should be the signal for the government to increase the volume of investment. This means lowering the rate of interest so that more investment projects will pass the test and reducing the net incomes of citizens (after taxes and subsidies) as much as may be necessary to keep total spending at the full-employment level. If there is net dissaving, the rate of interest should be raised. Investment would be reduced and net income should therefore be increased as much as is necessary to maintain full employment. (The effect of the interest changes on the propensity to save or dissave would of course influence the degree to which it is necessary to adjust incomes.)

In a mixed economy both fiscal and monetary policy should be used.

Investment in our existing economy is neither entirely private nor entirely collectivist. The optimum rate of interest is therefore neither that at which private saving is equal to total investment (at full employment) nor that at which private saving is equal to zero. It is somewhere in between, depending on the degree to which the government undertakes investment and adjusts the level of income, by taxes and subsidies, in order to prevent the investment from disturbing the level of total spending necessary for full employment. In a completely capitalist society in which all investment is undertaken by private enterprise, the appropriate instrument is a purely monetary policy in which the achievement of full employment by the adjustment of the supply of money ensures a volume of investment that corresponds to the preferences of the public between the present and the future. In a completely collectivized economy the appropriate instrument is a purely fiscal policy in which the achievement of full employment by the adjustment of net income, through taxes and subsidies, ensures the zero volume of private saving which indicates that in the opinion of the public the government is investing just the right amount. In a mixed economy like that in which we live it is appropriate to use both instruments.[9]

[9] Strictly speaking, it is only the *adjustments* in investment which are necessary for the full-employment policy that have to be considered. In a society which is mixed in the sense that certain investments are being undertaken by the government for reasons quite separate from employment policy, the purely capitalist adjustment via monetary policy will be appropriate if the principle is accepted that public investment is not to be increased (or decreased) in making the adjustment to full employment. The converse

It is interesting to observe that in the debates on this subject those who have a more capitalistic bias do in fact favor the use of monetary policy rather than fiscal policy, and those with a collectivist bias seem to favor fiscal policy rather than monetary policy. When both are used together, it is possible for each side to claim that the instrument which it favors is the really effective one and that the other is mere window dressing. The debate as to whether fiscal policy or monetary policy is more important is very much like the Talmudic debate as to whether the sun or the moon is more important. In that debate the conclusion was reached that the moon is much more important because it shines at night when the light is really needed.

Summary.

Functional Finance does not say that saving is bad. It says that *thrift* may be either good or bad, depending on whether we have too much or too little spending. Thrift is not responsible for saving which is entirely determined by investment. Saving is only the shadow of investment. There is no point in calling it good or bad because it is never a cause but always a result.

The liquidity-preference theory of interest, unlike the saving-investment theory, survives the introduction of the influence of changes in the level of income.

Consideration of the possibility of the economy maturing and not needing so much investment is falsely interpreted as condemning thrift. But this is the case only in the upside-down depression economy. The idea that economists who are concerned about economic maturity are pessimistic is also unwarranted, since

would be true for a society in which a certain amount of private investment was fixed and was not permitted to be changed for full-employment purposes. All the adjustment would then have to be in the public investment sector just as in a completely collectivist society. I am indebted for this correction to criticisms raised by Professor Alvin H. Hansen.

maturity means that we do not need so much investment and can therefore enjoy more consumption.

The multiplier is the number by which an increase in investment must be multiplied to yield the increase in income at which the public would be content, in accordance with its propensity to consume, to increase its saving by as much as investment has been increased.

Greater thrift (at the margin of income) means a smaller multiplier, since the multiplier is the inverse of the marginal propensity to save. But this is no good reason for a general condemnation of thrift. Only if we are in a deep depression and are prevented by some external force from investing more than a fraction of what is needed to restore prosperity is it unequivocally better to have a large multiplier (and therefore a smaller degree of thrift). In the absence of such an external force there is no point to the "economy" of bringing about the same increase in income with a smaller amount of investment.

The multiplier is sometimes thought of not as a condition of equilibrium, but as a process of income creation in successive time periods. This is unfortunate because in the present stage of economic theory we are not able to handle any real "process analysis," and the process approach can be developed only on the basis of a series of misleading implicit assumptions about the nature of our economy. It is best to assume some approximation to equilibrium without pretending to be able to follow the complex processes by which the equilibrium is approached.

In a depression thrift is bad because more spending would increase both consumption and investment. In full employment more consumption means *less* investment, and vice versa, so that we have a political problem in deciding on how to apportion resources between the two. This problem can be solved democratically in a capitalist society by the use of a purely monetary full-employment policy. In a collectivist society it can be solved democratically by a purely fiscal full-employment policy which so adjusts net income that net saving is zero at a rate of interest kept equal to the marginal efficiency of investment. In a mixed economy like our own it is appropriate to use both fiscal and monetary policy and fruitless to debate which is more "fundamental."

APPENDIX TO CHAPTER 17

1. Figure 16 shows what happens to the liquidity-preference formulation of the determination of the rate of interest if one takes into account the effects of changes in the rate of interest on the level of

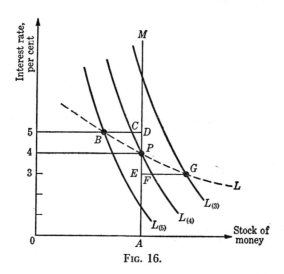

FIG. 16.

income. Instead of this destroying the argument, as it does in the case of the saving-investment formula, it only strengthens it.

$L_{(4)}$ is the original liquidity-preference curve, which shows that with a stock of money $0A$ the equilibrium rate of interest is 4 per cent. If we do not bring in the effect of changes in income we would say that if the rate of interest were 5 per cent the money in existence would exceed the money that the public wants to hold by CD, and this would push the interest rate down toward P. If the rate of interest were 3 per cent the demand for money to hold would exceed the amount of money in existence by EF, and this would push the rate of interest up toward P.

Bringing in the income effect we now say that if the rate of interest were 5 per cent, the liquidity-preference curve would change. There would be less investment and therefore less income. (The resulting decrease in consumption would make the reduction in income several times the reduction in investment in accordance with the multiplier. See pages 250–252.) With less income there would be less need for money to hold. The new liquidity curve corresponding to the new situation is shown by $L_{(5)}$. This is the liquidity preference corresponding to the level of income that corresponds to the level of investment that corresponds to a 5 per cent rate of interest. The result of this change is that there is a greater excess of the stock of money over the demand for cash to hold—BD instead of CD—and there is a greater pressure to reduce the rate of interest to the equilibrium level at P.

If the rate of interest were 3 per cent, there would be more investment, more income, and a greater need for money to hold in connection with the greater level of income. The liquidity-preference curve corresponding to the income level corresponding to the investment level corresponding to the 3 per cent rate of interest is shown in $L_{(3)}$. The excess demand for money to hold over the available stock of money is increased from EF to EG and there is a stronger force still pushing the rate of interest up toward the equilibrium level at P.

We can draw a new L curve that already has built into it the effects of income changes, showing at each rate of interest the demand for money to hold at the level of income corresponding to that rate of interest. This curve, marked by the broken line L in Fig. 16, would pass through B, P, and G. This gives us the same result as the more complicated construction we have been employing but it is liable to be misinterpreted and criticized as if it were not the L curve but the $L_{(4)}$ curve. Having the $L_{(4)}$ curve on the scene may perhaps prevent such mistaking of identity.

If we try to bring the income effect into the S curve in the saving-investment formula we do not get such a happy result. What happens is that the difference between supply and demand, instead of being increased, is reduced to zero in each case, and the S curve which takes the income into effect coincides with the I curve. We do not have any indication of the equilibrium rate of interest by an intersection between two curves because the two curves coincide throughout their

length. Some other explanation, namely, the one here given, is necessary to show how the rate of interest is determined.

2. In Fig. 17, P represents an initial point where consumption plus
investment make up an income of X. P lies on the 45-degree line
C + I = Y, as does every point representing an actual situation,

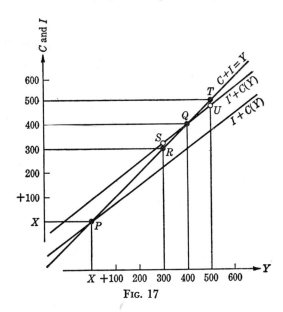

FIG. 17

because the consumption and the investment between them make up
and are equal to the income. The curve I + C(Y) represents the addition of the original investment to the propensity to consume. The intersection of this curve with the 45-degree line at P indicates that at
this point the propensity to consume is satisfied. The public does
not wish, at that income, to consume either more or less than it is
actually consuming.

If investment is increased by $100 from I to I', the I + C(Y) curve
is moved up vertically a distance representing $100 to the position
marked by the curve I' + C(Y). This curve now intersects the 45-degree
line at Q showing that the new equilibrium level of income is $400
higher than before. At this income the public is again consuming the
amount it considers proper for the new, higher income, namely, $300
out of the extra $400 of income, in accord with its marginal pro-
pensity to consume of ¾.

3. If income is increased by only $300, the actual position will be at R on the 45-degree line (Fig. 17), showing consumption increased by $200 which together with the $100 increase in investment constitute the $300 increase in income created. The $I' + C(Y)$ curve, for this level of income, however, does not pass through R but through the point S above it. This means the appropriate additional consumption when income has been increased by $300 is not $200 but $225 if the propensity to consume is $\frac{3}{4}$ as we are now assuming. The public would like to be not at R but at S. Their attempt to reach S consists of increasing their consumption, but this increases income at the same time that it increases consumption, so that the ensuing positions are represented by points along the 45-degree line. As R moves along RQ toward Q, S stays vertically above R moving along SQ toward Q. As long as income has increased by less than $400 above X, S will still lie above R and the movement toward Q will continue until Q is reached.

4. If income is increased by $500, $400 of this must be increased consumption. Such a position is represented by T on Fig. 17. T is, however, not in accordance with the propensity to consume, because with an increase in income of $500 the increase in consumption should be $375 as long as the propensity to consume is $\frac{3}{4}$. This objective is indicated by the point U, which lies directly below T. The attempt to reach U consists of reducing consumption. This reduces income together with the consumption, so that the actual point moves from T toward Q along TQ while the imaginary point sought by the public keeps on eluding their grasp as it moves along UQ, directly below T, toward Q. At Q it merges with the real position T.

5. The period analysis approach to the multiplier is illustrated in Fig. 18, which is an elaboration of Fig. 17. Starting with an income of X, represented by point P, we have an increase of investment of $100. This takes us to the circled point on $I' + C(Y)$ directly above P. But this is an imaginary point (represented by the circle being drawn hollow) because the increase in investment also means an equal increase in income. The actual point reached is directly to the right on the 45-degree line $I + C = Y$. It is the solid point marked J (for January), showing an increase in income of $100. In February the public consumes three-quarters of this increase in income, attempting

to reach the hollow circle directly above *J*, but in fact this moves them to *F* (in February). In March they try to get to the point directly above *F* but find themselves at *M*, and so on. Each month the income

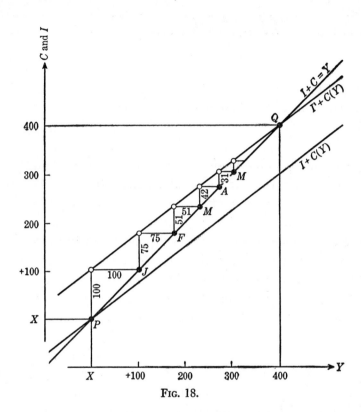

FIG. 18.

increases by the amount shown by the numbers in the diagram. Each step is just as high as it is long because it is built on a 45-degree line. Each step takes one a quarter of the distance (still remaining) toward *Q*.

CHAPTER 18

The National Debt

ONE OF the tenets of Functional Finance is that taxation should be undertaken only when the social effects of the taxes are desirable. If the government needs money it can print it or borrow it.

According to "sound finance" taxation is the normal and proper way for the government to get the money it needs, borrowing is only for emergencies, and printing money is unthinkable. This is based on an analogy with the individual in which tax collecting by the government is taken to correspond to an individual earning his income. An alternative analogy could consider tax collection as corresponding to stealing or robbery and the creation of money as a legitimate occupation of the government. This would lead to the conclusion that the normal way for government to get all the money it spends is to print it, that borrowing requires some special justification, and that taxation should be unthinkable. This would be no less logical than the sound finance approach, but neither would it be any more logical. Analogy should be used for inspiration, not for argument.

Another tenet of Functional Finance is that the government should borrow only when the effects of the borrowing are desired. For example, government borrowing may be used to check inflation by making it harder for people to borrow and invest or by inducing people to lend money to the government instead of spending it. But if its effects on the economy are not desired, borrowing, like taxation, should never be undertaken just because the government needs money. Nevertheless, Functional Finance is often called deficit financing and deficit financing is normally interpreted as regularly borrowing to meet current expenses and so incurring national debt.

The function of government borrowing is to check excessive investment.

The rejection by Functional Finance of the principle that the government should collect in taxes as much as it spends can just as well mean that the government would collect in taxes more than it spends as that it would collect less, and even if it collected less it need not borrow the difference. It can cover it by the issue of new money. But there are circumstances in which Functional Finance would lead to government borrowing and an increase in the national debt.

Functional Finance would lead to government borrowing if the government wanted to run a deficit, *i.e.,* to spend more than it collected in taxes, but did not want to cover the difference by the issue of new money. The deficit would be necessary only if in its absence total spending would have been too little. The borrowing would be necessary only if covering the deficit by issuing new money would lead to too much liquidity, too low a rate of interest, and excessive investment. Investment is excessive if it entails the elimination of some other and socially more desirable expenditure where permitting both would mean too much spending and inflation. Government borrowing then raises the rate of interest and cuts out some of the investment. It is then possible, without making total spending excessive, for the government either to spend more itself or to lower taxes and thereby enable others to spend more on the socially more desirable alternative. The resources that would otherwise be absorbed by the eliminated investment now go to produce the alternative goods consumed by the government or by the relieved taxpayer.

By far the most important alternative that is given priority over investment is expenditure for war purposes, and this is of course the main source of our national debt. Government borrowing might also result from the acceptance by the government of some criterion, democratic or otherwise, for determining how resources should be divided between consumption and investment. If consumption, perhaps in the form of better nourishment for children, is judged more desirable than some current investments, the government might borrow in order to raise the rate of interest and cut out these investments.

Not national but international debt is the true analogy to interpersonal debt.

But whatever the possible causes, Functional Finance can in certain circumstances result in a large and growing national debt, and it does not seem to be at all concerned about this. Is this a serious flaw in Functional Finance? Should there not be some additional rule to protect us from the dangers of excessive national debt? In this chapter we shall consider a number of the fears behind such questions and shall find that no further rule is needed.

Most people who worry about the national debt do so because of the analogy with personal debt. They know that it is imprudent for an individual to get into debt and they assume that this must also hold for the nation. This analogy is so inappropriate that economists are sometimes tempted to say that there is no need whatever to be concerned about the national debt, no matter how large it may be, because, as a nation, "we owe the debt to ourselves."

It is true that the "we" in this statement are not the same people as the "ourselves." Some of us owe some of the national debt to other citizens, and we shall consider some of the important effects of this in the present chapter. But it is still true that, as a nation, we *do* owe the debt to ourselves. This is why the analogy with private debt is inapplicable.

The analogy breaks down because when an individual is in

debt he is in debt to somebody else. The other person, the creditor, has claims which may become painful or embarrassing to the debtor. The proper parallel is, therefore, a debt by one nation to another nation (or to the citizens of another nation) to whom the debt is owed. The debtor nation is poorer because of such a debt just as an individual debtor is poorer because of his debt. The creditor nation, like the individual creditor, is of course richer for the same reason. Personal debt is a debt by one person to another person and should properly be called inter-personal debt. The proper analogy to *interpersonal* debt is not national debt but *international* debt or debt by one nation to an-other nation.

The 250 billion dollars owed by the United States government to the citizens who own government securities does not make the United States 250 billion dollars poorer any more than the fact that American citizens have among their assets 250 billion dollars' worth of government securities makes the United States that much richer. In exactly the same way the interest on the national debt and the repayments that the government makes to the bond-holders neither enrich nor impoverish the nation. But to see that interest payments do not constitute a subtraction from the national income seems to be even more difficult than to see that the national debt does not constitute a subtraction from national wealth.

The incurring of national debt is often denounced as unfair to our children and grandchildren who inherit it. The fallacy here is that if our grandchildren pay the interest or repay the debt, these payments can be made to none other than our grandchildren, so that *as a whole* they are neither benefited nor harmed by the national debt.

The analogy between interpersonal debt and national debt breaks down not only in the interest payments and the repayments but right in the beginning with the initial borrowing. An inter-personal loan or an international loan yields the borrower a real benefit. It enables him to consume or to invest more than he is earning or producing. And when he pays interest or repays the loan he must tighten his belt, reducing his consumption or his investment.

In the case of national debt we have neither the benefit nor the burden. The belt cannot be let out when borrowing and the belt need not be tightened when repaying. Incurring national debt does not increase the supply of available productive resources, and making the repayment does not destroy any of them.

"But surely there must be some limit to the national debt!" one is tempted to cry. Before one can deal with this protest it is necessary to distinguish between two meanings of the word "limit."

A natural limit to the debt makes an arbitrary limit unnecessary.

It may mean that we undertake not to let the national debt increase beyond some set size. When the national debt reaches that figure, we will not borrow any more no matter what is prescribed by Functional Finance. We will either balance the budget or finance a deficit by issuing new money. We may then suffer from depression or from inflation or from overinvestment and underconsumption (according to whatever criteria we may have of the best proportions between these two) but we will not permit the national debt to increase beyond the set limit.

On the other hand the limit to the national debt may mean that if we follow the principles of Functional Finance without considering what may happen to the national debt, the national debt will nevertheless not increase indefinitely but keep below some limit set not by us but by the conditions of our economy. We may call the first an "arbitrary" limit and the second a "natural" limit.

To impose an *arbitrary* limit on the national debt is to rule that at some point it is more important to prevent the national debt from growing than to maintain full employment and avoid inflation. It is difficult to see any more reason for preventing the debt from increasing when it is 47 billion or 55 billion or 200 billion or 400 billion dollars than when it is zero. If prosperity and stability are more important than balancing the budget when the debt is small, they are also more important than balancing the budget when the debt is large. The objection to a large or growing national debt is ultimately based on the belief that it would cause some vaguely defined economic harm. To sacrifice Functional Finance for the sake of preventing the national debt from growing is therefore to embrace the definite economic harm of depression or inflation for the sake of avoiding a possible cause of economic harm in the future—to jump into the lake in order to avoid a threatening shower.

But establishing no arbitrary limit to the national debt does not mean that the debt might grow indefinitely. There is a *natural* limit to the national debt. This is because the national debt constitutes *wealth* in the hands of the citizens who own it. It is true that the national debt is no addition to the real national wealth. There are no additional productive resources, and the additional assets held by individuals are balanced by the additional obligations of the government which may even descend on the citizen in the shape of additional taxes. Nevertheless the national debt makes the individual members of society feel themselves to be richer rather than poorer. Their desire to save, to add to their wealth, is not as strong, and their propensity to consume is greater. When the national debt has grown so large that people feel themselves so wealthy that they spend enough to provide full employment, there is no need for any further deficits. Functional Finance then prescribes the balancing of the budget and the national debt stops growing. It has reached an equilibrium level which is its natural limit.

There is also a natural limit to the issue of money, because of a liquidity effect as well as a wealth effect.

What we have observed about the national debt is also true of the quantity of money. The government may correct inadequate spending by deficits covered not by borrowing but by the issue of additional money. The stock of money would, however, not increase indefinitely but would tend to reach a natural or equilibrium limit. As the stock of money increased, further increases would become less and less necessary and would finally disappear altogether.

There are two reasons for this. In the first place an increase in money relatively to other assets increases liquidity, lowers the rate of interest, and induces more private investment. In the second place an increase in the amount of money is also an increase in wealth. It makes its possessors feel wealthy and therefore increases their propensity to consume. Both the increase in private investment and the increase in the propensity to consume mean more spending by individuals and therefore less need for government spending to maintain full employment and so less need for the issue of new money for this purpose. When the stock of money and the induced private investment and consumption have grown large enough there will be adequate spending for full employment even without any contribution by government spending of newly issued money. At that point Functional Finance prescribes an end to the issue of new money. An equilibrium or natural limit to the size of the money stock has been reached.

There is a similar limit if money issue is combined with borrowing.

The natural limits to deficits covered by borrowing and to deficits covered by issuing new money would also make themselves felt in the more normal case where deficits are covered in part by borrowing and in part by issuing money. The national debt and the stock of money would both be increased by the government deficit, and both would stop growing when the increased wealth (in government debt and in money) and the increased liquidity have between them raised private spending to the full-employment level where no further government deficits are needed.

"Money issue" often stands for *an excess of government spending over tax collection combined with the issue of new money,* and "borrowing" often stands for *an excess of government spending over tax collection combined with borrowing from the public equal to this difference.* If we separate the different elements in these complexes, we can say much more simply that Functional Finance prescribes a government deficit whenever there would otherwise be insufficient spending for full employment. The deficit naturally implies that the government pays out more money than it collects, that it issues money. (The converse, implied in the compound meaning of "money issue," namely, that an issue of money naturally involves a deficit, is not true, because it is possible for the government, *e.g.,* in repaying debt, to issue new money without having a deficit.)

Borrowing is a separate activity consisting of the substitution of government securities for cash in the hands of the public, leaving the budget unaffected. It has the effect of reducing liquidity without reducing private wealth. It therefore tends to raise the rate of interest and check investment while keeping constant the propensity to consume. The net effect is to reduce total spending by the reduction in investment. Greater deficits will then be needed to provide full employment if borrowing has reduced the amount of money in the hands of the public. These greater deficits mean either more spending by the government or more spending by taxpayers whose taxes are reduced. If these expenditures are considered more desirable than the investments which are choked off, borrowing is appropriate; otherwise it is not.

The combination of deficits with borrowing has the following effects: (1) the immediate increase in current spending and income, (2) the long-run effect of increasing wealth and liquidity by the issue of money involved in spending more than is collected in taxes, and (3) the canceling of the liquidity effect by the borrowing, leaving the long-run effect of increased private wealth (now in the form of securities instead of in money) and a greater propensity to consume. Because borrowing eliminates the liquidity effect, it postpones the day when deficits are no longer necessary. That is why the natural limit to the national debt (the stock of money being kept constant) is greater in dollars than the natural limit to the stock of money (the national debt being kept constant) and a combination of the two would have some intermediate natural limiting value.

The dangers of having too great a stock of money are exaggerated.

It is sometimes feared that too great a stock of money would be dangerous because the public might start spending it. There could then be a very sudden and large increase in spending which could not be offset quickly enough by the deflationary measures of Functional Finance. This does not seem to be a good enough reason for preferring depressions to Functional Finance. The stock of money needed for the convenient operation of a modern society is in any case so large that having a larger stock of money could not be much more dangerous. If there were a loss of confidence in the dollar, we could manage with as little as one-twentieth of our present money stock without going to the extremes of inconvenience that have been observed during hyperinflations. This means that we could have prices rising to twenty times their present level, a rise of 2,000 per cent, even without any further increase in the amount of money. It seems much more sensible to concentrate on the prevention of the loss of confidence than to try to keep the stock of money small enough to make a loss of confidence slightly less disastrous.

Budgets are useful, but only sections of an organization should be concerned with balancing them.

If there is no need for balancing the budget, why have any budget at all? The answer is that budgets can be very useful if one is not just obsessed with *balancing* them. In any complicated organization there are many things on which money needs to be spent. Except in the upside-down economy of depression, which Functional Finance tries to rule out, it is necessary to consider the limitation of resources. Every dollar should be directed where it can do most good and this means that in the optimum budget it is not possible to improve on the allocation by shifting any money from one purpose to another. The purpose of the budget is to prevent too much from being spent on any segment of the economy—"too much" meaning that some of the money could be put to better use somewhere else.

This is why it is necessary and appropriate for every individual person, family, firm, or local, state, or other governmental unit to keep within its budget, *i.e., balance* its budget. If it does not there will have to be less spent somewhere else in the economy. But for the economy as a whole this does not apply. There is no "somewhere else" which must be cut if the government, in the interest of obtaining full employment for the economy as a whole, finds it necessary to spend more than it collects in taxes. The government need not *balance* its budget but must *have* a budget to indicate how the total spending is to be allocated between the different uses. The segments must *balance* their budgets in their execution of this allocation.

National debt is inflationary, and this has to be offset by higher taxation, which has bad effects.

We can now consider the real as distinguished from the imaginary effects of the national debt. We have seen that borrowing is deflationary because it puts government securities into the hands of the public in place of money so that there is a loss of liquidity and a reduction of investment. But the larger the national debt the greater is the remaining wealth effect so that the propensity to consume is greater. We can therefore say that, although borrowing, or *increasing* the national debt, is *deflationary*, the *existence* of the debt is *inflationary*. And the interest payments that have to be made as long as the debt is in existence are also inflationary. A large national debt results in more spending both because of the wealth effect (people feel richer and will consume more out of the same income) and because of the income effect (the interest payments constitute additional income some of which is consumed).

With this additional spending a full-employment policy, keeping total spending at the full-employment level, will have to reduce spending elsewhere by a corresponding amount. Either the government will have to spend less or others will have to be induced to spend less, e.g., by having more of their money taken away from them in taxes. A larger national debt makes a higher rate of taxation necessary.

This looks like a return from Functional Finance to "sound finance," because "sound finance" says that more taxes will be needed to raise the money needed for the interest payments. But the resemblance is only superficial. What is needed is not the collection of more revenue but a higher tax rate that reduces spending by the public. An increase in a purchase tax, for example, which the public evades by spending less, will do the trick even if it *reduces* the amount of money raised by the government. On the other hand, a tax which raises revenue but does not reduce spending, e.g., a tax that falls on saving, is of no use.

We here have three real disadvantages which are more serious the greater is the national debt. The government will have to cut its own spending on matters which presumably were considered desirable, the public will have to be induced to cut their spending below what they considered desirable, and the tax will interfere with the proper working of the price mechanism. Against the first two disadvantages—reduction in government spending and in private spending (by the people subjected to the additional taxation)—we must set the advantages enjoyed by the owners of the government debt out of their increased spending. But there remains the third disadvantage, the harm done by the additional taxation in raising some prices in relation to others and in disturbing the proper incentives for economic activities.

It is true that only bad taxes have these bad effects. But in any modern economy all the good taxes, which are imposed because their effects are desired, will already have been fully utilized. Additional taxation needed not for their particular effects but only in order to reduce spending will have to be bad taxes of one degree or another.

One of the possible effects of taxation that is given very much emphasis in current political discussion is the excessive discouragement of *risky* enterprise which may be socially very valuable. If an investor has to pay the government a large part of any profits in taxes but has to bear all the losses himself, this makes him want to play safe and avoid risks. But it is not too difficult to correct this by having the government take the losses into account in one way or another. Much has already been done in the way of shifting the losses onto the government, by subtracting the losses from other income for taxation purposes, by carrying losses forward and backward, and so on. Much still remains to be done, and some of these problems will be considered in the next chapter. A complete loss offset would remove this particular evil from taxation.

More difficult to correct is the effect of taxes in reducing the incentive for *effort* below what is socially most desirable. In this way the existence of the national debt seems seriously to reduce the effectiveness of our whole economic setup. Everything else being equal, it is better for the economy if the national debt is smaller.

The bad effects can be prevented only by avoiding prosperity.

Nevertheless it is not at all useful to blame the national debt for these harmful effects! This is because there is no way of wishing away the national debt and leaving everything else unchanged, and there may be no way of preventing the national debt from increasing without permitting an alternative development which would be worse.

The government could indeed prevent national debt from growing by balancing its budget no matter how deep the depression. Because of the multiplier several hundred dollars of current income would be sacrificed by such a policy for every hundred dollars of investment that would have been financed by borrowing. Each $100 of national debt would earn about $3 a year in interest and might result in an increase in spending of $2 or $3 a year (including the effect of the greater propensity to consume because of the greater private wealth). This would have to be offset in part by a reduction in government spending and in part by increased taxes to induce a reduction in private spending. If the reduction is divided equally between these two, and if the multiplier is 3, this method of preventing the national debt from growing would mean sacrificing $300 of income in time of depression in order to avoid the harmful side effects in prosperous future years of the additional taxation needed to reduce private spending by $1.50 per annum. This method of avoiding national debt does not commend itself.

All this might seem to be unnecessary since it is possible to prevent the national debt from growing without having to suffer depression. But the *evils* of national debt can be prevented *only* by having depression. This is because these evils are really the results not of national debt but of *prosperity*, whether or not the prosperity is tied in with a policy that involves increasing the national debt.

We could have a full-employment policy and yet avoid national debt if we covered all the necessary deficits by the issue of new money, the liquidity thus created inducing investment sufficient for full employment. Or we might simply have full employment because there is sufficient private investment and no government deficit is necessary. But this would not avoid the evils we have been considering.

In the place of the national debt we would have the accumulation of *private* debt incurred by the corporations making the investments issuing securities. This private debt, just like the national debt, constitutes wealth to the people who own it. They even feel themselves richer than in the case of government debt because the rate of interest and profit is greater. There will be the same necessity for the government to reduce its own spending or to increase taxes in order to prevent inflation, and there will be the same evils on a somewhat greater scale. The evils are a result not of the national debt, but of the accumulation of private wealth that occurs when we have prosperity in a capitalist society, whether it takes the form of national debt or of private debt. The only way to prevent these evils is to maintain a state of depression in which people are too poor to accumulate wealth.

It is possible to prevent accumulation even in time of prosperity by taking the wealth away through extremely high income and inheritance taxes. But whatever other reasons there might be for such taxes, to impose such heavy taxes for the sake of avoiding much smaller taxes in the future is not to prevent but to precipitate the evils. It would surely be a case of jumping into the lake in order to avoid a shower.

The "self-liquidating" character of private investment does not avoid the bad effects. It disguises them and may increase them.

It has been argued that private investment is different from government deficits in that, parallel with the increase in income and of spending out of the income earned by the investors, there is an increase in the supply of goods to be bought. There is therefore no inflationary pressure that needs to be offset by additional taxation. But the expenditures by the government, if they are useful expenditures, also increase the productivity of the nation in the future. Productive private investment is certainly better than unproductive government investment, but by the same token productive government investment is better than unproductive private investment, or, even more generally, productive investment is better than unproductive investment—a true statement but not very much to the point.

Somewhat more to the point is the argument that private investment, even if it is not more useful socially than the alternative government investment, is "self-liquidating," which the government investment often is not. This means that the private investment charges enough for the product to absorb the additional spending induced by the distribution of dividends. Indeed it is only if the additional products are sold that the profits are made out of which the dividends can be paid. The government, on the other hand, undertakes investments which, even if they should be more useful than the private investments in increasing future output, often "do not pay" in the financial sense. In fact it is precisely because they do not pay private business to undertake them that they are recognized as public responsibilities. The spending induced by the non-self-liquidating government investment therefore has to be offset by taxes, while the spending induced by private self-liquidating investment does not.

This objection, while very plausible, misses the whole point of the matter. Private investment, because it does not and cannot be expected to undertake investments which are not expected to yield at least a normal profit, must charge a price for the product that is at least equal to the average cost. From the social point of view of obtaining the best allocation of resources it is desirable for price to be equal to marginal cost. The government investments which are "non-self-liquidating" are just those investments, like roads and parks, in which the marginal cost is less than the average cost, so that it is socially desirable to "run them at a loss." If they are not undertaken by the government but left to private enterprise, either they will not be provided at all or the services will be sold at a price sufficient to cover cost and normal profit and therefore *higher* than marginal cost. It is true that there is then no need for a tax to be imposed by the government to offset the increase in spending, but the harmful effects

of charging a price greater than the marginal cost does *exactly
the same kind of harm as the tax,* but to a greater degree.

Another way of looking at this is to consider the excess of
price over marginal cost as a tax. It is imposed by the firm on
the consumers of the product to cover the deficit that would be
caused by selling at the socially desirable price equal to the
marginal cost (which is what the price would be if the product
were produced by the government as a non-self-liquidating public service). This tax is almost certainly more harmful than the
tax which the government would impose to offset the excessive
spending because it is almost the worst of all the different kinds
of taxes available to the government although it is the only one
available to the private investor. Once more the attempt to avoid
the evils of national debt turns out to be a case of avoiding a
shower by jumping into the lake.

It is inappropriate to blame the national debt for inequality.

Most of the objections to national debt thus turn out to be
objections to prosperity or to wealth or to their implications.
They are also mostly objections made from a more or less capitalistic point of view looking for additional reasons for preferring
private to public enterprise. There is a socialistic objection, too,
that takes the form of charging the national debt with increasing
the inequality of wealth in the economy. This objection not only
involves the same mistake of attributing to national debt what
would be just as true of any other kind of increase in total
private wealth but is unjustified even when applied to wealth in
general. It is true that the national debt is held very progressively
(*i.e.,* the greater a man's income the greater will be his ownership of national debt even in relation to his income), but that is
only because wealth in general is held very progressively. Rich
people have much more money than poor people.

The increase in wealth due to the maintenence of prosperity
may also be very progressive (although we have given reason for

believing that a continuous maintenance of prosperity would result in a shift from capitalist to workers and therefore in a reduction in inequality). But we must also consider that the additional taxes made necessary by the accumulation of wealth are very progressive too, and the net result would depend on whether the additional wealth is more progressive or less progressive than the marginal taxes (which are likely to be much more progressive than the tax system as a whole). And in any case the socialist would hardly say that it would be better to avoid the increase of wealth by maintaining a condition of depression—unless he is not really a socialist but a communist who wants to make conditions worse as a means to obtaining power through mass discontent and social revolution. Anyone who is genuinely interested in reducing inequality of income and wealth should shift his gaze from the national debt and even from the accumulation of wealth that comes from prosperity and instead concentrate on measures for reducing inequality of income and wealth.

Summary.

Although Functional Finance rules that borrowing, like taxation, should be undertaken only when its effects are desired, it is often identified with deficit financing covered by borrowing. Functional Finance leads to borrowing (and so to increasing national debt) only when this is necessary to prevent excessive investment.

Concern about the size of the national debt is, however, based mainly on false analogies. The appropriate analogy with interpersonal debt is not national but international debt. National debt involves neither the benefits nor the burdens of interpersonal or international debt.

There is no need for an *arbitrary* limit to the national debt because there is a *natural* limit which is reached when the ownership of national debt makes people so rich that they spend enough to provide full employment. No deficit is then necessary and no further borrowing is involved. There is a similar natural limit to money issued by the government, if it should choose that way of financing deficits incurred for the purpose of maintaining full employment, and to any combination of debt and money.

Borrowing itself is deflationary because it replaces money by securities (government debt), thereby reducing liquidity and discouraging investment. Borrowing thus reduces the inflationary effect of money issue because the existence of national debt is less inflationary than the existence of cash. Dangers from the existence of much more cash than we already have are not too serious. Throwing out the principle of *national* budget balancing does not mean that budgets cease to be useful. Their function is to coordinate the different parts of any complex organization by getting each *section* of the economy to balance its budget.

The real effects of national debt derive from the inflationary nature of the existence of debt (not to be confused with the deflationary effect of borrowing). The inflationary effect has to be offset, to prevent inflation, by government economy or by private economy induced by taxation. The resemblance of this to "sound finance" is superficial. The real evil from national debt boils down mainly to harm done by the taxes needed for offsetting its inflationary influence. The taxes may discourage risky enterprise (though this can be corrected) and reduce the incentive for effort below the socially most desirable level.

The bad effects, however, turn out to be the effects not so much of national debt as of prosperity and can be avoided only by preventing the accumulation of wealth that goes with prosperity in a capitalist society. To do this by preventing prosperity makes no sense, and to do this by very heavy taxation is to get all the evils immediately instead of gradually and in the future.

The self-liquidating nature of private investment might be thought to avoid the evil because there is a flow of additional goods to sell corresponding to the flow of spending, so that no taxes are necessary to prevent inflation. But this overlooks the fact that the higher prices, which private enterprise must charge because (unlike the government providing social services) it has to avoid losing money, constitute the same social evils as the taxes, but in a greater degree.

The objection that national debt increases the inequality of wealth is questionable. Those genuinely concerned with reducing inequality should concentrate not on national debt or even on the total accumulation of wealth, with which it is here also confused, but on measures for reducing inequality.

CHAPTER 19

Functional Finance and Socialism

EXTREME ANTISOCIALISTS have called Functional Finance a socialist Trojan horse subversively smuggled into the unsuspecting citadel of capitalism for the purpose of betraying it to the socialists.

On the other hand Functional Finance has been denounced by socialists as a capitalistic antisocialist device because it would make capitalism work, sabotaging the advent of the brave new world by preventing the "inevitable" collapse of capitalism under the weight of its own "contradictions." And it is true that Keynes, the original source of the principles of Functional Finance, definitely called himself a capitalist. Some have even gone so far as to call it "fascistic," declaring that it sought to "cure the contradictions of capitalism at the expense of the working class."

The words "socialism" and "capitalism" should be abandoned.

The only thing that is clear in all these confusing statements is that "socialism" has different meanings to different people at the same time and different meanings to the same people at different times. And the same thing is true of the word "capitalism." When a word has become so swollen with meanings that any light endeavoring to penetrate it is converted into heat, it can sometimes be cut down to size by redefinition and once more be used as an instrument for communicating or clarifying thought. But when words are as far gone as socialism and capitalism, it is best to let them go and write them off and to use as many different words as may be needed for the many different meanings that the old words have swallowed and have not been able to digest.

289

We can consider the relationship of Functional Finance to seven objectives sometimes identified with "socialism."

The question: "Is Functional Finance socialistic?" is therefore best divided into a number of different questions, each dealing with a different social objective which may have been in the mind of the questioner. There seem to be seven such main objectives. In each case Functional Finance may be related to it in one of five different ways. Functional Finance may *include* or imply the objective, it may merely encourage or support its achievement, it may be *neutral* with respect to it, it may *discourage* it, or, finally, it may *exclude* or be directly contrary to the objective, preventing it from being reached. We may now consider in which of these ways Functional Finance is related to the seven main ideas or objectives called socialism.

Anticapitalism—rejected as too naïve and negative.

The first is the simple or even naïve idea that socialism is the abolition of capitalism. The simplicity is, however, dependent on the naïveté and disappears as soon as the question is made a little more explicit. It is not clear what it is that should be abolished—all private enterprise or only some private enterprise, or some particular instruments or institutions such as money, or banks or large corporations.

Such a purely negative approach to modern society is not always associated with socialism. Sometimes this approach is just as much antisocialist as it is anticapitalist. It sees the root of all evil in some existing instruments, techniques, processes, or social arrangements and thinks to improve society by just getting rid of this unhealthy root. Society would be made healthy by the abolition of money or machinery or steam engines or railroads or politics or nuclear scientists or Jews or bicyclists.

Functional Finance definitely rejects or excludes this attitude.

It tries to make use of any useful existing institutions and to make them work better. It is directly contrary to the idea that the way to make things better is to destroy what exists and to believe that a better world would automatically emerge from the ruins.

Extension of democracy—Functional Finance is neutral, but democrats cannot afford to be neutral to Functional Finance.

The second idea connects or even identifies socialism with extension of democracy. It is believed that inequalities of income, of wealth, and of economic power severely limit the amount of democracy we can have in a capitalist society and that abolition of these inequalities (under socialism) would make democracy much more real.

Functional Finance has nothing to say on the matter of democracy even though it may be the most important issue in the present-day world. Functional Finance can be applied just as well in a dictatorial society as in a democratic society and is completely neutral as between the two. The important thing for democrats to recognize is that if they do not make use of Functional Finance they will have no chance in the long run in the competition for the world with the dictatorships who will.

Equality—Functional Finance indirectly supports it via the increase in competition and mobility under full employment.

The third objective is equality of income and of wealth, not as a means of achieving some other end, such as contributing to the extension of democracy, but rather as an end in itself. Sometimes other objectives are aimed at only because they are expected to contribute to equality of income and wealth. These should be included under the present heading. Sometimes equality is considered as a means for achieving a greater efficiency in the utilization of economic goods than is achieved if rich people wastefully use goods that are needed more urgently by poor people. But this latter is so close to equality as a good in itself (perhaps only a more explicit spelling out of the basis for the objective) that it too must be included in the objective of economic equality.

Functional Finance has nothing to say directly on this issue either. It can be applied just as much in a society where there is the very highest degree of inequality as in a society where there is complete equality of income and wealth. There is, however, an indirect relationship. The maintenance of continuous full employment (which is not very likely to happen in the absence of a Functional Finance full-employment policy) will result in greater equality.

The relationship between the income of workers on the one hand and of capitalists or employers (in the widest sense) on the other is determined by the relationship between the wage rate paid to the worker and the price at which his product is sold. This relationship, which is very close to the notion of the "real wage" or what the worker can buy with his wage, is the rate of markup, the percentage that the producer adds to his cost to obtain the price at which he sells the product. The rate of markup is determined by a very complex set of institutions determining the degree of competition in each field.

The real wage cannot be increased by raising money wages, because, in the absence of any change in the degree of competition, there will be no change in the rate of markup so that prices will rise as much as wages, leaving real wages just as low and the inequality of income just as great as before. The way to reduce inequality and raise the real wage is to reduce the rate of markup.

In a capitalist society suffering from business cycles the rate of markup must be great enough to permit the profits of the booms to make up for the losses of the depressions. Enterprising people are always figuring they can make a good profit with, say, a 25 per cent markup for retail trade instead of the traditional 40 per cent, making up for the smaller profit per unit by a greater and continuous volume of business. But these are the people who perish by the thousand when depression strikes. They cannot sell the volume needed to break even at the low markup, and the old established businesses who declared all along that 40 per cent is necessary feel themselves vindicated. If we had the continuous full employment that Functional Finance could provide, the newcomers would survive and multiply until the oldsters were driven out or themselves accepted the lower markup brought about by the increased competition. Indirectly Functional Finance would have reduced the inequality of income between workers and employers.

This change may be considered the result of an increase in the mobility between work and business. Continuous full employment would also increase the mobility between different occupations and thereby reduce the inequality of income between different groups of workers. The resulting shift of income from highly paid workers or professional people to workers with very low pay may be much more important quantitatively than the possible shift from very rich capitalists to workers as a whole. It too is an indirect result of Functional Finance.

Public enterprise—Functional Finance is strictly neutral, even indirectly.

The fourth objective is the replacement of private enterprise "for profit" by public enterprise "for use," in whole or in part, and, according to some, for better or for worse.

Here again Functional Finance is strictly neutral. No matter how much or how little public enterprise there is, the same principles for regulating the rate of total spending are necessary for the prevention of depression and inflation.

There are of course indirect effects. A society in which enterprise is primarily public can hardly avoid recognizing the responsibility of the government for regulating the level of total demand by something like Functional Finance. A primarily private-enterprise society would be more likely to resist Functional

Finance because of the tendency of businessmen to see the government in their own image—to be caught by the false analogies between businesses and other segments of the economy where Functional Finance is inapplicable and the economy as a whole represented by the government where "sound finance" is inapplicable. Conversely a society in which Functional Finance is successfully practiced might look with more favor on other governmental activities in the social interest.

Functional Finance would also indirectly exercise a conservative influence. By making a private-enterprise society work better it would weaken such forces for collectivization as are built on unthinking discontent. Those who want public enterprise in any field would have to give good reasons for this and not merely say that things are bad and any change could not help being a change for the better. Functional Finance would also tend to conserve a public-enterprise economy by making it work better and putting more of a burden of proof on such as might want to change over to more private enterprise. Enthusiasts for private enterprise, who might at this point want to say that Functional Finance is more likely to conserve public enterprise than private enterprise, should recognize that if this is true it is true only to the degree that public-enterprise economies are more likely to make use of Functional Finance.

Functional Finance is not a spearhead of collectivism.

There are those who would stoutly deny the neutrality of Functional Finance and denounce it as a Machiavellian trick for the insidious collectivization of a private-enterprise economy or (though not so often) for the despicable protection of private enterprise from the dialectical decrees of "history." The second interpretation of Functional Finance is limited to communists and some negligible revolutionary sects. The first, however, is very widespread and influential.

The argument is that Functional Finance leads to increasing

national debt which leads to increasing taxes to raise the money to service the national debt. These taxes discourage private investment so that there is still more need for government investment to maintain full employment. The government investments have to be financed by deficits and these deficits involve more borrowing and a still greater debt. This completes a vicious spiral: More debt, more taxes, less private investment, more government investment, more deficits, and more debt again inexorably follow each other until private investment has been completely eliminated and we have unintentionally slipped into the collectivist society. Collectivism is then identified with the loss of all human freedoms in a society ruled by the secret police and the concentration camp.

This argument is widespread and influential even though almost every step in it is a *non sequitur*. The different links are just not linked to each other, so that there is no chain. A full-employment policy does not necessarily involve deficits. Deficits do not necessarily involve borrowing. Borrowing should be undertaken, according to Functional Finance, not when there is insufficient private investment but when private investment is judged to be excessive. A larger national debt does involve higher tax rates[1] but an appropriate policy of permitting adequate loss offsets, which we shall discuss later in this chapter, would leave investment just as attractive as in the absence of the taxes. Maintaining full employment would make private investment *more* attractive than permitting depression to occur from time to time and to cloud the horizon all the time. Even if all investment should be undertaken by the government for other reasons, this would not mean the end of private enterprise. By far the greater part of our economy consists not of investment but of production of goods and services for current consumption. And even if the whole economy were collectivized and private enterprise prohibited, there is no necessary interference with any of the basic human

---

[1] Here there *is* a link between two steps but, as we have seen above (p. 280), not the one imagined by opponents of Functional Finance.

freedoms: freedom from fear and want, freedom of movement, of expression of opinion, of political organization, and so on. The only freedom that is curtailed by the prohibition of private enterprise is the freedom to practice private enterprise. The letter of Functional Finance has nothing to say about this freedom or indeed about any other, but the spirit of Functional Finance would say that any particular freedom should be supported if (like, say, political freedom) it increased the sum of human freedom, and should be suppressed if (like, say, the freedom to own slaves) its suppression resulted in a greater sum of human freedom. But this is to expand from Functional Finance to the larger social philosophy of Democratic Functionalism.

Planning—Functional Finance has no place in completely centralized planning but is an essential part of sophisticated, decentralized, informational planning.

The fifth objective is planning. Originally it was centralized planning to take the place of the "anarchy" of capitalism and to introduce order. More recently decentralization has been accepted as a good thing and almost all planners try valiantly to combine the two. But there remains the essential idea that planning of some sort is necessary, or at least desirable, such as does not exist under capitalism but which could exist under socialism.

Functional Finance again has nothing directly to say. Nor has Functional Finance anything directly to say on the degree of decentralization. Indirectly Functional Finance would help decentralization, because the existence of continuous prosperity is even more helpful to the small manager, just as to the small businessman, than it is to the great commissar or to the great business tycoon.

If planning means supplanting the price mechanism by governmental regulation of the details of the economy, there is no place for Functional Finance which is a part of the price mechanism.

More recent planners almost unanimously favor both the use

of the price mechanism and the maximization of decentralization. Prices then constitute the guides which tell the decentralized managers just how important it is to produce more of the various products and just how important it is to economize in the use of the various factors of production. The result has been a change in the form of planning until it is reduced to the collection and dissemination of information and the establishment of a framework within which the price mechanism and the disseminated information could most effectively be utilized. Functional Finance would form an integral part of such a framework.

With Functional Finance to provide full employment and with the price mechanism and the optimum collection and dissemination of information to guide workers, employers, and investors in their decisions, having a plan is cut down to having a policy. The government may have a policy of encouraging investment as against consumption, or of self-sufficiency as against making the best use of international division of labor, or of social security as against the "ill-fare state," and so on. Functional Finance is neutral with regard to such policies once the policy of full employment has eliminated the upside-down economy of depression where most of the problems that these policies are directed at either do not exist at all (there is no need to choose between investment and consumption as long as it is possible to have more of both) or are fundamentally changed (no real social security is possible if severe depressions are rampant). The only policy that Functional Finance is directly concerned with is the policy of maintaining full employment.

Antimonopoly—Functional Finance is neutral but indirectly helps. Monopoly should not be blamed for unemployment.

The sixth objective is the reduction of the restrictions perpetrated by monopolies. This is closely related both to equality and to planning. Monopoly is significant economically because it means a higher rate of markup and therefore a smaller share of the national income going to labor. We have seen how full employment can reduce markups. The elimination of monopoly is also one of the residuals that remain when plan is collapsed into policy. Monopolistic restrictions should be removed wherever possible in the interest of the more effective working of the economic system. But Functional Finance can prevent inflation and depression just as well when there are monopolies as when there are none.

It is true that the restriction of output in any particular industry, which monopoly always practices for the sake of the higher price that can be obtained when the output is reduced, does reduce employment in the monopolized industry. But to suppose that this must result in less employment in the economy as a whole is only another example of the fallacy of supposing that what is true of any segment of the economy must also be true of the economy as a whole. If Functional Finance is practiced, a restriction of output and employment in one section of the economy causes an increase in output and employment in the other parts of the economy where there is no monopolistic restriction or where there is relatively less monopolistic restriction. The evil of monopoly is not unemployment, but the inappropriate allocation of resources, not enough resources being used (because of too little output) in the monopolized industries and too much being used in the others. This evil is completely separable from the evils of depression or inflation with which Functional Finance is directly concerned.

Governmental responsibility—Functional Finance favors and exemplifies this.

The seventh and last of the objectives is the acceptance of governmental responsibility for seeing that the economy as a whole operates smoothly and also that it operates in the general interest and not for the benefit of purely sectional private interests. This is perhaps the most concentrated essence of planning that is left when the various modifications and sophistications we have been considering have all run their course.

Functional Finance definitely encourages governmental responsibility. It is itself an evidence of the acceptance of responsibility by the government for maintaining full employment, and it may suggest by example that the government accept responsibility in other fields.

We have now considered what seem to be the main economic objectives that people have in mind when they speak of establishing socialism, and most of the time it was not too clear on which side of any particular issue one would expect to find the people who call themselves anticapitalists or socialists or the people who call themselves antisocialists or capitalists. What this means is that the words "capitalism" and "socialism" are not any use any more.

William James once tried to show how an ambiguous word can obstruct both thought and communication by telling the story of a hunter who walked completely around a tree on the other side of which a squirrel was circling, keeping the tree between himself and the hunter. He then asked, "Did the hunter go round the squirrel?" The answer depends on which of two meanings of "going round" is intended. If "going round" means being first south of the squirrel, then east, then north, then west, and then south again, the answer is yes. But if "going round" means facing the squirrel, then being on his left, then behind him, then on his right, and then in front of him again, the answer is no. He was facing the squirrel all the time (with the tree between them). This story did not, however, completely clarify the point to those of William James' students who wanted to know, after class, whether he "really" went round the squirrel or not.

In the same way some people will continue to argue as to whether Functional Finance is prosocialist or antisocialist and will accuse of hairsplitting those who *refuse* to answer this meaningless question and who are satisfied with "merely" knowing what is its relationship to the practical problems of our times.

Functional Finance fits into Democratic Functionalism.

The general point of view to which Functional Finance is most sympathetic is that which accepts the humanistic and democratic objectives held in common by the first prophets of liberal capitalism and the first prophets of libertarian socialism and which regards issues like private or public enterprise as instruments, and not as goals. The only goal is the welfare of people; everything else is the means for serving it. This point of view, which judges all instruments by how they function to serve the needs of people and which accepts the democratic postulate that all people are equally worthy to be served, is what I like to call "Democratic Functionalism."

The first thing that must be done to permit a rational approach to the problems of men living together is to stop talking about socialism and capitalism, whether as objectives or as bogies. Every device can then be examined to see whether it serves to raise the standard of living, to maximize the freedom of the individual, and to give the greatest opportunities for the development of the members of society. Every institution and every proposal can then be judged in the light of these criteria instead of by the heat generated in their association with those semantic hotboxes, capitalism and socialism.

The bad effects of taxation in discouraging enterprise can be corrected by having complete "loss offset" for everybody.

The semantic confusions of capitalism and socialism come out very clearly in connection with the problem of "loss offset." This is the problem, mentioned in this chapter and in the preceding one, arising from the discouraging effects of taxation on risky enterprise.

When a large corporation is making enough profit on its regular activities, it can undertake new investments without being at all disturbed or discouraged by the high tax rate. It is true that, if the new investments are successful, the government will take away a large part of the profits, but it is also true that, if the new ventures should fail, the corporation will be able to subtract the losses from the profits on its regular activities and will get a part of the losses back in having to pay less tax to the government. Their possible net loss is reduced in the same proportion as their possible net profit; the ratio between the two is unaffected.

This means that, up to the amount of their income-tax obligations, corporations have complete loss offset. They are not discouraged from making investments, no matter how high the tax.

What is needed is an extension of this effect to everybody. Income taxes would then not be discouraging to investment, and one of the evils of taxation would be eliminated. One way that is rapidly developing now is to permit businesses and individuals in certain circumstances to carry forward profits and losses from year to year for income-tax purposes. This is a clumsy and inefficient way which involves a lot of bookkeeping and possible illicit manipulations. There is a much simpler way of bringing about the desired effects.

If the government is collecting in income taxes, say, 60 per cent of the high incomes of the people who own the corporations, the government is in effect the owner of 60 per cent of the corporations. We do not like to admit that our economy is really socialized to this extent, but if the corporations were to come to an agreement with the government whereby all future taxes were commuted in return for the issue to the government of additional (nonvoting) shares which would give it 60 per cent of the shares in the corporation, there would be no change in the essence of things. Everything would go on exactly as before, the previous owners getting 40 per cent of the profits and the government getting 60 per cent, and in all new ventures undertaken by the corporation any losses would be deducted from the other profits so that 40 per cent of the losses would be borne by the previous owners and 60 per cent by the government.

The desired effect can be made applicable to all business if this effective participation by the government in the profits of business is consciously recognized and generalized. The government could then shoulder its share in all business losses by simply reimbursing a fraction of them by a government check, just as it accepts its share in all profits.

The chief obstacle is our unwillingness to recognize legally the degree to which we are a socialist society in effect.

At the present time, our reluctance to recognize the degree to which our private enterprise is really socialized permits us to do this only where we can disguise the shouldering of losses by calling them *deductions* for income-tax purposes from other profits made by the same taxpayer on other activities or at different times. We hesitate to apply the algebraist's trick of subtracting a larger number from a smaller number in this matter because the resulting negative tax, which would come out wherever an investor's losses exceeded his profits, is given the disparaging name of "subsidy." The result is that the government carries its share of the loss only for those taxpayers who are rich enough to be paying enough in taxes on other income from which the losses can be subtracted. Those who are not rich enough are just doubly unlucky.

The extension of the right to carry forward profits and losses increases the opportunities for such loss offsets, but there remains a serious discrimination against those who do not have other profits or enough of them from which losses can be subtracted. If the government would simply *pay* each year its share of *all* losses in the same proportion as it takes its share of profits, the inequity would be ended and the discouraging effects of taxation on investment would be eliminated throughout the economy.

Complete loss offset would make investors just careless enough.

It might be objected that such action, apart from being very unorthodox, would make investors too careless. They would not care so much about losing money in any venture because they would have to bear only a fraction of the loss, the rest being shifted onto Uncle Sam. If this argument were valid, it would also be valid against permitting the loss offset where it now exists. The successful corporation or businessman is *now* shifting onto the government the losses which are deductible from other income for tax purposes. But the argument is not valid. The induced "carelessness" is exactly what is needed. The incompleteness of loss offset makes investors *too* careful—as is natural if the investor is made to bear a larger share of the possible losses than he is permitted to enjoy of the profits. Government underwriting of the same fraction of *all* losses as it takes of the profits would correct the over-carefulness. Instead of the bad word "carelessness" we should use the good word "enterprise."

It would be possible to combine the advantages of capitalism, socialism, and feudalism.

Even complete loss offset would still leave the evils from taxation in discouraging the net reward for effort. This cannot be corrected as easily as the discouragement of risky enterprise. But the necessary expenditures of modern government seem to be greater than the amount that the public wants to save out of even a full-employment income, so that some taxation is necessary for the prevention of excessive total spending.

In the Middle Ages, when taxation was more difficult than now, the problem was solved by the government *owning* large blocks of property, the income from which provided the means for the government's expenses. With Functional Finance we do not think of the government having to impose taxes in order to raise money, but it has to impose taxes in order to prevent excessive spending. If the government owned more of the property of the country, less income from property would be earned and spent by citizens and need to be offset by taxation. The acquisition of legal title to sufficient additional property by the government via very heavy income or capital taxation might do more harm than the taxes it was designed to make unnecessary. But an increase in the rates of taxation on income from property, if combined with complete loss offset, has all the real effects of the acquisition of property by the government. It reduces the incomes and the expenditures of property owners without interfering at all with the utilization of the property. Less taxation is then necessary on earned income where taxation would still be interfering with the optimum efficiency of the economy. The effect would be like the feudal arrangement where the government got most of its income from the ownership of property.

The principle here suggested of complete loss offset by government accepting negative income taxes on all negative incomes, or losses, is no finished plan for immediate application. There are serious difficulties of fitting in the progressiveness of income taxation that is so well established as a social objective. There is the problem of the extent to which the taxation of income from property would be an indirect tax on the effort to earn income for the purpose of acquiring property. But these do not seem to be insoluble problems. We may say that the acceptance of the principle of complete loss offset would permit a greater reliance on virtual government ownership by the taxation of income from property with a reduction in other taxes and an increase in the efficiency of the economy. It would give us the effects of feudal ownership of property by the government reducing the need for harmful taxes, of capitalist freedom for individual enterprise, and of socialist participation by the government in industry. But it is best to forget all about these types of government, concentrating on the effectiveness of the various devices in serving the purposes of a democratic society, leaving it to the metaphysicians to argue whether the society in which we live, and which is moving in the direction of Democratic Functionalism, is capitalist, socialist, feudal, or what not.

Summary.

Functional Finance has been denounced both as antisocialist and as anticapitalist. This is because the words socialism and capitalism have too many meanings to be useful any more. We may, however, consider the relationship of Functional Finance to the following seven different objectives which are at different times meant by socialism.

1. The *abolition* of capitalism or of some basic institutions. This is too negative an idea to find support in Functional Finance.

2. The extension of democracy. Functional Finance is equally applicable in democracies and dictatorships, but democrats cannot afford not to apply Functional Finance.

3. Equality of income and wealth. Functional Finance has nothing directly to say about this, but the application of Functional Finance would indirectly reduce inequalities through the effect of full employment in increasing the degree of competition and of mobility.

4. The replacement of private by public enterprise. Functional Finance is neutral. It is more likely to be used in societies with more public enterprise but would tend, by making it work more satisfactorily, to conserve whatever form of society made use of it. The charge that Functional Finance would lead a free-enterprise economy down a slippery slope to collectivism (and totalitarianism) does not stand up to examination.

5. Planning, centralized or decentralized. Functional Finance would help in decentralization but has nothing to say about planning unless it means planning everything and throwing out the price mechanism. Functional Finance has no place and is incompatible with that kind of planning. When a plan is used in con-

junction with the price mechanism, decentralization, and Functional Finance, it boils down to the collection and dissemination of *information* and the laying down of policy. Functional Finance is directly concerned with no policy other than the policy of maintaining full employment.

6. Countering monopolistic restrictions. Functional Finance is neutral about this too, but full employment tends to reduce monopoly. The belief that monopoly is responsible for depressions is another case of the fallacy of illicit generalization.

7. Governmental responsibility for the smooth working of the economy in the public interest. Functional Finance favors this, being itself an example of the exercise of such responsibility.

The discussion shows some of the confusions hidden by the words socialism and capitalism. Functional Finance fits best into Democratic Functionalism.

An examination of the "loss-offset" problem of how taxes may be prevented from discouraging risky investment shows how socialistic we are without knowing it, how our refusal to admit it to consciousness prevents us from dealing rationally with this problem, and how we could combine the benefits of capitalism, socialism, and feudalism, if we would concentrate on the real problems of human cooperation and leave these words to the metaphysicians.

CHAPTER 20

The Business Cycle

THE BUSINESS cycle is what happens to the level of income and employment if there is no full-employment policy. The parable of Chapter 1 is mostly designed to turn attention away from the task of explaining business cycles to the task of preventing them.

It is not necessary to know why there is too much or too little spending in order to be able to correct it.

It may seem to be unscientific to hope to prevent business cycles without fully understanding their cause. Surely, it might be said, knowledge must come before action! The answer is that we need know no more than that depression is caused by insufficient spending and inflation by too much spending, to know what must be changed to prevent inflation and depression. It may be true that we do not know what causes the spending to be too great or too little, but if we knew these causes we might not know the causes of these causes, and in any case we must at some time come to an end unless we prefer to stop the regress by postulating some first cause that must not be questioned. If Functional Finance can keep spending from being too low or too high, it is as scientific as anything can be. To refrain from using the cure until one has gone to some deeper level of causation is no more reasonable than to refuse to wear glasses until one knows what has caused a person to be shortsighted or to refuse to provide crutches until one knew how the patient became lame.

Nevertheless it is not foolish to study business cycles as long

307

as one does not consider this a substitute for action to prevent them. The study may even have some useful practical results.

Economic expansions and contractions show a certain stability. Neither the regularity nor the irregularity of business cycles should be exaggerated.

What is shown in the study of business cycles is that when employment and income are increasing there is a tendency for the movement to continue in the same direction and for the movement to be rather gentle so that it may go on for several years before bringing the economy from depression to full employment. The same is also true in reverse. When a contraction is under way, it has a tendency to continue, and this can also go on for several years before reaching severe depression. We do not go in a few days or weeks or even months from full employment to severe depression or from severe depression to full employment. It usually takes several years. There is that measure of stability.

There is also a tendency for the movement to come to a stop and reverse itself, so that the expansion does not always reach full employment before there is a recession or downturn, and often there is an upturn before the contraction has proceeded very far. There is rarely a stable, continuous level of employment and income at the top of the expansion, but there is often a fairly stable bumping along at the bottom of the contraction.

There are then four elements which go to make up the business cycles: expansion, downturn, contraction, and upturn. The expansion is usually accompanied by a rising level of prices and the contraction by falling prices. The different elements of the cycle vary very much in length and consequently the cycles themselves do too. Some economists seem to have been too much impressed with the averages of the cycles over the recorded period and speak as if there were a law about the length of the cycle which has been compared with much more definite periodicities in astronomy. Others have gone to the other extreme, stressing the unevenness or the uniqueness of each expansion and contraction and of each boom and depression and denying that there is such a thing as the business cycle at all. It seems more reasonable to take a middle view and to say that there are fluctuations with sufficient regularity to warrant their being called cycles, but not sufficiently regular to be of importance.

The regularity would be important if it enabled anyone to make reliable predictions about the future course of the cycle. This is not possible and can never be possible, because anything thus foreseen would be changed by the very fact of the anticipation. If it were known, for example, that the depression were going to end in six months' time so that prices would then begin to rise, everybody would immediately want to take advantage of this knowledge by buying now to sell in six months' time, and the result of this anticipation would be to make prices and employment rise now and to prevent them from rising in six months' time.

Booms do not have to be followed by busts.

An exaggerated respect for the regularity of the stages in the business cycle is responsible for one of the most effective and most frequently used arguments for checking an expansion. This is the argument that if we do not stop the inflation we shall have to suffer from the depression following it—that if we permit the boom we shall have to suffer the bust.

The alliteration in this phrase seems to be extremely powerful, but unfortunately the logic is very weak indeed. There are very many good reasons for not having inflation: injustice to people with fixed or only slowly adjustable incomes, waste of resources and frustration of private as well as social plans, and the ruin of masses thereby rendered easy prey to the demagogues of revolution and counterrevolution. But we are not necessarily punished with a bust just because we have had a boom.

There are no good reasons for not having an expansion of economic activity up to the level of full employment. But the alliterative phrase is used indiscriminately as much against the one as against the other.

It is a pity to have to reject so powerful an argument against inflation when other more reasonable and more honest arguments may fail to induce the necessary action, but it must be admitted that this argument is not sound and may easily be applied not to prevent inflation but to prevent correction of depression. If a boom is followed by a bust, that may be owing to faulty methods of stopping the boom; it is not owing to the fact of having permitted the boom.

*Business-cycle students often assume an automatic
full-employment mechanism that just needs "fixing."*

Interest in the causes, or very often in a supposed "cause," of business cycles often stems from a belief that there is inherent in the capitalist system some equilibrating force that should give us full employment all the time but that there is some one thing wrong which, if corrected, would result in our economic machine automatically giving us full employment all the time. The search for this flaw—this loose screw which just needs to be tightened—is really what is meant by the dissatisfaction with Functional Finance as not going to the root of the trouble.

Functional Finance is based on the view that the trouble is not a loose screw in the mechanism but rather that there is no practical mechanism at all—it has to be invented and introduced into the economy. There is a theoretical mechanism which could conceivably give full employment automatically, but we have seen above that it depends on a degree of price and wage flexibility that is not only unreasonable but dangerous.

As is to be expected, the belief that capitalism would not have any business cycles but automatic full employment if only we could find the loose screw and tighten it has its counterpart in the view held by all socialists before Keynes, and still held by nearly all of them, that the business cycle is an inherent and essential part of capitalism. Some even go so far as to declare that if the business cycle were eliminated what we would have could not be called capitalism. We have dealt in Chapter 19 with this kind of semantic problem.

Other students are seeking to develop a dynamic economic theory.

There is a more sophisticated reason for studying the business cycle than the search for the secret of the failure of automatic full employment. This is to try to discover the nature of the time lags and reactions throughout the economy which would enable us to see the effects through time of anything that we do or that we can see happening to the economy.

It would certainly be good to know the effects through time of expenditures, taxes, borrowing, and so on. In our discussion of the multiplier we saw how useful it would be to be able to conduct a process analysis which would tell us what would be the course of the economy from moment to moment. But unfortunately, as we saw in that connection, there does not seem at present to be any prospect of success. Meanwhile we can practice Functional Finance by the more modest light of equilibrium analysis, which depends on the real world not being too different from the equilibria that we can derive from our simple assumptions about the propensity to consume and so on.

Some extreme devotees of the process analysis approach have stressed very much the difficulty or even the impossibility of carrying on a full-employment policy without taking into account all the complications that are necessary for process analysis. The frightening picture is drawn of Functional Finance, or indeed any full-employment policy, making things worse rather than better because by the time any policy begins to have its effects, conditions have changed and the opposite policy would be more in order. An attempt to cure a condition of insufficient spending might begin to operate only when the trouble had changed to one of too much spending. Attempts to correct this might then be undertaken only to find that they started to work when conditions had again been reversed. The cures would thus have the effect not of mitigating the "natural" fluctuations but of aggravating them.

There are two things to be observed here. The first is that this objection to Functional Finance is not based on the business cycle but on the study of the economy in the details in its processes. This would be possible, and no less difficult, if there were nothing like the business cycle at all. The criticism is nothing but a plea for holding up policy until the crude equilibrium economics has been supplanted by a refined dynamic economics which so far has not yet been developed.

Economic policy cannot and need not wait for dynamic economics to be developed.

The second thing is that if the dynamic analysis were developed, it would almost certainly be so complicated as to seem to prove that policy is impossible after all. The case is very much like that of the mathematician who proved that it is impossible to ride a bicycle. The calculations that have to be made to figure out with sufficient accuracy the exact pressures to be applied to the pedals and the handle bars and the position of the various members of the body to keep the bicycle on any chosen path for 10 yards would take the greatest mathematicians many months or years to figure out.

This does not mean that every child who rides a bicycle is a still greater mathematician who can work the problem out in fractions of a second. What it means is that the problem is irrelevant and does not need to be worked out for riding a bicycle. It would be necessary if every muscle in the cyclist had to be given detailed instruction by a master mathematician who would have to know also the exact contours of the pebbles met on the road and just what gust of wind would be encountered at every moment through the ride. The bicycle rider does not do that or anything corresponding to it. He merely sees or feels what is happening and corrects the errors from moment to moment. (Recently some mathematicians have caught on to the nature of this trick and have developed Cybernetics.) The recognition of error, or of the current position from time to time, and the adjustment of action to this position, is what makes it possible for even a very slow-witted nonmathematician to ride a bicycle and for ordinary mortals to apply Functional Finance to prevent inflations and depressions.

There is no disputing that a knowledge of the time lags and repercussions involved in economic actions would make a nicer adjustment possible and would permit a better use of resources through *anticipatory* adjustments to offset fluctuations that otherwise can be corrected only when they show themselves. But it is not *necessary* to graduate in this higher skill before being able to do anything about practical economic problems. What saves us, and what indeed has made our economy able to operate at all, is the stability in the nature of our economy which prevents sudden jumps from full employment to deep depression even if nothing is done about the level of economic activity.

In the absence of better prognosis, we could simply assume every month that conditions of demand, except for the contribution by the instruments of Functional Finance, will be the same next month as they are this month. This would enable us to keep pretty close to our goal, for we would not deviate from it by more than the change in the private section of the economy in the course of a month. And this is not to take into account the greater stability in the private sector when a full-employment policy eliminates the expectations of continued increases or decreases in demand that develop if the economy is allowed to run the erratic course which we call the business cycle.

Obsession with business cycles leads to the assumption that we still have them when we have got rid of them.

The study of the business cycle does not, however, always lead to the relatively harmless conclusion that a better understanding of the dynamics of our economy would be a good thing. It often leads to a hypnotic obsession that makes one unable to look at the economy without seeing cycles before the eyes. It leads to the proposition, intended to be a concession to Functional Finance, that it may be all right to iron out the business cycle by inflationary fiscal and monetary policy in the depression and deflationary monetary and fiscal measures in the boom, provided that the deficits of the depression are made up by the surpluses in the boom.

One thing wrong with such formulations is the assumption that the general level of economic activity is just right and all that is necessary is to shift some of the activity of the boom to the depression and all will be well. It would be something of an improvement to have the same average level of employment all the time without the fluctuations, but the greater evil is not in the fluctuations but in the low level of employment when we *average* good times and bad times. What we want is not merely to even out our unemployment over time but to eliminate it.

But the more serious objection to the formulation is that it assumes, apparently quite innocently and unconsciously, that, like the poor, the business cycle will always be with us. It assumes that there will still be a depression and a boom, with deficits in the former and surpluses in the latter—in short, that when we have succeeded we shall still have failed to eliminate the business cycle.

The view that we must have a depression to justify a deficit would permit depression to be alleviated but never cured.

This strange kind of defeatism has its origin in a precursor of Functional Finance called "priming the pump" and is closely connected with the notion of a screw or some other little thing that needs to be tightened. Or perhaps it does not even need to have a screw tightened. It is like a watch that has stalled somehow on dead center and just needs to be shaken to get it going again as good as new. The pump just has to be primed, or started off, and then it will work well.

Functional Finance is not priming the pump. It cannot fit in with the notion that the machine for maintaining prosperity needs only to be pushed and then will go on by itself, because it denies that there is a motor in the machine. Nevertheless it is continually criticized, even when used in the mild manner in which it has so far been used in the United States, as if it were a policy of priming the pump that had not kept the promise that it would not be needed once the pump had been primed and the depression overcome.

The December, 1949, *Monthly Letter* of the National City Bank of New York provides a clear example of this everyday complaint of city editors. The first half of the *Letter* cheerfully comments on the high level of economic activity, current and prospective, after the recession and the pessimistic outlook of the previous year and explains it as mainly due to government deficit spending for military and other purposes. The second half of the *Letter* is a tirade against deficit spending *in a time of prosperity*. The National City Bank is outraged by the admissions of government spokesmen that business and employment are good. Deficits during depressions may be condoned, though not commended, but deficits when prosperity is brazenly admitted. . . ! That is not according to the rules of the game, and dire though vague consequences are threatened.

The rest of the *Letter* is full of very useful and sound information and analysis. It is the self-hypnosis with the business cycle as an eternal category that makes such competent economists, and the businessmen whose thoughts they reflect, put themselves in the position of the patient who thought it sinful to take his vitamins or his insulin except when he was sick. The modern view is that the function of medical treatment is to keep people well and not to condemn the doctor or accuse the doctor of practicing dangerous black magic on the ground that the patient is in good health.

The obsession with business cycles may even lead to an attachment to depressions, crediting them with the benefits of the competition they stifle.

Perhaps the most interesting of the quirks arising from the self-hypnosis of some economists with business cycles is the tendency to attribute to business cycles useful social effects which are really due to competition and which would be enjoyed in a much higher degree if depressions did not operate to kill off competitive attempts to reduce profit margins. As an example of this I can do no better than to quote from Stanley Edgar Hyman in *The New Yorker* of October 27, 1945: [1]

> Our favorite watchdog of public morality, the *Nation,* has been keeping a wary eye on *Opinion and Comment,* the quarterly organ of the College of Commerce and Business Administration of the University of Illinois. Recently it paid off, and the *Nation* reported gleefully that a man named Ralph Blodgett had written an article for the magazine entitled "We Need Those Depressions." It quoted Blodgett as saying:
>
> "It is to be hoped that depressions are never abolished, for they have many desirable features. Those who learn to 'ride the business cycle' can find as many advantages in depressions as in

[1] Reprinted from *The New Yorker* by permission. Copyright, 1945, The New Yorker Magazine, Inc.

booms. . . . That very name 'depression' is inappropriate. It horribly maligns those great periods so full of splendid opportunities. . . . Let us keep those periods but abolish only the name. . . . Some economic research foundation might well offer prizes for suitable names and select the best one."

As far as we know, no research organization has yet offered such a prize, but the idea is a good one. Our suggestion for a name is "blodgetts." We would define a blodgett as "a great period full of splendid opportunities, when the man of the house can get lots of fresh air, exercise, and a chance to know his family better."

Summary.

It is more important to prevent business cycles than to explain them, and it is not unscientific to act to prevent them without knowing the causes of the prevented fluctuations in the level of spending and the causes of these causes and so on.

The study of business cycles shows a degree of stability in the expansions and contractions of the economy, although there is a tendency for these movements to reverse themselves. The business cycles have no regular periods or amplitudes, but it is too much to say that there are no business cycles at all. The business-cycle movements are by their nature unpredictable because successful prediction would destroy the events predicted, nor are booms the cause of following busts.

Much study of business cycles arises from a search for a "loose screw," tightening which would restore to working order a mechanism for the automatic maintenance of full employment. Functional Finance is based on the view that such a mechanism never existed. A more sophisticated approach is an attempt to build a dynamic economic theory which would be superior to equilibrium economic theory. Functional Finance is based on the view that there is no reason to wait for this development, that its success does not appear to be imminent, and that it probably would not be of much help to a full-employment policy although it could be useful for other purposes.

To suppose that it is necessary to know the dynamic inter-relations of all economic events in order to be able to have a full-employment policy is like arguing that it is impossible to ride a bicycle because the mathematical treatment of this project is very difficult. In Functional Finance, as in riding a bicycle, it is sufficient to see the direction in which correction is necessary and to have some notion of the general order of magnitude of the correction. We can rely on the same stability of the system which has made it workable even without Functional Finance.

Obsession with the business cycle leads critics of Functional Finance to assume that booms and depressions continue even when trying to imagine their being eliminated, speaking of what would have to be done in the depression and what in the boom. This defeatism arises in part from a confusion of Functional Finance with priming the pump. It leads to especially angry condemnation of government deficits if they occur in times of prosperity, even when the prosperity is seen to be caused by the deficits. In other cases, obsession with the business cycle has led to many benefits of competition being attributed to depressions.

Part VI

International Aspects

CHAPTER 21

International Trade and Capital Movements

UP TO NOW we have completely disregarded the existence of countries other than our own. But our economy is not closed and completely self-sufficient. We do have economic relations with the rest of the world and we must consider how these would affect our conclusions about Functional Finance or other employment policies. And for other countries international economic relations are much more important than for the United States.

Functional Finance is not affected by the existence of a "foreign-trade industry."

Fundamentally we may say that international economic relations make no difference to the general principles we have been developing right through this book. Foreign trade can be considered as just another industry. The "foreign-trade industry" is the means by which we obtain for our own use goods that are manufactured abroad. The *input* of the foreign-trade industry consists of the effort involved in the manufacture of our exports which can be considered as the raw materials and intermediate products which the foreign-trade industry converts into our imports. The *output* of the foreign-trade industry consists of the imports which it yields to us for our use.

An increase in the output of the foreign-trade industry naturally goes with an increase in its input. If we want more imports we have to sell more of our exports to get more foreign money with which to buy them. At the same time the dollars that we

321

spend on our imports constitute the dollars earned by other countries with which they can buy our exports, and the more dollars we spend on our imports the more dollars they will have to spend in buying our exports. In every industry a greater demand for the output means a greater input of labor and raw materials. In the foreign-trade industry a greater demand for our imports, which are the output or product of our foreign-trade industry, involves more exports, *i.e.,* more input into the foreign-trade industry in the form of labor and raw materials devoted to the manufacture of exports. If we spend more money on our *imports,* this will increase employment in the manufacture of our *exports.*

This may seem to be upset by the possibility of our spending more on our imports than is spent by foreigners on our exports. And conversely there may be more spent on our exports than on our imports. But in this the foreign-trade industry is not different from any other industry. Any industry may spend more on its input of raw materials and factors of production than it receives from the sale of its output of finished products. The difference is called "investment" if it corresponds to accumulated stocks or equipment, and it is called "loss" to the extent that the excess of input over output, or of expenses over revenue, is not so covered. If an industry spends *less* on its input of factors and raw materials than it receives from the sale of its output of product we call the difference disinvestment (if it is due to the reduction of stocks and equipment) or profit.

An export surplus constitutes an investment or a gift.

In the foreign-trade industry an excess of our exports of goods and services over our imports of goods and services, or an "export surplus," is an excess of input over output. This is a sacrifice on our part and constitutes either an investment by this country in the rest of the world or a gift to the rest of the world. Corresponding to the *investment* in accumulated inventories or equipment in a domestic industry is the accumulation of claims on the outside world for that part of our exports which has not been paid for by our imports. Corresponding to the *loss* in a domestic industry is an excess of exports over imports for which there is no claim or obligation outstanding because it was a gift or a loss. (The latter may be considered an involuntary gift, in this case, because, unlike a loss in a domestic industry, from which nobody need gain, a loss in the foreign-trade industry is a benefit to the other side where it appears as imports which are not paid for by exports.) An excess of exports over imports therefore means that we have acquired a claim on (or made a gift to) the rest of the world. The excess of exports over imports may therefore also be called a *capital export*.

All this is seen exactly in reverse by the people in the rest of the world, since their exports constitute our imports and their imports constitute our exports. If we have an export surplus they import more than they export and they enjoy an "import surplus." The output to them by their foreign-trade industry is greater than the input by them. In enjoying this benefit they acquire an *obligation* to us unless we make it a gift. They have a capital import, which, unless it is a gift, constitutes *dis*investment.

If instead of exporting more than we imported we had done the opposite and imported more than we exported the roles would, of course, have been reversed.

An export surplus (an excess of exports over imports) has acquired the name of "a favorable balance of trade," but a favorable balance of trade may not be at all favorable in actuality, and an unfavorable balance of trade (an excess of imports over exports) may be extremely favorable. In 1949, for example, almost the whole world outside the United States wanted to have as unfavorable a balance of trade as possible, because that meant capital imports which would enable them to build up their productive equipment without having to cut so much into their current consumption. The extent to which they could have an unfavorable balance was, however, limited by the degree to which the United

States was willing to have a favorable balance, exporting more than she imported, for the sake of the acquisition of foreign investments or for humanitarian or political reasons.

By means of an export surplus a country can "export unemployment."

In times of general depression and unemployment, however, everything is the other way around. An export surplus, or favorable balance, whether it takes the form of a gift or of a foreign investment, may really seem very favorable because of its effect on employment. It has the same effect on employment as domestic investment. It creates income without providing goods for current domestic consumption. A part of this extra income is spent on consumption goods and this results in more income being earned, so that the multiplier comes into operation, and income increases by several times the export balance.

If there is anything less than full employment any increase in investment increases not merely the money income of the economy but the real income and the volume of employment. An export balance does the same. There is therefore pressure in times of depression for achieving an export balance by restricting imports. If imports are restricted and there is no resulting change in exports, we do have an increase in (foreign) investment and an increase in employment.

Since an export surplus from our point of view is an import surplus from the point of view of the other countries involved, a restriction of our imports will cause them to suffer a *diminution* in foreign investment (or an increase in foreign *dis*investment) and a decrease in their real income and employment. This decrease is equal to their import surplus multiplied by their multiplier. The total effect is that by means of the import restriction and the resulting export surplus we have *exported some of our unemployment* to other countries. Naturally they do not like this.

The amount of additional unemployment suffered in the other

countries need not be exactly equal to the reduction in our own unemployment. Although their import surplus must be exactly equal to our export surplus, their multiplier may be different from ours so that they may have a smaller or a larger change in income. There may also be a different relationship between income and employment in the other countries—it may take more people or fewer people to earn the same income. But the reduction in their income and employment will be of about the same order of magnitude as the increase in our own so that we may expect them to take some measures to defend themselves from an unfavorable balance of trade when it takes the form of our dumping our unemployment on them.

Exporting unemployment invites retaliation.

The most obvious thing for them to do is to retaliate by imposing tariffs or other restrictions on their imports from us. If this cuts our exports by as much as we have cut our imports, they have no import surplus, we have no export surplus, and none of our unemployment is exported. The unemployment situation is the same as if neither we nor they had restricted imports, but both we and they are poorer. Output per man employed is less because some of the international trade has been cut off. Both we and they are reduced to making domestically items that can be obtained more economically via international trade or to doing without some of them altogether.

But even if the other countries impose no restrictions on their imports, our exports will have to be cut if we cut our imports, simply because the other countries will be getting fewer dollars for their exports with which to buy our exports. They cannot buy more from us than we buy from them; that is to say, they cannot have an import balance (and we an export balance) unless in one way or another we lend them or give them the additional dollars they will need to pay for the difference. (They may acquire some dollars by selling off their foreign assets.)

This granting of gifts or loans is another aspect of the capital export that is implied in an export surplus. This is also the way in which an international obligation is more real than an obligation within a nation. Our export surplus means that the other countries are able to consume and invest more than they produce, we providing the wherewithal by our unrequited exports. If they should ever have to repay the debts or pay interest on the debts, they would then have to export more than they import. They would then have to consume and invest less than they are producing while we would be able to do the opposite. They would have to tighten their belts while we could let ours out.

We can export some of our unemployment only if we are in the upside-down economy of unemployment and furthermore only to the extent that we give or lend the outside world the dollars with which to buy the excess of our imports over our exports. In the same upside-down world the other countries would object to our making these gifts or loans to them because that would entail the exporting of some of our unemployment to them. They would resist by imposing restrictions on their imports (which are our exports) by tariffs, by import quotas, by foreign-exchange controls, and by many other less direct interferences with trade. We would have the futile struggle of each country trying to export more than it imported, trying to give away more goods than it receives in the attempt to export some of its unemployment. Naturally there can be no general success in an enterprise of this kind. Total exports cannot be greater than total imports. The only certain result is the indirect damage done to all by the reduction in the volume of and in the benefits from international division of labor.

It is not true that capitalism must "export or die."

Such scrambling by countries trying to shift their unemployment onto each other in times of general depression has given rise to the Marxist notion that a capitalist country must export more than it imports if it is to be in a state of health. The slogan is that a capitalist economy must "export or die." But the basis for the whole conception is the continuance of the upside-down depression economy. It is always possible for any country to create the necessary spending for prosperity without going in for foreign investment. It can always go in for domestic investment. And even if there are no useful domestic investments, completely useless domestic pretended investment, like employing men to dig holes in the ground and then to fill them up again, would be just as effective in maintaining domestic employment as producing the most useful things for foreigners to consume.

Nor would it even then be necessary to indulge in such foolish pretended investment. All the beneficial effects on employment can be brought about by the same spending on consumption. The production of consumption goods provides employment in the same way as the production of investment goods or of exports. There are the same repercussions, via the multiplier. And there is never any lack of need or desire for some consumption goods or services by some section of the population. The idea that a country can cure unemployment *only* by developing an export surplus is completely baseless unless the society has developed a taboo against every other way of increasing the level of spending. Unfortunately some societies have shown a tendency to be influenced by just such taboos, but then it is the taboo which says that the country must export or suffer depression and not the capitalist system, which does not in any way depend on the observance of the taboo.

There are countries which indeed must export or die because only by exporting can they get the foreign currencies that they need in order to be able to buy essential imports. But the real necessity is for *imports;* the exports are only the means of obtaining the imports. It would be more correct to say that a densely populated industrial country that cannot produce its own foodstuffs must "import or die." It must export in order to be able to import its food and raw materials, unless, that is, there are other countries who are so convinced of *their* need to export that they are willing to send the food and raw materials without asking for anything in return.

The "export or die" myth both helps and discredits rehabilitation plans.

The Marshall Plan of economic help by the United States to certain European countries is supported by some people who are not very keen about helping Europe but believe that the Marshall Plan exports are necessary for prosperity in the United States. Many Europeans also hold the belief that the Marshall Plan exports are necessary for American prosperity and this belief is exploited by the communists in their endeavor to poison any friendly feelings toward the United States by the European populations who benefit from the Marshall Plan. When they fail to persuade the beneficiaries that the Marshall Plan is an evil trick by which the American imperialists are enslaving and exploiting them, they fall back on argument that the Europeans, by permitting the Americans to send them the Marshall aid, are doing a greater service to the Americans than the Americans are doing to them. By enabling the Americans to export more than they are importing they are saving the American economy from being choked by its excessive productivity.

It is hardly necessary to point out that the same effects on the American economy could be produced by dumping the excess exports in the Atlantic or in the Pacific or anywhere in between or more simply still by permitting the producers of the exported goods to enjoy themselves on vacations with pay instead of making these goods to be destroyed or given away. There are very good reasons in terms both of morality and of expediency why the United States should help the poorer European (and other) economies to recover and rebuild their economies. It is not necessary to add to these the false argument that the favorable balance or export surplus is necessary for the health of the American economy. This argument is no sounder when it is used by advocates of the Marshall Plan to help and establish world peace and prosperity than when it is used by agents of Russian imperialism in the "hate America" campaign. But as long as we in this country are influenced by taboos against making use of alternative devices for maintaining domestic prosperity, the unwarranted belief that an export surplus is good for us can provide political support for two extremely worth-while objectives: the maintenance of prosperity in the United States and the provision of the economic help which we owe to our poorer neighbors and which will yield us rich dividends in strengthening the free world against Russian totalitarianism.

Group interests exploit the employment promises of protectionism.

We have been considering the Marshall Plan here because of its relationship to the argument that export surpluses are helpful or even necessary for the maintenance of high employment. While protectionists pleading for tariffs on imports often argue that the protection would help the employment situation by creating an export surplus, there are many other causes of protectionism. Behind almost every proposal for a tariff or quota or any other restriction on imports there is some special group interest which would be enabled by the limitation on foreign competition to charge their fellow citizens a higher price for something or other. The higher price paid by the buyers is enjoyed only in part by the domestic producers, since much of this is lost in the higher costs of our producing goods which can be produced more efficiently abroad. (If they could not be produced relatively more efficiently abroad it would not have been worth while importing them in the first place.) There must be added to this the further loss by those buyers who cut out or reduce their purchases of the commodity in question because of the higher price. The losers by the restriction must therefore lose more than the gainers gain.

The rest of the world of course also suffers in the same way from the reduction in the volume of foreign trade.

There is an exception to this general rule that both we and the rest of the world must lose from our restrictions on international trade. This is where our restriction, by limiting the market for our imports, results in such a lowering of the prices we pay for the imports we still buy relative to the prices we get for our exports that this improvement in our "terms of trade" more than offsets the loss described above. In such a case, however, other countries will be suffering the loss not only from the reduction in the amount of trade but also from the worsening of *their* terms of trade. If our imports have become cheaper relatively to our exports, their imports have become *dearer* relatively to their exports in exactly the same proportion. This double loss is practically certain to cause them to retaliate and then it will be quite certain that both we and they have lost by the restriction in trade.

Full employment would give free trade a fair chance.

For two centuries economists have fought against restrictions on trade but without any lasting success. In explanation of their failure they have pointed to the greater political effectiveness of the small groups of producers who gain from particular restrictions as compared with the diffused and unorganized consumers who lose more than the producers gain but who do not apply so much pressure on legislators as the lobbies maintained by the interested producers. There is undoubtedly much truth in this explanation, but there is another element which seems to be even more important. That is the absence of a full-employment policy, so that even in times of prosperity there was always the fear of depression and unemployment.

In an atmosphere of unemployment and fear of unemployment the lobbies maintained by the interested groups can make the proposals for tariffs and other restrictions on imports look much more respectable. They can argue with much greater plausibility that they are concerned not for the extra profits to be made by their employers by charging higher prices to other citizens, but for the maintenance of a higher level of domestic employment. The protection is made to look like the protection of employment rather than the protection of profits. And this is what is responsible for the general support given to measures that impoverish the community. It is naturally just another aspect of the upside-down economy of depression, and this is why restrictions on imports proliferate most rapidly when there is a decrease in economic activity and employment.

If there is full employment and the expectation of the continuation of full employment the protectionist lobbies cannot use this camouflage. There is then not a shortage of jobs but a shortage of goods. It becomes apparent to everybody that the economy cannot be benefited by preventing foreign supplies from helping out. The selfish endeavors are seen for what they are. With the establishment of a full-employment policy there are prospects of this part of our economy also being put right side up and the whole world benefited by the abolition of all restrictions on international trade.

Functional Finance is proof against foreign depressions.

But will not a full-employment policy by a single country be spoiled by what happens in other countries? Will not a depression, for instance, originating in some other part of the world necessarily bring about a depression in our country despite Functional Finance?

The answer is a categorical no. By Functional Finance we can always maintain adequate dollar spending on the goods we are engaged in making for ourselves. There can never be any reason for our doing without things we can make for ourselves just because there is something wrong in some other part of the world. And if there is prosperity in the industries catering for the domestic market there can be no general depression in the economy as a whole. We may have difficulties in the export industries if for any reason the foreigners will not or cannot buy our exports, but that is quite a different thing from having to suffer from depression in the industries that produce for domestic consumption.

Foreign depressions can, however, invade our land if we permit them to frighten us away from Functional Finance. And there is a real danger of just this happening.

If there is a depression abroad and we maintain prosperity at home we shall find ourselves with an import balance. The depressed foreigners will not be able to afford to buy so much of our exports, but we, continuing to be prosperous, shall be able to continue to buy our imports (which are their exports) as before. We shall be checking the depression abroad by keeping their export trades in a flourishing condition. We shall not be getting enough foreign currency in payment for our shrunken exports to be able to pay for our healthy imports, but for as long as the depressed countries are willing to lend us the difference there need be no further repercussions. They will be investing the difference in claims on this country, and this investment, which constitutes a capital export by them to us, will operate, in conjunction with their multiplier, to increase their level of employment and national income, checking the severity of their depression.

Functional Finance dissolves any "imported unemployment."

They will in fact be exporting some of their unemployment, but here it is dissolved, without harm to our economy, by our exercise of Functional Finance. Our capital import (which is what the capital export by the depressed countries is from our point of view) is indeed a disinvestment and would by itself cause depression and unemployment in a measure multiplied by our own multiplier. But Functional Finance does not permit this.

Other investment or consumption is increased to offset the dis-investment and so to prevent any depression from emerging.

This is not to say that our economy is not damaged at all by the depression in other countries. We are damaged. There is a reduction in employment in our export industry, and although we make it easy for the workers displaced there to find employment elsewhere in our economy, they are not likely to be as efficient or to be able to earn as much in the alternative occupations. Some of them may even be unsuitable for any other kind of work and remain unemployed for a while. But as long as the other countries are willing, by giving us credits, to maintain their exports to us while their imports from us are kept down by their depression, there is no need for our country to suffer at all from the depression abroad. We can continue to keep paying the wages and salaries of the men who are displaced from producing the exports which the outside world now cannot afford to consume, and anything that these displaced workers can contribute to the production of things for our own consumption or investment is a net profit for us as far as the immediate effects are concerned.

In the longer run we must take into account the effect of our getting into debt to the rest of the world. This means a net reduction in our wealth. Even if we were to direct all the displaced workers into increasing our capital equipment to increase our wealth we would be less wealthy in the end because the displaced workers and other resources were probably more efficient in the production of exports than in anything else. They would produce less if employed in the production of additions to our capital equipment even if they should minimize this loss by choosing the alternative occupation in which they are relatively most efficient and letting those factors be released for the purpose of making the investments which would do this most effectively.

But there is no need to worry much about this particular manifestation of the damage done to our economy by the existence of depression abroad, because it is not likely that we would for very long be able to enjoy such an import balance financed by the depressed economies abroad. We are more likely, with our greater prosperity, to want to give than to take credits. Our exporters, in attempts to maintain their exports in a depressed market, are more likely to offer extended credits than are their exporters to us, for their exporters will be doing pretty well. And unless the principles of Functional Finance have been very thoroughly absorbed in this country, any attempts by the governments of other countries to sustain their export surplus (for the sake of checking their depression) by giving us credits in one form or another are likely to be resisted by competitors in this country as unfair competition.

Depression abroad depreciates our currency and reduces our foreign trade.

If the depressed countries do not finance our import surplus there will be a scarcity of their currencies. We shall want to spend just as much as before on our imports, but the amount of foreign currency available to us is limited by the amount that the foreigners are paying for their imports from us, and this is reduced by their depression. The natural result is for the prices of foreign currencies to rise as the demand for them exceeds the supply. As the foreign currencies become more expensive, we are discouraged from importing so much because the cost to us of our imports rises in the same proportion as the appreciation of the foreign currency. At the same time the appreciation of the foreign currencies appears to the foreigners as a depreciation of the dollar and this makes our goods cheaper for them to buy. It takes less of their money to get the dollars needed to pay for any item imported from us. The result of the appreciation of the foreign currencies (which is the same thing as the depreciation of the dollar) is an increase in our exports and a decrease in our imports. As long as we still have an import balance there will still be a shortage of foreign currency. The exchange movement will therefore continue until the import balance disappears. Our imports will fall and our exports will rise until they are equal to each other.

In this situation both the imports and the exports will be less than they were before the depression hit the foreign countries. We shall be importing and exporting less than before. This is the way the depression abroad affects us. Economically the depressed countries are now shrunken. We cannot do as much trade with them when they are depressed as when they are prosperous, and consequently we cannot gain as much from international trade. We have to make some things for ourselves that we could have got on better terms via the "foreign-trade industry." Our export industry will have to be contracted and will meanwhile be depressed, but the industries competing with our imports will be correspondingly expanded. There is no need for our economy as a whole to suffer any of the depression that may be raging in foreign parts.

Alternatives to depreciation are deflation, import restrictions, and depression.

There is no need for us to participate in the depression, that is, *if we are willing to permit the dollar to depreciate* as just described. But if we are not willing to permit the dollar to be depreciated this kind of adjustment is ruled out. We cannot prevent the dollar from being depreciated as long as our demand for imports exceeds the demand for our exports. As long as this is the case the supply of dollars (which is the demand for foreign currency to pay for our imports) will exceed the demand for dollars (by the foreigners who offer foreign currency for the dollars they need to pay for our exports) and the dollar will depreciate. We can prevent the dollar from depreciating only by somehow preventing the demand for imports from exceeding the demand for our exports.

There are three ways of doing this. The first way is to bring about a reduction in our domestic prices, money wages, and money incomes (without reducing the real employment and real income). If these are reduced in the same proportion as the dollar would have to be depreciated to eliminate the import balance there would be the same effects on our imports and our exports. Our imports, though unchanged in price, would be *relatively* more expensive when compared with our lower wages, prices, and incomes, just as in the case of the depreciated dollar. Our exports would be just as much cheaper to the foreigner. It is just the same to him whether our prices are reduced while the dollar is maintained or our prices are maintained but the dollar is depreciated.

The second way is to impose governmental restrictions on our imports. Tariffs or quotas or restrictions on international payments or other ways of interfering with our imports can reduce our effective demand for imports to the level of the reduced demand for our exports.

The third way is for us to bring about sufficient depression in our country to cause demand for imports to fall as much as demand for our exports has fallen.

Depression may be suffered as a means of inducing deflation.

The least objectionable of the three is the first. It would have no harmful effects at all. It would permit the enjoyment of full employment as well as the enjoyment of unrestricted international trade with the maximization to everybody of the benefits therefrom. The only difficulty is that it is not feasible. The extreme wage and price flexibility needed for this solution does not exist (and would be very dangerous to economic stability if it could be brought about). The only known way in which the reduction in money wages and prices can be obtained in a modern democratic society is to have a very serious depression for a long time. Such a depression would constitute the third method of preventing the depreciation of the dollar and could perform this service until the money wages, prices, and money incomes are reduced by the required amount. This third method is clearly the most objectionable of the three. It is more objectionable than the second method—imposition of restrictions on imports of one kind or another—which would permit domestic prosperity to be maintained though with an additional diminution in the volume of international trade and in the benefits that all parties can derive from it.

It seems difficult to believe that anyone would make use of the third method—sacrificing prosperity for the sake of maintaining the international value of a currency—but that is just about what was done by Great Britain from 1925 to 1931, when monetary policy directed at preventing the outflow of gold which would force a depreciation of the pound sterling maintained a severe depression in Great Britain with 2 to 3 million unemployed.

In this situation the second method is a lesser evil than the third. J. M. Keynes, who like all respectable economists, had been a free trader all his life, nevertheless suggested that, granted the desirability for political prestige or other reasons for maintaining the international value of the pound sterling, Great Britain should make use of the second method and impose a revenue tariff which would permit full employment within the country without the excessive demand for imports. The import balance was in this case caused not by depression in the rest of the world but by the loss of foreign markets and in income from foreign investments as a result of World War I, but the effects are just the same as those we have analyzed in this chapter.

Keynes' "revenue tariff" would not have done any more harm to other countries than the actual policy which was being followed of preventing the depreciation of the pound by fostering a depression in Great Britain. The demand for imports would have been just as great with the "revenue tariff" and full employment in Great Britain as it was without the revenue tariff and with depression in Great Britain. But the proposal was not put into effect until the pound had been devalued and all the good reasons for it were no longer valid.

Only if we abandon Functional Finance in endeavoring to resist depreciation do we get into serious trouble.

The first solution, which would be harmless, is impossible and the other two are harmful to prosperity or to international co-operation. But there is no real need for despair because the whole problem arises only if there is a compulsion to prevent the natural depreciation of the currency. If we can get rid of this compulsion we can achieve all the desirable effects, maintain prosperity, *and* continue to make the best use of the international division of labor by following the extremely simple procedure of doing nothing at all and letting the foreign value of the currency move to its natural level.

If we would only concentrate on maintaining domestic full employment no matter what happens to the foreign value of our money we can take advantage of the existence of this easy alternative method of reaching equilibrium. Instead of adjusting our whole structure of wages, prices, and incomes, which can be adjusted only through a long and severe depression, and suffering the domestic inconveniences and injustices that a change in the price level causes between debtors and creditors, we can simply let the foreign value of our currency find its own level.

Such a disregard of the rate of foreign exchange encounters very strong resistances of various kinds and some of these will be considered in the next chapter. If we do disregard the value of our foreign exchange we can apply Functional Finance just as well in an economy that has economic relations with other countries as in a closed economy. It is only if we put the maintenance of some established value of our currency in terms of foreign currencies above the prevention of domestic inflation and depression that we can run into serious trouble, and if at the same time we refuse to offset a decrease in the demand for our exports by other measures for decreasing our demand for our imports, we are forced to bring about the balance by engineering a depression in our own country. The excuse that this is forced on us by the foreign depression is very thin.

We have considered the difficulties arising from a depression abroad. A tendency for the currency of a country to depreciate can be caused by other things too. An excess of the supply of our currency over the demand for it may be the result of a fall in foreign demand for our exports or an increase in our demand for some imported item instead of something produced domestically. It may be the result of capital exports, residents of our country exchanging their dollars for other currencies in order to invest them abroad, foreigners being repaid capital invested by them in this country, or residents emigrating to other countries taking their property with them and exchanging their dollars for foreign currencies. No matter what the cause of the tendency for the dollar to depreciate, all the effects we have been considering in this chapter are the same as when the tendency to depreciation is due to a depression abroad.

We may be damaged in many ways by these occurrences. We may be made poorer. We may lose some of the benefits of foreign trade. We may lose from changes in the terms of trade against us, the prices of our exports falling relatively to the price of our imports, so that we have to work harder and yet have a lower standard of living. But unless we are frightened away from Functional Finance by one taboo or another there is no need for us to suffer any general depression. The danger is only that strange as it may seem we might find ourselves *engineering* depressions as a means of preventing currency depreciations.

Summary.

In an open economy foreign trade can be considered as the industry that produces imports, our exports being the input of the foreign-trade industry. As in any other industry an excess of input over output constitutes either investment or loss, and an excess of output over input constitutes disinvestment or profit.

Investment also appears as export surplus, as a loan or gift to foreigners, and as a capital export. What is a loss in other industries is a gift in the case of the foreign-trade industry because our export surplus is an import surplus for other countries, so that what we lose they gain. Everything is reversed from the foreigner's point of view. An export surplus is also called a "favorable balance of trade" although it may be far from favorable in reality.

If we restrict our imports and thereby create an export surplus or foreign investment this increases domestic employment in the same way that domestic investment does. For the other countries this appears as an import balance or as foreign *dis*investment which similarly reduces employment. The result is that we export some of our unemployment, and we may expect the other countries to retaliate by restricting their imports (which are our exports). The net result is mutual impoverishment.

Unemployment can be exported only to the extent that a country exports goods and gets nothing back for them in return. This makes sense only in the upside-down world of depression, but on it is based the Marxist notion that a capitalist economy must "export or die." A full-employment policy based on domestic spending is just as easy and foreign investment is unnecessary for prosperity. Some countries must import or die, but there is never any need to have an export surplus for economic health. The belief that we must is no sounder when it is used by well-meaning but confused people to support the Marshall Plan for rehabilitation and world peace than when it is used by the communists to discredit American generosity.

Protectionism is usually fostered by groups who gain much less from it than other fellow citizens lose from it. Even in the exceptional case where the country as a whole gains from protection by reason of an improvement in the terms of trade, retaliation is almost certain to turn the country's net gain into a net loss. The failure of economists to persuade nations that they lose by protection is largely due to the existence of depression and fear of depression and the idea that jobs rather than profits are being protected. With the establishment of a full-employment policy this item may also be put right side up.

Depression in other parts of the world cannot spread to our economy as long as we practice Functional Finance in our domestic economy. Even if foreign countries develop an export balance and export some of their unemployment to us it would be dissolved here by our use of Functional Finance. We would be able to *increase* our real income although by less than the indebtedness that we would be incurring in the capital imports.

The foreign countries cannot, however, be expected to continue to maintain their export balance. In the absence of their export balance their currency will appreciate (and ours depreciate). A new equilibrium will be reached in which we gain less than before from international trade, but we need not suffer any general depression. But if we refuse to allow our dollar to depreciate we may be frightened away from Functional Finance and then we will find that the depression has invaded our land.

We can prevent the dollar from depreciating if we reduce our imports to the level of our reduced exports. We can do this by import restrictions, by deflation (reducing the price and money level), or by depression. Deflation can usually be achieved only after a long and serious depression. Depression is much more harmful than import restriction but may, as in England in 1925–1931, be the result of refusing to permit the currency to depreciate.

If we do not worry about the possible depreciation of the dollar, however, we do not get into these troubles. We can then maintain domestic prosperity by the same rules of Functional Finance as a closed economy. This applies also where there is a tendency for the currency to depreciate for any other reason. Changes in the outside world may reduce our income or our wealth in various ways, but unless we are needlessly frightened away from Functional Finance, we can always maintain domestic full employment.

CHAPTER 22

International Currency
or Sentimental Internationalism

"FIRE," SAYS the ancient proverb, "is a good servant but a bad master." This is true not only of fire but of every instrument that has been devised for helping man to achieve his ends. But when the use of some instrument becomes habitual, one tends to forget the purposes for which it was established, the means usurps the status of the end, and we often have the end itself sacrificed to the means originally devised to serve it.

Foreign-exchange stabilization has become a fetish.

The elevation of a means to an end may constitute the basis for the tragedy of fanaticism or idolatry. In the personal sphere we see this human aberration in the extravagances of the miser who has forgotten that accumulation was for the purpose of enriching and anchoring a better life and he sacrifices life to accumulation or the fresh-air fiend or the hypochondriac who sacrifice health and comfort to the oxygen or the warmth which at the proper time and in the proper amount could serve to increase health and comfort. In the national economy we have seen it in the elevation of the *device* of budgeting from an instrument which has a part to play in economic health to a *principle* of balancing the budget at whose feet the very health of the economy may be offered up as a pious sacrifice. In the international economic field a similar deification has overtaken the principle of fixing or stabilizing the international exchange rates between the currencies of different countries.

Soon after World War II the Bretton Woods agreements established the International Monetary Fund as part of a scheme for determining the exchange rates between most of the national currencies. In the initiating discussions almost everybody declared the primary purpose to be the establishment of stable exchange rates.

In the course of the negotiations several provisions were written in, permitting countries to devalue their currencies to a limited extent and providing for permission to be given by the authorities of the International Monetary Fund for further changes in the rate of exchange of a country in case of "fundamental disequilibrium." Since the signing of the agreement several countries have devalued otherwise than provided for by the agreements, while the authorities have found it necessary to say nothing about such *faits accomplis*. But these flexibilities, legal as well as illegal, are contrary to the expressed philosophies of most of the writers on the subject, including the preambles to all of the original proposals out of which the agreement was constructed. The expressed philosophy was to put the stabilization of the exchange rates and the prevention of competitive currency depreciation very high among the objectives and in many cases right at the very top.

Perhaps the clearest of these expressions, though not in the least untypical, was Professor Jacob Viner's. He declared that

> There is at least one monetary principle, however, on which almost all persons who believe in international economic collaboration would now agree. Exchange rates are properly matters of international concern. They should not be fixed unilaterally by particular countries regardless of their consequences for other countries. Above all they should not be deliberately manipulated either as weapons of economic aggression or as beggar my neighbor instruments of economic defense.[1]

Professor Viner goes on to clinch the matter with a quotation from the most eminent authority possible.[2]

[1] "Two Plans for International Monetary Stabilization," *Yale Review,* Autumn, 1943.

[2] *Ibid.*

Alfred Marshall, the great English economist, writing in 1887 at the heyday of Victorian utopianism, forecast that "the time will come at which it will be thought as unreasonable for any country to regulate its currency without reference to other countries as it will be to have signalling codes at sea which took no account of the signalling codes at sea of other countries." That time has not come yet. As recently as 1932 it was stated as a matter of course by an international conference, the Stresa Conference, that "decisions touching upon monetary policy belong exclusively to the sovereignty of each country." But if the postwar world is to handle its monetary problems satisfactorily the Stresa doctrine must give way to the Marshallian one.

In the light of this axiom the essential nature of the original intention of the International Monetary Fund is clear to see. It was to be a device for getting sovereign nations, in exchange for international credits, to give up their power over their rates of exchange so that these could be adjusted only in accordance with the rules of the Fund. The facts of life have already dealt rather cavalierly with these intentions, but the same basic doctrine is still to be found in almost all respectable financial journals repeated *ad nauseam* as a self-evident axiom.

The basic condition for international economic cooperation is not fixed exchange rates but economic prosperity.

Nevertheless the axiom is false. It is not true that the stabilization of foreign exchanges is essential or even helpful for international economic cooperation. Like other "self-evident truths" the axiom is acceptable only as long as one does not think of questioning it. When we do question it and ask what is the purpose of exchange stabilization we are reminded that the primary purpose is facilitation of international economic cooperation and we become aware of the danger of international economic cooperation being sacrificed on the altar of the cult of exchange stabilization. What we need, to take the place of the axiom, is a scientific statement of the proper place of exchange stabilization in any international arrangements, agreements, or organizations that are directed toward increasing or facilitating international economic cooperation.

The first condition for the success of any such endeavor is that national policies for maintaining full employment are helped and not hindered. Just as Functional Finance must not be hindered nationally by considerations like the balancing of the budget, so it must not be hindered internationally by the necessity of maintaining some specific foreign-exchange rate.

One reason for this condition is simply that no country can be relied upon to sacrifice domestic prosperity for the sake of maintaining foreign-exchange rates even if that were necessary for greater international economic cooperation. But, as we shall see, just the opposite is fortunately the case. Concentration by a country on domestic full employment never *has to* take a form that interferes with international economic cooperation. No other country need be hurt by a country's concentration on domestic prosperity and stability. In fact, the sacrifice of domestic prosperity for the sake of exchange stability could only diminish and endanger the degree of international economic cooperation.

Given the maintenance of domestic prosperity in the different countries, the first objective of international economic arrangements is the freeing of international trade from restrictions of all kinds, quotas, tariffs, exchange controls, and the rest, so that there can be the greatest benefit all around from the international division of labor. Second is the freeing of international payments from bureaucratic interference. Third, and this is a necessary condition for the second point, is the prevention of excessive disturbances to national economies from sudden flights of capital. Fourth is the convenience to business of having foreign-exchange rates that are expected to remain stable.

The stability of the exchanges is last in this list because the other items are all more important than this convenience. Some of them are so much more important that a policy which endangers them for the sake of the maintenance of exchange stability is explicable only in terms of the unthinking acceptance of an axiom or dogma. But exchange stability *has* become a cult whose devil is exchange depreciation and whose archdevil is "competitive exchange depreciation."

The cult of exchange-rate fixing rests largely on a sentimental internationalism.

The convenience of fixed exchanges consists in the importer or exporter being saved the trouble of worrying about possible losses (or gains) on account of a change in the value of a foreign currency when a payment has to be made in a few weeks' or months' time. This inconvenience cannot at the most be more troublesome than the bother of a simple and inexpensive hedging or insurance operation. It is clear that the convenience to some traders of not needing to undertake hedging transactions in connection with some of their international transactions cannot be the reason for the tremendous popularity of exchange stabilization. Some other explanation must be sought.

First in the explanation of this cult is the sentimental feeling that any international organization is "a good thing." This is associated with the notion that a single international money is desirable, if impracticable, as a step toward "one world." The next best thing is to have firmly established rates of exchange between the different currencies so that, for the purposes of international payments at least, one currency can be translated into another as confidently as dimes can be translated into dollars. This is indeed just what the old gold standard did. For a century it succeeded in linking the currencies of the major countries by fixing the values of different currencies in terms of gold and so, indirectly, in terms of each other.

But this is sentimental and not practical internationalism. It does not contribute to the ends which are really important. Any scheme which does this, such as the gold standard or the

International Monetary Fund, says in effect that if there is any change in the world economy which would naturally be corrected by a shift in the relative value of the different currencies, this shift is prohibited and some other way must be found of making the adjustment.

For example, suppose that everything has been going smoothly when one country suddenly finds that the foreign demand for some of its exports has fallen. The American demand for, say, French wine is undermined by advertisements for Coca-Cola so that the demand for francs (by American wine importers who have to pay the French wine growers in French francs) is less than before. The natural result is that the franc falls in terms of the dollar. This will have the effect of making all French goods cheaper to Americans, and so Americans will buy more of other French goods. At the same time the fall of the franc will mean in France that all imported goods are more expensive—more francs must be paid out for each dollar's worth of imports—and so the French will tend to substitute domestically produced goods for their imports. In this way the situation is straightened out. France imports less and exports more of other goods. France loses from the decreased demand for her wines, but her loss is limited to the inevitable deterioration in the terms on which she can obtain imports in return for her exports.

Price and income deflation could substitute for currency depreciation.

But if the gold standard or the International Monetary Fund does not permit the franc to depreciate, this solution is not available. When the demand for francs falls below the supply, the franc does indeed begin to fall, but the fall is checked almost immediately. If the gold standard is in operation the fall is stopped at the "gold export point." At this point gold dealers find it profitable to take the excess of francs off the market, exchange them for gold at the French Treasury at the French fixed gold standard parity, ship the gold to the United States, and there sell it to the United States Treasury at the United States fixed gold standard parity. They can get more dollars for francs in this way than at the market rate, and the difference is profit. Thus there arises a flow of gold from France to the United States.

The theory of the gold standard was that the decrease of gold in France leads to a decrease in France in the amount of money based on gold. This leads to a fall in French prices and then Americans buy more of the cheaper French goods. The French themselves, whose money incomes have fallen, prefer to buy cheaper domestically produced goods instead of imported goods because these have not become any cheaper and so are dearer *relatively* to the French goods. This second method sets things right in exactly the same way as the decline of the franc. French goods are relatively cheaper for the American. It makes no difference to him whether this is because he gets more francs for each dollar or because he gets more French goods for each franc. American goods are relatively dearer for the Frenchman and it makes no difference to him whether this is because he has to pay more francs for each dollar or because the prices of French goods have gone down and his income in francs has gone down with them, so that he has fewer francs, each having a greater value in France, with which to buy dollars. (At the same time the inflow of gold into the United States is supposed to raise prices and incomes in the United States so that there is a double reason for the Americans to increase their purchases in France and for the French to reduce their purchases in the United States.)

With prices not perfectly flexible, exchange rigidity can cause depressions.

If this second method of adjusting to the decrease in the demand for French exports worked as smoothly as might be supposed from this account, there would be no disadvantages to off-set the conveniences of having a fixed rate of exchange between the franc and the dollar. Unfortunately it does not work anything like so smoothly. The outflow of gold from France does not automatically reduce French prices in general. What it does is to reduce the level of economic activity in France and it is the reduction in the level of activity that tends to reduce prices. But prices, wages, and incomes are not easily reduced. There is great resistance to their reduction. And all the gold in France could be exported before there is much impression on the wage, price, and money income level. If the gold is all gone the franc could no longer be maintained at the old parity with gold and with the dollar and we would have the first kind of adjustment after all. But that is not what is intended on the gold standard, and when the French monetary authorities notice that there is an outflow of gold and a danger of their finding themselves off the gold standard simply by virtue of having no more gold, they engage in ways and means of checking the gold flow.

These ways and means consist essentially of stepping up the decline in economic activity in France. By raising the rate of interest, balancing the budget if it was unbalanced, raising tax rates, and reducing government spending in any case, a more severe state of depression is brought about. This depression, by making the French too poor to spend more on imports than they are receiving for their exports, eliminates the export balance. There is then no tendency for the franc to fall in relation to the dollar, it is no longer profitable to send gold from France to the United States, and the outflow of gold is cured.

Practical internationalism is hindered *by the elimination of exchange flexibility.*

It is of course not intended to have this depression as a permanent solution. It is hoped that after a while the depression will have the effect of reducing wages and prices and money incomes, and when that has come about there will no longer be any need for the depression. Nevertheless it takes even a severe depression a long time to have the required effect on wages, prices, and incomes, and until this is achieved it is necessary to suffer the depression. A secondary result of this depression is a reduction in the degree of international cooperation and a sharpening of international conflict in the endeavors of the different countries affected to export the unemployment to each other. An international gold standard which prevents the easy adjustment of the exchange rates hinders rather than helps practical internationalism.

The International Monetary Fund does not work very differently from the gold standard. International credits and balances with the Fund take the place of gold. One of the inducements to get countries to join the Fund was the offer of quotas of international credits which would permit a country to maintain its exchange rate just as if it has so much gold to bolster it with under the gold standard. But a country running out of credits would have to take the same steps to prevent its quotas from being exhausted that it takes to prevent its gold reserves from being exhausted. It would have to undertake the same kind of domestic restrictions and reduce the level of domestic economic activity and employment in undertaking the second method of adjustment—adjustment via a depression to reduce wages, prices, and money incomes.

This depression, which is necessary as part of the mechanism of the second method of adjustment, may last a very long time before it has the required effect on wages, prices, and money incomes. Meanwhile it can spread to other countries and lead to countless harmful repercussions, economic and political, until the original problem of adjustment has been lost in the general catastrophe. Clearly it is much more reasonable to let the adjustment take the form of a depreciation of the franc in terms of dollars (and other national currencies) than to force a similar fall in all the domestic French prices. The adjustment of the foreign value of the franc is easy and immediate. The adjustment of all French incomes and prices comes up against tremendous frictions and dangers to economic stability. We have to choose between the stability of the economy and the stability or rather *rigidity* of the rate of exchange.[3]

Fixity of exchanges does not protect investments in foreign trade.

In the face of these frictions enthusiasm for currency rigidity would soon wane if it rested on sentimental internationalism alone. But the cult of exchange rigidity is also supported by the belief that rigid exchanges safeguard foreign investments and investments in industries working for export. Such investments are subject to great loss in the event of depreciation of the currency of the country in which the investment is made or for which the exports are intended. It is not practical to insure against these losses by hedging against exchange depreciation. But it is hoped that rigid exchanges would protect such investments and in this way increase the level of international economic cooperation. Unfortunately, adopting the hard way of making adjustments to changes in international conditions (by keeping the exchanges fixed and forcing the adjustments onto domestic wages, prices, and incomes) does not improve matters at all.

If there is a general fall in French prices and incomes the products of the American export industries will be just as much beyond the reach of the French consumers as when the franc goes down (and the dollar goes up) in the same proportion. And if the

[3] Stability is not quite the right word to describe the maintenance of the foreign value of a currency at some established level, especially as it contributes to *instability* of economic activity, employment, and real income— indeed of our whole social order. Rather should it be called exchange *rigidity*. Both words refer to the failure of some quantity to change. If we regard this as desirable we usually call it a stability and if we regard it as a nuisance, *e.g.*, if prices refuse to change when we believe that a change in them would be beneficial, we speak of rigidity. Since a fixity of the exchange rates means that an easy adjustment is prevented from taking place and a difficult and painful one must be suffered instead, enthusiasm for fixed exchange rates should perhaps rather be called the cult of exchange *rigidity*.

prices in France refuse to fall the attempt to make them fall means a depression in France that is cold comfort to the American exporter. He will still be unable to sell his goods in France, but now it will be because his customers are unemployed or going bankrupt.

The investor in French securities who would lose from interest payments in depreciated francs can safeguard himself by lending in terms of dollars and stipulating that his interest payments and capital repayments shall be in dollars too. This may involve a strain on the borrower if there is a depreciation of the franc (which to the Frenchman looks like an appreciation of the dollar). But this strain will be no greater than if the loan were in francs but the maintenance of the dollar value of the franc forced a general reduction of prices and incomes in France in terms of francs. If the price and income deflation is resisted there will be the still greater danger to the investment from the depression that must continue until the resistance is overcome. Safeguarding investments by maintaining the dollar value of the franc is entirely illusory.

Import restriction is a "beggar-my-neighbor" policy.

A third support of the cult of exchange rigidity lies in lumping currency depreciation with import tariffs as a "beggar-my-neighbor" policy.

We have seen that France, in our example, by letting her currency depreciate can avoid the depression that would result from trying to keep her exchanges stable. A third choice for France is to impose a tariff which decreases her demand for imports by as much as the demand for her exports fell in the first place. There will then be no tendency for the franc to fall and no call for deflation of French prices and incomes with its danger of depression.

The imposition of the tariff can be regarded as an attempt by France to shift the employment problem to other countries. It reduces the demand for *their* exports and they are consequently faced with the same problem that faced France in the first place. If they do not wish the foreign value of *their* currency to fall they must either reduce their domestic price level or shift the problem onto a third party by imposing a tariff themselves. The initial problem of unemployment is not eliminated but *aggravated* by the increasing interference with foreign trade. Such policies are properly called beggar-my-neighbor policies. Each nation tries to snatch some employment from its neighbors, to export some of its unemployment, with the net effect of making conditions worse all round. The further this game is carried the greater the impoverishment of all concerned.

In a condition of general depression the *similarity* between tariffs and currency depreciation is very striking. Any country, by depreciating its currency, can increase its exports and decrease its imports, thus gaining in employment at the expense of its neighbors just as in the case of tariffs.

Mutual depreciation is impossible.

The *difference* between tariffs and exchange depreciation is seen when one considers the effects of retaliation. In the case of tariff retaliation the benefit disappears and there remains the net harm to both countries of the interference with the international division of labor. *This is not true for currency devaluation.* Retaliation is strictly speaking impossible. The dollar cannot fall in terms of the franc at the same time that the franc falls in terms of the dollar. It *is* possible for two countries to impose and to increase tariffs on their imports from each other, but it is *not* possible for two countries to depreciate their own currencies in terms of each other's.

Although this consideration should logically settle the argument it looks to many like too slick a trick which breaks off the argument by catching the opponent off balance. It is therefore useful to come back to currency depreciation and consider (1) what happens if two countries permit their currencies to depreciate and

(2) what happens when the governments of two countries deliberately try to depreciate their currencies.

Natural *depreciation cannot be competitive.*

The more important of these is the first. Whenever the level of economic activity and of employment in a country is increased, whether this is the result of Functional Finance *or of anything else,* the increase in employment and prosperity results in an increase in the demand for all sorts of goods *including imported goods.* The additional demand for the additional foreign currency needed to pay for these will tend to depress the rate of exchange. If the country cannot permit its exchange to depreciate, cannot afford to lose gold or use up its foreign-exchange holdings and credits in preventing the depreciation, and does not want to resort to tariffs (perhaps because of fear of retaliation), *it must prevent any increase in domestic prosperity.* Currency depreciation is the *natural* concomitant of an increase in prosperity. Would such a depreciation result in a tendency to competitive depreciation? Would the dollar tend to depreciate if the franc depreciated because of an increase in French prosperity?

Just the opposite would happen. The French prosperity, which caused the depreciation of the franc, would increase the demand for American goods and this would mean an increase in the demand for dollars to pay for them. The tendency would then be for the dollar to *appreciate;* this should not surprise us since the appreciation of the dollar is merely another aspect of the depreciation of the franc. The tendency for the dollar to appreciate is a result of an increase in the demand for American goods, and this would tend to enrich rather than to beggar us. The appreciation of the dollar is necessary to prevent the French from buying more from us than they sell to us, but they will be buying more from us and we shall be buying more from them than before. We shall be able to carry on more trade with France and on better terms for ourselves. In effect there has been an increase in the size of

France, economically speaking, and this is what provides us with increased opportunities of beneficial international exchange.

If there is full employment in France to begin with, an increase in domestic spending will bring about not an increase in employment and economic activity but an inflationary price rise. Both we and the French will want to buy more of our goods, which have not gone up in price, instead of the dearer French products, and so the franc will depreciate as in the case just considered where there was unemployment to begin with and the increase in domestic spending increased employment and real income. When the franc has fallen in the same proportion as prices and incomes in France have risen everything will be the same as before in real terms. We do not gain from the depreciation of the franc, but neither do we lose. There might be some discomfort to us during the transition period while French prices were rising and nobody knew exactly what was going to happen (or we might be able to make great profits in the course of the inflation) but the discomfort to the French from the inflation would be so much greater than it could possibly be to us that we may rely on their trying to avoid the inflation if they can. At any rate France does not gain at our expense, and there is no tendency for the dollar to fall in competition with the franc. On the contrary the natural tendency is for the dollar to rise.

In the two cases we have considered, the devaluation was the natural though possibly unexpected effect of an expansion of domestic spending. What happens if there is no expansion of domestic spending but a country nevertheless *deliberately* devaluates its currency?

Deliberate *depreciation cannot harm other countries if they practice Functional Finance.*

The depreciation of the franc can be brought about in this case only by buying up dollars on the foreign-exchange market and hoarding them. The immediate effect is that our export industries are depressed because their products become more expensive for the French to buy. At the same time those of our industries which compete with French goods are depressed because the customers buy the cheaper French goods instead.

This loss of employment is not in itself a loss to our country as a whole. France will be sending us more goods than before and will be taking less goods from us than before, the difference between our exports and our imports being what she is giving us in exchange for easily printed dollar bills. Even if this is a temporary arrangement, we shall be getting a substantial loan from the French without interest.

But this gift or loan from France *does* mean that there is a decrease in employment in our export industries and in our import-competing industries. As the people in these industries are put out of work they will have less to spend on the products of other industries and the decrease in demand may lead to unemployment there. In this way unemployment may spread throughout the land so that we really would be hurt by the depreciation of the franc.

Fortunately there is no need for permitting any such harmful results to come about. If we follow the Functional Finance policy of maintaining adequate domestic spending we shall be able to maintain the demand for the other industries and enable at least *some* of the displaced workers to find some other occupation. Whatever they would add to production would be a net addition to the national income.

All this is true even if the French government gets all the francs for buying the hoarded dollars out of current taxes. But if there is not full employment in France and the French government conducts the operations with newly printed or borrowed money, this may lead to a further increase in French economic activity and a greater demand for our exports (among other things). We shall be able to do more trade with the French and we shall benefit from having a larger country, economically, with which to trade. This is an additional gain to us, over and above their hostile gift.

If this analysis is correct all concern for protecting countries from harmful effects of currency devaluation by their neighbors is quite unwarranted. Currency devaluation is never unneighborly in its effect on any country which practices Functional Finance and is thereby immune to domestic deflation.

One of the greatest deterrents to the application of Functional Finance by any country is that the prosperity it engenders, by increasing the demand for imports, may tend to reduce the foreign value of the country's currency. The solution is to set each country completely free to let the foreign value of its currency move to the level at which it finds equilibrium, whatever this level may be, subject only to the prevention of unnecessary fluctuations by the pegging procedure described on pages 360–362 below. Thus by permitting currency freedom for every country it would become impossible for any country to be hurt by anybody else's currency devaluation. The whole evil would be completely eliminated.

Such a freedom from concern about currency devaluation is in the economic sphere what has been vainly sought in the military sphere. It is a weapon so much stronger in defense than in attack that if everyone is armed with it nobody is in danger. Those who would oppose a general rearmament of a kind that rendered everyone immune from attack would be *endangering* peace. In the same way it is the sentimental internationalists, in their attack on the freedom of currency devaluation, who are dangerous for real international economic cooperation. It is these sentimental internationalists who will be responsible for the tariffs and other real restrictions on trade and capital movements to which countries will resort if denied the natural and harmless automatic adjustment by currency movements.

The International Monetary Fund is not as bad as might have been suggested. It does provide for adjustments in the rates of exchange to correct "fundamental disequilibria." But fundamental disequilibrium has no authoritative interpretation. It may be that the managers of the Fund will be wise enough to grant permission for depreciation of a currency in every case where its maintenance would have the harmful effects we have been considering. But that would mean giving permission whenever it is asked for or encouraging a national practice of depreciating first and asking for permission afterward when it could hardly be withheld. If that should be the case the Fund would do no harm, but in that case the exchanges might as well be recognized as not "stabilized" but free.

Except where there is high mobility of population, exchange-rate fixing is unnecessary and dangerous.

The analysis just given still leaves one with an uneasy feeling. If it is always better for a country to depreciate its foreign exchange than to try to reduce its domestic prices, why should not every state, county, city, and village have an independent currency which it can depreciate when necessary instead of trying to reduce its local prices and money incomes by force of depression? Is not the argument punctured by this *reductio ad absurdum?*

The argument can be saved only by establishing a principle which will tell us where currency depreciation should be permitted and where not. Fortunately this principle is not very difficult to establish. Where there is *great mobility of population* between two areas, rigidity of the exchanges can cause no great harm. As soon as it brings about a contraction of employment and profit opportunities in France, there will be a migration of *people* from France to America. This is a far *better* solution than the adjustment of either domestic prices or exchange rates.

Such a movement of population, by increasing the supply of goods in America and decreasing the supply of goods in France, would tend to correct and make unnecessary the relative decline in French prices. It is then possible to enjoy not merely the stability of foreign exchanges but the still greater convenience of a single money for the two areas. *The condition for a successful single currency area is that there be a high degree of mobility of population within the area.*

Where there is not such mobility, the best solution is not available and our concern can be only to prevent further aggravation of the trouble by a depression. If unemployment is to be avoided in France it is necessary that its prices be reduced as compared with American prices so that those who should have moved to America but had to stay in France will be able to find some other, even if inferior, employment. The reduction of French prices (including money incomes) relatively to American prices may take the form of reducing French prices in France. This is very difficult and normally can be reached only after a long and severe depression. It may also take the form of a reduction of the value of the franc relatively to the dollar. This is simple and natural and has all the advantages of the former without the difficulties of bringing it about.

This then is the answer to the attempted *reductio ad absurdum.* Where there is great mobility of population there is no need for relative price adjustments and so the conveniences of a single currency can be enjoyed. Where there is not real mobility of population, whether because of natural obstacles or legal prohibitions or conservatism of the population or anything else, a relative reduction in prices is necessary to bring work to those who do not go where the work is to be found. Where in addition to the resistances to movement there are also resistances to price and income reduction, the depression that would be necessary to force these prices down can be avoided by permitting the foreign value of the currency of such an area to fall relatively to the currency of the other area. This is the justification of different currencies and this is how they are instruments for easing the adjustments necessary in international economic cooperation rather than devices for hindering it.

Our conclusion is then that any attempt to fix the rates of exchange between the currencies of the different countries is unnecessary and dangerous. It is unnecessary because a country whose own foreign-exchange rate is free will not be frightened away from a policy of Functional Finance for maintaining domestic prosperity and preventing domestic inflation and so cannot be harmed by any other country's exchange depreciation. It is dangerous because it can force a country, in protecting its exchange rate, to keep domestic money demand below that needed for prosperity or to resort to real hindrances to international economic cooperation and beggar-my-neighbor devices like tariffs, quotas, exchange controls, and the rest.

Stability is possible without rigidity if the Fund merely pegs *exchange rates against day-to-day fluctuations.*

A further difficulty confronting exchange stabilization is the threat of capital flights from one country to another—especially when it becomes obvious that a particular rate of exchange cannot be maintained much longer and a devaluation is imminent. Attempts to solve this problem usually rest on a distinction being made between legitimate payments on current trading accounts, which are to be free (in accordance with the second objective of international monetary arrangements), and capital flights, which might have to be prevented by administrative machinery. But this latter must in effect destroy the freedom of payments on current account. There would be needed a complete system of bureaucratic checking on all international payments to make sure that they are really payments on current account and not devious means for smuggling capital out of the country. The impossible task would have to be undertaken of distinguishing between speculative movements of capital which are disturbing to regular international transactions and the legitimate capital movements which are essential to the free development of the world economy. Probably the most serious objection to such supervision of international payments is that it establishes a dangerous governmental power over individuals who may seek to move their property to other countries in attempts to escape discrimination or persecution. This surely conflicts with at least one of the Freedoms we publicly proclaim.

It is possible to avoid such dangers and difficulties arising from the cult of exchange rigidity while enjoying the benefits of maximizing international economic cooperation. In fact it is possible to hope to add to these benefits the benefits of *stable* as distinct from *rigid* exchange rates. If all countries follow a policy of Functional Finance for maintaining domestic prosperity and preventing inflation and avoid sudden changes in their tariffs, etc., the exchange rates, even if completely free to move, will not move very much once the disturbances of the war and the postwar emergency measures have come to an end and the exchanges have found their natural level. After that they will move only in response to changes in population, in techniques of production, in consumers' tastes and the like, all of which are slow in their aggregate effects for most countries. Free exchanges do not mean violently fluctuating exchanges. It is rather when attempts are made to fix exchanges and hold them at unnatural levels that pressures accumulate which, when they burst the bonds, show spectacular explosions.

These benefits could be achieved if the Fund would behave like the various national exchange-stabilization and -equalization funds from which it is descended. If the Fund had been able to escape the traditional association of international money with gold, it could have asked each country to make its contribution entirely in its own currency. Since this can never cause any country any difficulties, the size of the contributions could have been based on considerations of pride rather than parsimony. All that is needed is that the contributions be large enough to permit the Fund, by *pegging* the rates of exchange at what it believes to be the equilibrium level, to offset any day-to-day fluctuations. If the Fund finds that there is persistent pressure on the exchange rate in one direction it will change the rate to one which it can maintain without buying (or selling) unlimited amounts of a particular currency, for that would mean that the country concerned is importing in excess of its exports (or exporting in excess of its imports).

Changes in the rates of exchange maintained by the Fund would have to be unannounced. To prevent speculators from making large and easy profits at the expense of the rest of the population, it would be necessary for the transactions of the Fund to be secret so that there will be no clue as to whether the exchange rate will have to be changed and in which direction. Large changes would not be necessary once the initial disturbances of postwar relief and rehabilitation grants have come to an end, nor will the changes have to take place frequently when some experience has been developed as to the natural rates of exchange at which the supply of each currency is equal to the demand.

Capital movements could also be free, and freedom of trade encouraged.

Individuals can then be completely free to make payments abroad without any control. If there should be large flights of capital from one country to another, say for political reasons, these can be prevented from interfering with the normal working of the economy. If there is, for example, a large flight of capital from France to the United States that is expected to return to France later, this would tend to bid up the dollar and depreciate the franc and this could cause considerable disturbance to both the French and the American economy. The opposite would happen when the time came for the return of the capital, with similar disturbances. The Fund could prevent all these disturbances if it were prepared to provide out of its own stock the dollars demanded by exporters of capital from France, keeping the francs it received for them until the time when the capital would fly back. It might have to ask the American government to help it out if it ran short of dollars, and the French government might have to print more francs to replenish temporarily the diminished stock of francs in France (unless the Fund would lend it the francs it had accumulated). The dollars paid out by the Fund would naturally flow into the circulation of the United States, but any inflationary pressure would be checked by the normal application of Functional Finance (in taxation or governmental borrowing to withdraw the excessive dollars from circulation—and perhaps to lend them to the Fund to continue its operation). If the capital movement is expected to be permanent the Fund could cushion the effects by absorbing most of the currency offered on the market and releasing it gradually, thus preventing serious dislocations.

The Fund could also provide a futures market on which traders could hedge against movements of exchange rates, charging them a small fee just adequate to cover the cost of running the offices (unless this service was provided by private speculators at still lower charges). Each country could be perfectly free to buy or sell or hoard gold if it so wished with no restrictions whatever. The Fund would be no more interested in gold than in any other metal.

The primary advantage to a country from subscribing to the Fund is that it could give up all concern for its foreign-exchange value and concentrate on keeping domestic money demand (by Functional Finance) at the level which gives prosperity without bringing inflation. The Fund could also be used to free international trade from existing or potential restrictions. It could be made a condition of membership that the country undertake not to impose any new tariffs or other restrictions on trade, not to increase any existing restrictions on trade or international payments, and to remove some or all of these in ten or twenty years— perhaps by gradual stages.

The inducement for a country to agree to these additional conditions is that the other countries will remove their tariffs against its exports, a benefit that it would not enjoy if it stayed outside. (Or this part of the plan could be optional.) At the same time it would be advisable for the Fund or for some sister agency such as the International Trade Organization to undertake an educational program to make it more commonly understood that the loss to particular industries from the removal of tariffs is always less than the gain to the rest of the country so that those hurt by the freeing of trade could be compensated by governmental grants which would still leave the rest of the country benefiting from the removal of the tariff. There is an exception to this where a country imposed import restrictions which change the terms of trade sufficiently in its favor but these would be cases of definite monopolistic exploitation of other countries which should be recognized not merely as unfair but as a "beggar-my-neighbor" benefit that would be destroyed by retaliatory restrictions.

It would be preferable, at least as long as gold continued to be generally accepted as a store of value, for the initial exchange rate of the dollar to be too high rather than too low (as far as the equilibrium levels can be estimated in the beginning). This would permit the exchange to be stabilized for a long time, even if it were considerably out of line, by the export of gold out of the United States' enormous stock. We would get some useful goods in exchange for some of the yellow metal which would be useful for other countries that psychologically need larger gold reserves before they can bring themselves to the monetary expansion they will need for maintaining prosperity after the reconstruction period. It would also hasten the beginning of the *stability* of foreign exchanges (as distinct from *rigidity*) that will be a symptom of the success of the Fund.

A single currency is a symptom of unity achieved, not a road leading to it.

It is conceivable that when this position of stability has been reached the price adjustments necessary to keep the international system in equilibrium with fixed exchanges would be small in comparison with the individual price adjustments called for by particular changes in tastes, in the availability of the factors of production, and in the techniques of production. If this should be so we could have a real single currency with the same coins and bills for all the countries for which this is true. The psychological advantages of this in encouraging feelings of international solidarity and in furthering the removal of barriers to the movement of goods and of people might be sufficient to warrant giving up the flexibility of the exchanges. But it is doubtful whether it would be advisable to *fix* the exchanges, even if virtual stability would seem to have been reached, in the absence of the advantages of a really uniform currency. At any rate this is a matter only for a future in which all the disturbances of the war and the reconstruction are over and everything is running smoothly. None of the conditions for a successful regime of fixed exchanges would seem to be in evidence for the immediate future.

In the foreseeable future there is no visible prospect of a world so united that a single currency would be feasible. In such a divided world the best thing is to be clear about some general principles of the beginnings of international cooperation. In the absence of the clear application of such principles the best of intentions can lead to unfortunate results—as in the case of sentimental internationalism.

The fundamental principle of *social order* or cooperation between individuals is that *public acts,* which are acts that affect other people, shall be so regulated that whoever undertakes them will give due consideration to the benefit or hurt to other people. The fundamental principle of *freedom* is that *private acts,* which are acts that do not affect other people, should *not* be regulated, so that every individual can do what is best for himself without being frustrated to no purpose.

In the relations between nations the same general principles hold. Public acts in this case are acts by a nation which affect other nations, and private acts are acts which do not affect other nations so that there is no reason why they should be regulated.

The imposition of a tariff by a country is a *public* act because other countries are affected by it. Tariffs must therefore be regulated in any satisfactory greater society. Whether a country adjusts itself to a change in international conditions by reducing the foreign value of its exchange or by reducing the domestic level of prices is a *private* matter which does not directly affect the inhabitants of other countries. The only exception to this is where a domestic inflation and parallel currency devaluation is brought about as a means of evading payment of just debts to foreigners even at the cost of similarly defrauding domestic creditors.

A depression in one country hurts other countries by threatening a spread of the depression (against which the other countries can safeguard themselves by Functional Finance) and by lessening their opportunities for foreign trade (against which the other countries have no remedy). Having a domestic depression is therefore a *public act*. It is the international duty of every country to maintain domestic prosperity and avoid domestic inflation. These duties are sufficiently in the country's own interest to make any international sanctions quite fruitless and free exchanges only make it easier for a country to carry out these duties.

Marshall was wrong in his analogy (page 344 above) between the rates of exchange and the signaling codes at sea. International exchange rates, when they are free all around, are private and not public matters; and the energies which sentimental internationalists have devoted to the cult of exchange rigidity properly belong to efforts for the removal of real hindrances to international cooperation and real beggar-my-neighbor policies which, by tariffs and quotas and the like, restrict the international movement of real goods and capitals.

The cult of exchange rigidity, even though it prefers to speak in terms of stability and is based largely on a sentimental internationalism, is a hindrance, not a help, to the maintenance of domestic prosperity in all countries; and on domestic prosperity alone can international economic cooperation firmly be built. When the "one world" that the sentimental internationalists have in mind has been firmly established and there is economic stability, free trade, and personal mobility throughout the whole world, an automatic stability of the foreign exchanges will have come about and a single currency can then be established everywhere. It would be an ornament fitting to a smoothly working "one world" —a symbol of unity and a sign of success. To attempt to establish this symptom before the real unity is there can only delay the day of its achievement.

Summary.

The principle of stabilizing exchange rates has been improperly elevated from a means to an end. In the proposals which led to the establishment of the International Monetary Fund exchange stabilization was a top objective. Nevertheless it is not true that exchange stabilization is necessary or even helpful for international economic cooperation.

International economic cooperation depends in the first place on national prosperity and full employment. Of the further objectives the stability of the exchanges should be at the bottom of the list. Fixed exchanges are only a minor convenience to the international trader. The cult of exchange stability rests on a sentimental internationalism which sees in exchange stability an approximation to a single money and a step toward "one world." But in effect it divides rather than unites the world by eliminating the most satisfactory way of adjusting to economic changes.

The gold standard operated on the theory of domestic prices instead of the rate of foreign exchange being adjusted to economic changes. But the domestic prices can often be adjusted only by means of long and severe depressions, while the adjustment of the exchange rate, which does the same job, is easy and quick. Preventing the easy adjustment so as to necessitate the difficult one should rather be called exchange *rigidity*.

The belief that fixed exchanges make foreign investment safer is based on a failure to see that the forces which would cause a depreciation would reveal themselves in other and usually more objectionable forms if the depreciation is prevented.

Currency depreciation is unjustly lumped together with trade restrictions of various kinds as a beggar-my-neighbor policy. This is incorrect because, unlike import restrictions, currency depreciation cannot lead to mutual impoverishment through retaliation. It is impossible for currencies to be depreciated in terms of each other.

A *natural* depreciation results from an increase in a country's domestic spending (relatively to another country) which brings with it an increase in demand for imports. The other currency will then tend to *appreciate*. We do not have any *competitive* depreciation in this case. Where the increased spending increases employment and real income the other country gains from increased opportunities for international trade. Where the increased spending is purely inflationary the other country is unaffected. In no case is the other country hurt by the natural depreciation.

A *deliberate* depreciation can be engineered by a government buying and hoarding foreign currency. This cannot harm but can only benefit a country practicing Functional Finance. If everybody practices Functional Finance and cannot be frightened from this by currency depreciation nobody can be harmed.

Where there is great mobility of population, freedom of currency to depreciate is unnecessary. Movement of people is a better solution than any of the adjustments so far considered, and a single currency is in order.

Leaving the exchanges free does not mean that they would fluctuate greatly once an equilibrium had finally been reached. Stability as distinct from rigidity could be further helped by the Fund *pegging* exchange rates so as to offset day-to-day fluctuations. Capital movements could be free too, the Fund protecting the national economies from dislocations. The Fund could also encourage international economic cooperation in other ways. When a final equilibrium has been reached it might be desirable to institute a single world currency but that is not a matter for the near future. A single currency, even in the form of fixed exchange rates, would be a symptom and symbol of the united world attained. It is not an instrument for helping to bring about the unification.

Part VII

Conclusion

CHAPTER 23

Economics, Politics, and Administration

WE HAVE now concluded our treatment of the *economics* of employment, but a word or two must be added on the *politics* and the *administration* of employment policies in general and of Functional Finance in particular. This is especially necessary because of the frequency with which opponents of measures like Functional Finance move from economics to these other fields. They very often agree, after protracted argument, that "the economics is perfectly correct." But since "a man convinced against his will retains the same opinion still" this agreement does not prevent them from continuing their opposition. They then try to justify the continued opposition on different grounds. No longer able to charge economic illiteracy, they take refuge in charges of political impossibility or administrative unfeasibility.

The central purpose of the book is to help remove the confusions and misunderstandings that are in the way of a wholehearted utilization in our society of the economic steering wheel referred to in Chapter 1. The rest of the book is an amplification of Chapter 1, developing explicitly the income analysis on which it is based, considering some of the objections and difficulties in the way of its full application, and considering some closely related issues like the national debt, the international aspects of employment policies, and the problems that would arise *out of* the achievement of full employment. All through the book it has been necessary here and there to touch on political and administrative aspects of employment policies. In this chapter we shall try to pull some of these elements together.

The political philosophy of Democratic Functionalism shows that there is no conflict between freedom and order.

The social and political philosophy of Functional Finance is that of Democratic Functionalism, of which Functional Finance is a part. Democratic Functionalism calls for the application of the humanistic principles of classic liberalism to modern problems and to modern techniques of dealing with them. It consists of the *functional* principle that all social institutions—ancient or modern, actual or potential—should be judged only by their effectiveness in carrying out their functions in the social interest and the *democratic* principle that in estimating the social interest, there should be no discrimination between different men or groups of men, for that would be undemocratic, but that all men should be considered equally worthy.

One corollary of Democratic Functionalism is that the much spoken of conflict between freedom and order in society is a delusion and a snare. It is *never* necessary to choose between freedom and order. It is not even necessary to look for a *compromise* in which some of each is sacrificed for some of the other. Order is nothing but an instrument for maximizing the total freedom in society by lessening the freedom of some people to do what they want to do when that limitation increases by *more* the freedom (which includes the ability) of others to do what *they* want to do. It follows that the maximum or order is identical with the maximum of freedom. A sacrifice of freedom for the sake of order is as senseless as any sacrifice of an end for the sake of the means for its own achievement.

The acceptance of a rule can turn political into economic problems and make them solvable.

There is, of course, often a conflict between the interests of different people or of different groups of people. In such conflicts it is inevitable that some interests, some freedoms should be sacrificed for the sake of others. Unless there is some accepted principle or rule that determines the nature of the settlement, the conflict of interest gives us a *political* problem. This means that the settlement is nothing but a resultant of the forces that the interested parties can bring to bear on the issue. The settlement is then truly a *compromise,* with complete disregard of the interest of one or other of the parties as a limit of the range of possible compromises.

Where there is a generally accepted principle or rule for determining the nature of the settlement, a genuine solution is possible which is not a mere compromise or resultant of immediate forces. If the rule is one which limits freedom only where the limitation is necessary for the sake of greater freedom, then both freedom and order are maximized. The limitation of the smaller freedoms constitutes the order necessary for the enjoyment of greater freedoms.

The principle or rule necessary for providing a genuine solution must be directed at the *content* of the settlement and not merely at the *manner* in which the settlement is reached. The institution of democratic procedures for resolving differences by majority vote does not change the basically political nature of conflicts or the compromise nature of their settlement. The substitution of ballots for bullets diminishes the amount of naked violence but does not constitute a principle or rule to take the place of the pressure of the conflicting forces in determining the content of the settlement of the issues voted on.

The principle of freedom is such a rule.

An important step toward the replacement of arbitrary compromise by a rule is to be found in the principle of freedom. This is the principle that anyone may do whatever he prefers to do as long as this does not affect the ability of other people to do what *they* want to do. This principle enables purely economic problems to be separated out from the complex of social relations, and to the purely economic problems we can apply relatively simple procedures of getting optimum solutions in terms of maximization of the benefit to those who are affected.

The principle of freedom is seen most clearly in the imaginary case of the distributist society in which individuals can produce the things they want by themselves in their own houses or gardens. In the absence of interdependence in production there is no political problem involved. Nobody else is affected by anyone's industry or laziness. We get the optimum solution by permitting each individual to maximize his satisfaction by working just as hard and as long as seems best to himself.

In a modern economy where industry must be highly integrated if it is to be productive enough to keep us all alive, let alone maintain our high standards of living, the principle of freedom still permits us to extract purely economic problems and to solve them by a maximizing process just as in the imaginary distributist society. This trick is done by establishing markets and prices and paying for effort at a money rate equal to the value of the marginal product of the worker. Paying anyone the value of his marginal product means that whether he works more or works less exactly the same is left over for the rest of society to enjoy. The social benefit is maximized by permitting each worker to work just as hard and as long as he finds it best to do in his own interest. Society is not interested in applying any pressure on him to work more or to work less, and he is not able to apply any pressure on society by threats of working more or of working less. Freedom is maximized.

What all this means is that we can convert a political problem into an economic problem by applying to it some generally accepted rule that makes the solution determinate rather than arbitrary. We can then solve the problem by a process of maximization. Economists can show determinate solutions not because they are smarter than political scientists but because the economic problems are just those problems for which a generally accepted principle has become applicable so as to make its solution determinate.

The principle of democracy is another.

The opportunities for solving political problems by turning them into economic problems are, however, severely limited by the condition that nobody may be harmed by the solution that maximizes the benefit to those affected. This is still true even after making full use of the principle of compensating (out of the benefits yielded by the maximizing procedures) those who would otherwise be harmed. (Whether such compensation is considered as an extension of the principle of private property or as replacement of private property by other institutions may seem important to those who like to think of themselves as devotees of capitalism or of socialism but is not of interest to Democratic Functionalism.) In all cases where some may be benefited (*i.e.,* have their freedom increased) only by methods which would hurt others (*i.e.,* diminish *their* freedom to do what they want) the problem is still political and can be settled only on the arbitrary basis of a resultant of the forces brought to bear by the interested parties.

This remaining jungle can be reduced to order by the general acceptance of an additional principle or rule. This is the principle of democracy. The general acceptance of the principle that all men are to be considered equally worthy would permit the benefits and the damages to be put in a single scale. A determinate solution emerges if we let the greater outweigh the lesser.

The combination of the principle of freedom with the principle of democracy tells us, for example, how the total income of society should be divided among the population. Effort should be paid for at a rate equal to the value of the marginal product, and the rest of the national income should be divided equally among all the population (except for clear cases of special need such as blind persons or those requiring special medical attention).

Any other income, unless it is indirectly necessary in applying the principles of freedom and of democracy, can be justified only on the basis of other principles overriding Democratic Functionalism. For example, income from property may be defended where it permits a man who has earned some income by his effort to save some of it and enjoy the interest on his savings, which he can do without diminishing anyone else's income, in complete accordance with the principle of freedom. In such a case the justification is that the protection of such property income is a corollary of Democratic Functionalism. Income which is not justifiable on the principles of Democratic Functionalism may, on the other hand, be justified on other principles, such as the satisfaction of established expectations or the special rights of selected sections of the population.

The principles of freedom, functionalism, and democracy are very closely related.

It should be noticed that the principle of freedom is hardly distinguishable from the principle of functionalism, so that Democratic Functionalism may also be considered as consisting of the principle of freedom and the principle of democracy. Furthermore the principle of freedom can also be considered as the limiting case of the principle of democracy, where the smaller freedom that is sacrificed to the greater freedom has the limiting value of zero. The closeness of these principles to each other means that Democratic Functionalism is an integrated and closely woven system. It is not given its proper due as such by those who have called it the mixed economy just because they cannot resist attaching labels to its different institutions and the only labels they have available are old ones marked "capitalism" and "socialism."

Functional Finance can achieve political acceptance as common sense.

Functional Finance is most likely to be put into regular practice not as the distinguishing policy of a particular party but as the obvious thing to do, irrespective of party, and therefore not of any interest to the writers of political pamphlets. Functional Finance is not likely to become the center of a religious movement like communism or fascism. There was perhaps a possibility of its becoming that a few years ago when it was easier to hope that world peace could be guaranteed by a demonstration, over several decades, that it is possible for capitalist countries to maintain prosperity without going to war with Russia or even with each other. The atomic armaments race and the sharpening of the international situation as a result of the demonstration by Russia that she is not likely to allow concern for world peace to frustrate her missionary-imperialist ambitions have taken away the time needed for the demonstration of capitalist full employment as well as much of the meaning of such a demonstration to the communist world. But the greatest obstacle to the development of Functional Finance into a religion is the fact that it relies on a rational element in the conduct of human affairs.

Reformers naturally underestimate social rationality.

To reformers and radicals who normally have not the great patience necessary to see the gradual adoption of many of their projects, the irrationalities of society loom larger than they are. The rational activities go on smoothly in the production and the distribution of goods and services that constitute the great bulk of human activity. It is the interruptions in rational activities that absorb our attention and it is the failure to adopt the new and better procedures that occupies our field of vision. This leads the critics of our society to a most uncritical exaggeration of the degree of irrationality in our social life and the difficulties of bringing about acceptance of a rational program like Functional Finance.

In fact the principles of Functional Finance have already been accepted to a very high degree. In practice administrators and legislators, who would certainly not recognize themselves as "Keynesians" or as "Functional Financiers," find themselves justifying government deficits as necessary to prevent depression and maintain prosperity, or refusing to reduce taxes, even though the budget is in surplus, because they see that the country is in an inflationary condition and that the tax reduction would make total spending too great. And in the academic field, it is now very fashionable to support all sorts of "Keynesian" measures after making solemn declaration of an anti-Keynesian faith.

Functional Finance has in fact been partially adopted already.

No matter what government is in power in the United States, it is quite certain that *severe* depression will be prevented by government deficits if necessary. The complexion of the party in power will only show itself in the number of anti-Keynesian speeches that will accompany it. The prevention of *moderate* depression has not yet been generally accepted as simple common sense, but the gradual extension of the same principle from more severe to less severe depression is inevitable as our skill in the use of the corrective measures develops in the course of its practical application.

The reason for the relatively rapid acceptance of this part of Functional Finance is to be seen in the absence of any real interests that are opposed to the maintenance of prosperity. Without the support of important interests the dogmas of sound finance cannot last very long.

It will be more difficult with the measures that need to be developed to prevent the great bargaining power of labor to cause inflation when there is a high employment. But here too there is reason for restrained optimism. Some labor leaders have caught glimpses of the problem. They are aware of the dangers to the labor movement from a coalition of other elements in the society against them if in the course of the race of each union to keep its wages abreast of the others they should turn prosperity into inflation. They will therefore be prepared to listen to reason and to cooperate in techniques, like the principle of wage determination suggested in this book, which would yield stability to society without working injustice on labor. In the establishment of this stability it will probably be necessary to make use of the normal procedure in political democracy of mobilizing the political pressures of other groups to overcome the power of such labor organizations as would resist them. Liberals will learn and are now learning to overcome their tendency to identify the interests of labor organizations with the interests of labor or even with the interests of society or of humanity.

Of great importance in the integration of Functional Finance into our society is the possibility of adopting the different measures slowly and piecemeal. There is no necessity for a sudden and complete adoption of the whole program. The different parts of it can work and do good even when alone, experience can improve on them, and time can lead to the whole being gradually adopted as it is seen to fit into the natural order of things. Future statesmen will then discover that they have been practicing Functional Finance just as they have been talking prose. It will be adopted not as liberal or as progressive but as common sense.

Special-interest pressures are not made more dangerous by Functional Finance.

By the politics of Functional Finance is frequently meant not only the task of getting it accepted by the authorities who can put it into practice, but the difficulties of applying it in practice because of pressures by particular groups that would work toward perverting its proper application in the general interest. Of special interest is the suggestion that the resistance to such pressures must lead to dictatorship.

Many of these suggestions that Functional Finance must lead to dictatorship are based on misunderstandings—and sometimes one is even tempted to believe deliberate misunderstandings—of the essential nature of Functional Finance. The creation of employment by the government through deficit financing is sometimes denounced as a kind of bribery by which a political party buys votes with jobs and in this way destroys the democratic society. This kind of condemnation, if valid, would constitute a condemnation of the whole democratic principle whereby politicians are tempted to do what is best for the people not out of the goodness of their hearts but out of a desire for reelection. It is a criticism which fails to distinguish between democracy and bribery. Or perhaps one should say that democracy is nothing but the bribing of the voters with good government. Would that there were much more of that kind of bribery.

Another confusion is more reminiscent of the kind of "amalgam" that is produced by the governments of Russia and its satellite nations for their show trials when they energetically and almost inextricably tie up suspected political deviationists with spies, traitors, mass murderers, and hydrophobic snakes. In the amalgam produced by the prolific "Fighters for Freedom" (of the Committee for Constitutional Government) deficit financing is identified with socialism and socialism is identified with communist totalitarianism and the slave labor camps of Siberia. This disgraceful device of condemnation by association, with the association invented by the condemning judge and jury, would not be worth mentioning were it not that perhaps the greater part of the propaganda of the "Fighters for Freedom" is highly commendable and really would help the freedom and the efficiency of our society. It is a pity that these excellent parts of its work should be vitiated by the association with the shameful distortions in its campaign against any suggested departures from the most rudimentary forms of sound finance.

Much more deserving of respect are the genuine fears of liberal-minded men concerning the dangers to liberty that may result from the government's being freed from the necessity of keeping its budget balanced at all times. It seems to many that if the government could not defend itself by declaring that it must balance the budget, only the establishment of a dictatorship would enable the government to resist the perennial pressures for more expenditures and tax reductions. Functional Finance is supposed to give the government a degree of discretion that fatally weakens its defense against the lobbyists.

Preventing inflation is a stronger maxim than balancing the budget.

This view is based on the error of supposing that the substitution of Functional Finance for sound finance constitutes the substitution of unfettered discretion for a firm rule. But Functional Finance is rather the substitution of one rule for another rule. Instead of keeping government spending at a level where it is equal to tax receipts, the government is enjoined to keep its spending at a level where total demand in the economy results in neither depression nor inflation. There may have been a time when the necessity of balancing the budget was a more effective counter to excessive demands on the government than the necessity for preventing inflation. But the wolf-crying of the budget balancers has so much damaged the effectiveness of the cry that even the most regular lip servers of sound finance are now ready to grant temporary exceptions at the drop of a hat. The prevention of inflation is not only a more important matter in reality, it is even recognized as such in dealing with practical issues by government officials, by legislators, and even by columnists and newspaper editorial writers who, when they are not considering any concrete situation, automatically proffer verbal obeisance to sound finance. With the substitution of the Functional Finance's rule of reason for the budget-balancing dogma, there is not more but *less* call for the development of dictatorial methods to resist the lobbies of special interests.

The real dangers to liberty are reactionary authoritarianism and revolutionary ignorance.

The real dangers to free society are two, neither of which is related to Functional Finance or Democratic Functionalism. The first danger comes from those who simply do not believe in democracy and would prefer to live in an authoritarian society, such as existed in olden days, although nowadays it would be streamlined with the much more efficient modern techniques of totalitarian suppression of all dissension. In this conflict clarity demands that the issue not be clouded and that it be recognized that those who want to maintain and extend human freedom should concentrate on the fight for the maintenance and the extension of human freedom and not let their energies be dissipated in irrelevant crusades against imaginary bogies invented by the enemies of freedom for this very purpose.

The second danger comes from those reformers who are blind to the degree to which the freedoms already achieved are based on the use of the market and price mechanism in implementing efficiency, decentralization, and freedom of choice. Attempts to improve the economy by throwing out the price mechanism instead of developing and perfecting it can result in breakdowns unexpected by ignorant revolutionaries and in a cancer of more and more administrative emergency measures which keep on aggravating the disorders they are intended to remedy. Functional Finance is based on a complete recognition of the necessity and of the possibilities of the price mechanism on which modern economy is built so that it is in no danger of the paralysis that would follow a policy of dispensing with the price mechanism. Functional Finance is often charged with constituting just this threat to democratic society, but the charge can only be the illegitimate offspring of the indefensible identification of Functional Finance with doctrinaire socialism and totalitarian communism.

Functional Finance leaves the world full of problems.

There remains a class of objections to the institution of Functional Finance that are much more sober than any of those discussed so far in this chapter. Objections to Functional Finance may be divided into those which are brought up by people who are looking for objections and those which really would make the life of the administrators of Functional Finance difficult. The former objections, while claiming to be part of the political problems of the *operation* of Functional Finance, really belong to the political problem, discussed earlier in the chapter, of overcoming the resistances to the *establishment* of Functional Finance. The latter are really problems of the administration of Functional Finance when it has been politically accepted.

Here we have such problems as choosing between the many different methods of maintaining an adequate level of total spending, deciding on the division of the national resources between consumption and investment, balancing the interests of the different segments of the economy which will be applying pressures for government expenditures or subsidies to be directed in ways which would benefit them rather than some other segment of the society, overcoming particular pressures for more spending or lower taxes where these would result in too much total spending and inflation, and so on and so on.

Then there is another set of problems such as the difficulty of forecasting future expenditures by other parts of the economy so as to have just the right degree of compensatory spending arranged beforehand or the difficulty of figuring out all the repercussions of any government act of spending throughout following future periods so that future compensatory plans will not be disrupted by the remaining repercussion of old activities of the same kind.

Yet another set of problems is provided by the necessity of obtaining agreement to such plans as the scheme for prevention of inflation through the operation of wage bargaining in times of full employment when the "reserve army of unemployed" is no longer available as a stabilizer of the general level of wages.

And throughout all these different kinds of problems there are purely administrative tasks like the collection of index numbers of various kinds to help determine the trends of prices and wages and output and employment or the collection of the basic statistics for determining the "indices of relative attractiveness" of the different occupations.

Reactionaries and revolutionaries both treat problems as objections.

All these different sets of problems are genuine. They will make life difficult for the administrators of the economy under Functional Finance. But there is no reason for supposing that life will be any more difficult than in any other financial system which does not give the society the benefits of Functional Finance. We have considered some of these tasks in earlier chapters in this book. We have seen that much of the concern about, say, the difficulty of forecasting the future expenditures of the different sections of the economy or of the future repercussions of government contributions to total spending (or for that matter the future repercussions of *any* contributions to total spending) arises from the mistake of supposing that it is necessary to know the future course of spending with great accuracy in order to be able to stabilize total spending. We used the analogy of the bicycle which can be ridden successfully without any accurate calculation of what would happen to it in the next minute in the absence of corrective action by the rider.

This example is typical of the general tendency to treat administrative problems as if they were administrative impossibilities. The introduction of a new element like Functional Finance seems to create an atmosphere in which familiar problems which are dealt with daily and with adequate success suddenly seems to assume the proportions of unscalable obstacles. Our economy has all along been providing some solution or other to conflicting interests and will continue to do so whether we have Functional Finance or not. The solutions have not always been the wisest in the past and they will not always be the wisest in the future. A kind of failure of nerve leads to a hysterical perfectionism in which the extremes of conservatism and revolution meet. To the conservative the fact that a proposed change will not cure all ills is a reason for rejecting the proposal in favor of changing nothing. To the revolutionary the fact that a proposed change will not cure all ills is a reason for rejecting the proposal in favor of changing everything. The sane view recognizes that perfection is not for the world of actuality, that we may improve forever without reaching perfection, that we will always have problems with us. The sane view considers the continued existence of problems not as an objection to any proposal for betterment but as a reassuring sign that we are talking of the world of actuality and not of some never-never land of irresponsible dreams.

The only security is in making haste slowly.

Functional Finance will not inaugurate a problemless world. Life will not be effortless. There will still be struggles and conflicts and difficulties and defeats. But it is an important step forward. It is a disturbing step to the conservative who sees only the difficulties remaining even if they are nothing but the old difficulties we have with us all the time magnified and made terrible by their association with something new. It is an unsatisfying step to the revolutionary with his vision of dissolving all problems by a sufficiently bold rejection of everything we have painfully acquired over the centuries in a blind jump into the unknown. But for those who see the future as a continuation of the dynamic development of the past, with a learning from our past experience and the expectation of the further continuation of the painful process of learning, Functional Finance is a step which society is now engaged in making. It has already been made in part and will be completed when it ceases to be somebody's theory but is seen by almost everybody as the simple common sense of avoiding the upside-down economy of depression or the dizzy fever of inflation.

The progress must be gradual, for only gradually can a new theory become obvious common sense. But this gradualness is the fastest way of sure progress, providing always that we do indeed "make haste slowly" and avoid the opposite danger of making "gradualness" a pretense for standing still. For the one thing we cannot do in this world of ours is to stand still. If we do not go forward in the further development of the free society but permit depressions and inflations to torment and harry the lives of millions, the eagerly waiting totalitarians will inherit the earth and wipe out all the remaining freedoms.

Fortunately there is not the slightest need for such a failure of freedom by default if only the immediate dangers of planetary destruction by modern war can be held off for several decades. The strengthening of the democracies and the demonstration to the people in the totalitarian countries (who also would rather live than die) that democracy can yield both peace and prosperity will make the earth safe for the practitioners of human freedom. But a basic element in the strategy of freedom is the establishment, as rapidly as possible, of stable prosperity in the free countries of the world.

Summary.

In lieu of a summary of this chapter and indeed as a means of bringing into closer focus the scope of the whole book, the reader who has been persevering enough to read to this point is asked to read again the first chapter of the book "The Economic Steering Wheel, or the Parable of the People's New Clothes."

Index

387

DATE DUE

SEP 8 0 1964			
MAR 22 1977			
GAYLORD			PRINTED IN U.S.A.